M000190304

Out of the Fog!

To Donna &
Something to read
while you recover
from the "fall" (so sorry
about that). Sandra
2·24·22

A Story of Survival,
Faith and Courage

Sandra CH Smith

OUT OF THE FOG!
A Story of Survival, Faith and Courage

This is a work of non-fiction. Events and experiences detailed herein are all true and have been faithfully rendered as the author has remembered them, to the best of her ability. Some names, identities and circumstances have been changed to protect the privacy and/or anonymity of the various individuals involved.

OUT OF THE FOG! *A STORY OF SURVIVAL, FAITH AND COURAGE* Copyright © 2020 by Sandra CH Smith. All rights reserved. Printed in the United States of America. No part of this book may be used, reproduced or transmitted in any manner whatsoever by any means, electronic or mechanical, including photocopying and recording, or by any information storage and retrieval system without written permission expressly from the publisher except in the case of brief quotations embodied in critical articles and reviews. The scanning, uploading and distribution of this book via the Internet or via other means without permission of the publisher is illegal and punishable by law. Please purchase only authorized electronic editions. Your support of the writer's rights is appreciated. For information and/or requests for permission should be made via email to: BookBaby Publishers, address, BookBaby. com

BOOKBABY PUBLISHING, FIRST EDITION PUBLISHED 2020.
Book designed by BookBaby Publishing
Cover photo from author's collection

The Library of Congress has catalogued the e-book edition as follows:
Smith, Sandra CH
Out of the Fog! *A Story of Survival, Faith and Courage/* Sandra CH Smith – 1st ed.
ISBN #978-1-09834-778-9 (e-book)

The Library of Congress has catalogued the softcover edition as follows:
Smith, Sandra CH
Out of the Fog! *A Story of Survival, Faith and Courage /* Sandra CH Smith – 1st ed.
ISBN #978-1-09834-777-2 (softcover)

Author's Contact: Sandra@SandraCHSmith. com , Po Box 13, Bisbee AZ 85603-0013

l. Smith, Sandra CH Smith – Mental health – Self-Help. 2. Writers, American–21st century—Autobiography. 3. Recovering Alcoholics—United States—Autobiography. 4. Women's Issues. 5. Alcoholism—United States. 6. Smith, Sandra CH—Childhood and youth. 7. Family problems. 8. Sailing. 9. Women sailing

Also by Sandra CH Smith:
A Cook's Tour of Epicuria…One Woman's Adventures

(Published 1999 by Capricorn Press, Eureka Springs AR)

For Carl F. Rohne…my beloved husband
With gratitude for all your wisdom, inspiration and encouragement.

For Ian Tannahill Theophilos Smith…my brilliant and caring son
Thanks for your patience, tolerance and wit

For all past, present and potential members of 12 Step programs
around the world…without you I wouldn't be here!

And lastly, thanks to all the seagulls who followed
me from port to port and never stopped buoying me up!

When you come to the edge of all the light you have known,
and are about to step out into darkness,
faith is knowing one of two things will happen:
there will be something to stand on, or you will be taught to fly.

— *Richard Bach,*
Jonathan Livingston Seagull

Contents

Chapter One

Decisions, Decisions...How I Hate to Make Them!

Here Comes the Sun was playing in my head as I watched Apollo glide his golden surfboard down the Moss Landing Harbor channel on the last wave of the afternoon high tide. Jonathan Livingston then swooped in and perched atop the tallest mast in the harbor.

"Hey, there," he whispered down to me. "The gossip du jour around the docks this morning was about some 43-year old gal who bought a 35-foot sailboat and she doesn't even know how to sail. They say she's crazy. I think she must be kinda cool, but heck...what does an old seagull know."

Having just taken possession of the boat he was perched on, I whispered back, "Normally, I wouldn't give a damn what those Salinas cowboy sailors think. But at this moment, I might tend to agree with them. Ever since I almost drowned as a kid out there in the Big Blue, I've been scared of that powerful ocean and I'm sure not ready now to end up in Davy Jones' locker. I'm going to take things easy: one step, one day at a time."

Jonathan Livingston winked at me, nodding in agreement. "Whatever happens," I announced to him and the Universe, "I'd rather the last half of my life be an exhilarating Adventure with a capital 'A'. No more monogrammed designer duds, tailored skirts and cashmere sweaters for me. Goodbye to vapid dinner-party chatter and that boring suburb of Philadelphia. Poseidon, here I come!"

I never dreamed personal freedom and growth meant I'd end up alone on a sailboat in Monterey Bay, and more terrifying, maybe someday even far out beyond the safety of the harbor.

Circumstances that would change my life often appeared on the horizon without warning. Occasionally, I was the moth being obsessively drawn to the flickering flame which would eventually destroy her; other times, the butterfly taking wing towards a fragrant but deadly blossom. And sometimes, just a fat and sassy frog sitting on a lily pad, soaking up rays waiting for her next adventure. A few months before arriving in California, I began to suspect the Universe, hiding behind a silken veil, and without my knowledge, request or even consent, was creating a divine plan for me. How dare it!

After 16 years of juggling motherhood, marriage, charity do-goodery and a successful journalism career, I faced a decision to either continue unhappy, sinking beneath the surface of those roles I was playing, or to give notice to some or all of them. Who could have imagined I'd even consider leaving life as a full-time mother and wife, walking away from a gorgeous home in the suburbs, and giving up everything a woman could possibly ever want. It would be *adios* to summers at our beach cottage, *au revoir* to winters in exotic destinations; goodbye to esteemed positions on various charity boards, and farewell to a so-called glamorous social life. It might even mean the end to a career where I had worked my way up from obituaries and cub reporter to night editor of three suburban Philly newspapers. Who'd have guessed I'd be grabbing my well-worn beloved beatnik threads stashed too long in the attic, my world-travelled collection of French perfumes (some already turning to alcohol) that I had carried with me through years of prior adventures, my favorite coffee mug, and be escaping to downtown Philly.

"You're crazy," said my suburban friends. "It's too dangerous down there…you'll be murdered in a week…or worse! And besides, what will people say?"

The fears of those gossipmongers weren't going to scare me, nor would their rumor-spreading insinuations! I had a new-found faith that things would be fine if I left even though all I had to my name was $600, the total of my last newspaper paycheck. Already, $300 of this was ear-marked for the first-month rent on the tiny third-floor apartment I'd just found downtown by magic. The realtor had said on the phone that the apartment was right next to what I understood as "Fiddler Square". Wow, a sign! How perfect! A fascinating fiddler will be lurking somewhere nearby to entertain me in the moonlight. When I finally was ready to move in, I discovered it was really, "Fitler" Square. Oh, well…at least the neighborhood sounded elegant in spite of the austere grimness of the apartment.

The somewhat autobiographical farewell feature story I handed in to the editor the day I quit I had entitled, "Her Skid Row Was A Beautiful Tree-lined Street In The Suburbs." Maybe it would help other women who were stuck in that same suburban dead-end.

I thought to give everything up would be the toughest decision I'd ever have to make. I didn't know then that not too long later, there would be many even more difficult ones. What I did know, however, was that I was tired of having all aspects of my life controlled and manipulated by a husband who wouldn't even put my name on our bank accounts, who made me feel less than that one-legged water-bug scurrying across the damp basement floor.

For the six years before we had children, I helped him run the real estate business he had taken over when his father retired. I worked long hours every day in the office, doing bookkeeping, managing over 200 rental properties of our many owner-clients, handling the advertising, answering phones, charming clients, reminding him of all the things he had forgotten to do on his side of the desk…and never got a penny. It was humiliating having to almost beg him for money just to buy Kotex. I couldn't figure out how my life had taken such a radical downward spin. Things just sort of crept up on me like that homeless black cat stalking its prey in the dark shadows of the old weed over-grown cemetery I had grown up behind so long ago where the Grateful Dead's Jerry Garcia would later be buried. But I did know it was time to muster the courage to do something really frightening…leave everything behind and simply walk out.

No more coming home from interviewing someone for a feature story or from covering a Municipal meeting to find an open bottle of his Canadian Club sitting on the coffee table, a half-empty bottle of wine in the fridge, or a martini pitcher still half-filled with ice sitting in the dining room. No more listening to the chink of ice cubes being put in a whiskey glass at 5:30 p. m. when he arrived home, announcing it was cocktail time. I was almost one-year sober, still hanging on to my recovery program for dear life, and I was not going to let any of his subterfuge lure me back to that damned bottle!

I met the children's father on the Canary Islands. That year, I was attending L'Université de Grenoble, situated conveniently at the foot of the French Alps. I didn't choose the Sorbonne because I knew it would be crowded with American students and I was determined to learn French well enough to speak it like a native. I also wanted to spend spare time skiing the Alps. It was Europe's worst winter on record and people were dying in the streets. Almost daily, old folks were found curled up and frozen to death in the dark corners of stairwells. No trucks, boats or barges came into or left Grenoble as all roads, rivers and canals were frozen over most of that winter. Fuel for heating stoves was seldom available and if at all, at exorbitant black market prices. I'd walk for hours through the slippery streets of Grenoble, carrying a five-gallon can, searching, begging for stove oil, often, after dark, returning, empty-canned, to my tiny dreary freezing apartment. I finally gave up hunting and just stayed under the blankets, shivering in my bed when I didn't have classes.

To find the nearest warm spot for Christmas break from classes, I hitchhiked down to Barcelona and asked a travel agent where the closest place was to swim in the ocean. His answer? The Canary Islands. I had no clue where they were but went to the shipping lines office to get a ticket on the next banana boat headed there. I stood in a long line and at the ticket counter was told the boat was sold out. I went three mornings in a row, always to be told, "Sold out." As time was passing, I gave in and returned to the travel agent who said if I paid him in advance for the roundtrip tickets and for the two weeks I'd be staying in a hotel, plus meals, he'd get me a roundtrip ticket. Yeah, sure, I thought, but agreed and said I would have the money in the morning. He quoted the two second-class boat tickets the same as the shipping company's price; the mid-range hotel with meals would be $20/day. It would be taking all I had, leaving me just $25, but it would be worth not having to worry about finding a place to stay and places to eat. The next morning, the agent handed me the one-way ticket for the next boat leaving that afternoon. He said his agent would meet me at the dock in Las Palmas with the return ticket and lead me to my hotel. At 5:00 p. m., I was on a small banana boat headed to Las Palmas de Gran Canarias.

When I came aboard, a crew member led me to a dark and dingy little one-cot room down in the bilge area next to the engine. It was one half-step below steerage accommodations under deck in an area reserved for cargo. I immediately went back upstairs to the Purser's office.

"I paid the Barcelona travel agent for second-class accommodations," I said to the man behind the desk. "I've been given something worse than steerage class. I want to be shown this very instant to a better cabin and at least, a second-class one."

He smiled, put a "closed" sign on his door, and took me to a first-class cabin which was much larger, had a sink in the corner and a porthole I could open for fresh air.

"No extra fee, Missy," he said with the kind of smile that hinted of future "business".

I got the feeling it would be wise to lock my door tightly every night as I was not about to be exchanging favors with this guy or any other he might try to foist on me.

The Canary Islands, also known informally as *the Canaries*, are a Spanish archipelago and the southernmost autonomous community of Spain in a region known as Macaronesia. Comprised of eight main islands and many smaller islands and islets, the Canaries are 62 miles west of Morocco at the closest point. Gran Canaria, my destination and one of the larger islands is, as the seagull flies, 1,392 miles from Barcelona. As I always used to say when asked where the heck the Canaries were, "Head out of the Med, hang a soft left into the Atlantic and they're the first sandy beaches you come to."

We'd be making several short stops to drop off or pick up cargo or passengers along Spain's *Costa del Sol* including at Cartagena, Malaga, then past Gibraltar, and the last stop before arriving at the Canaries would be Cadiz. I would have a short time to explore all these places I had been reading about ever since I was a kid. I was always (and still am) enthralled with stories about the Spanish Empire, one of the most powerful empires of the 16th and 17th centuries and known as, "The empire on which the sun never sets." My destination was the main stopover in those days for Spanish galleons on their way to the Americas as they came south to catch the prevailing north-easterly trade winds. Wow! Maybe someday, I'll be sailing the High Seas in search of those very same trade winds!

Once the cabin issue was settled, I put on a big pair of dark glasses, my most alluring smile, and went up to the highest deck to watch the boat pulling away from Barcelona. Next, I strolled up to the bridge to introduce myself to the Captain.

"Sir, my name is Sandra Smith and I will be travelling alone on your fine ship to Las Palmas on Gran Canaria. I will greatly appreciate your kindness and consideration in making sure, as a single woman, I will safely enjoy the experience."

"Mademoiselle, avec plaisir," he replied, apparently thinking I was French. "May I invite you to join me at my table for dinner this evening, and perhaps, even the next?" Naturally, I accepted and then took off wandering around the boat as I now had full access to all areas as a first-class passenger.

In the main lounge, I met the other passengers…all five of them. Brad was an American about 50 who had been head of the USDA in Panama until he came home and found his wife in bed with his best buddy. He quit the job, contacted an uncle who captained a large steamer to the South Pacific, got a one-way ticket, bought a unicycle and sailed off. Once he arrived in French Polynesia, he somehow acquired a pet chimpanzee and proceeded to cover as much of the area he could on his unicycle with the chimp on his shoulder. Brad eventually ended up in Barcelona (*sans* chimpanzee) teaching English at Berlitz. When soon bored with that, he palled up with another teacher, David, an Irish fellow about 30 who left his career as an accountant in Dublin to see the world. They both quit teaching, then went down to the Barcelona docks to look for work, claiming Brad was a famous chef from New York City and David, Ireland's most celebrated sous-chef. Both got jobs on the luxurious yacht owned by Bảo Đại, the 13th and final emperor of the Nguyễn dynasty, last ruling family of Vietnam, who cruised around the Mediterranean on his private *yacht*, one of the largest ever docked in the Monte Carlo harbor. Less than a week later, they were fired as neither even knew how to boil water. Onto the banana boat, they hopped. The chimp and unicycle were long gone and now, Brad's prized single possession was an antique short-wave radio he took with him everywhere to keep up with world news.

Sitting at the bar next to David and Brad (whom I would dub, "Uncle Brad") was Pim, a fellow my age from Amsterdam who had gotten his girlfriend pregnant and decided to get outta Dodge pronto. The fourth passenger was Richard, an American, slightly older than me, who had just been discharged from a two-year stint with the U. S. Navy's Sixth Fleet. He had up to a year to take advantage of the free return passage back to the United States and decided to see more of the world before going back to reality. The fifth passenger was Mrs. E. P. Brown, a 72-year old Scottish lady from "Sunning Hill" somewhere in the Berkshires, who was well-traveled, well-preserved, pleasant and rather reserved.

We all enjoyed sharing stories during the voyage at sea and when docked at the various ports of call, each went off separately to explore. I found it amusing when we passed Gibraltar with the British ashore frantically flashing signals for our Captain to identify his vessel he just stood on deck with his arm around me, laughing.

"I never respond to those damned British," he said, downing a triumphant gulp of Spain's most elegant brandy, *Carlos Primero*. The flashing continued until we were around the corner and out of sight.

When I wasn't dining at the Captain's table and being toasted with *Dom Pérignon* Champagne, I had meals with the other passengers. They asked where I was staying in Las Palmas and I told them about my experience with the travel agent. They started taking bets against anyone showing up at the Las Palmas dock to give me a return ticket and lead me to a hotel as promised by the travel agent.

They were wrong – a respectable man did show up an hour after we arrived and said to me, in perfect English, "I am here out of courtesy to tell you I received a cable from some Barcelona travel agent to get you a return boat ticket and a second-class hotel with meals for $10 a night and of course, I couldn't get anything for that cheap amount. He wired barely enough to even cover the boat ticket. I did not accept the wired money and sent it all back with a reply that I would not be able to assist. I'm so sorry and best of luck." Off, he walked.

When our "little family" (a name we had taken on halfway to Las Palmas) heard this, Mrs. Brown surprised me by saying I could sleep as her guest in the spare bed in the room she had reserved at a *pensione*. The boys, as I called them, said I could eat meals with them. They found a room for all four at a down-market place above a bar where Uncle Brad proudly set up his radio and invited us all to be there every night at 5:00 p. m. for the nightly world news.

Other than the four daring Swedes and two bold Germans we kept running into, tourism had not yet discovered the Canaries and Las Palmas. There was only one hotel and two places to eat dinner downtown – one, a Chinese hole-in-the-wall and the other, an overpriced once-but-no-longer-elegant cavernous dining room in The Santa Catalina Hotel which was built in 1892 and last refurbished in 1923. I later learned that after many renovations and restorations, it became known as, "The Royals Hideaway Hotel" because of the stellar list of famous celebrities and royalty who stay there. When I was in Las Palmas, it was just another dilapidated and outmoded has-been hotel that never seemed open. For budgetary restrictions, our "family" chose to eat at the Chinese restaurant which was nothing more than many mismatched tables jammed together, often unwiped, with remnants of the previous diner's meal, and one greasy menu tossed on a table no matter how many diners were seated at it.

That first night, we all met at 5:00 p. m. at the boys' place, listened to the radio for an hour and then decided we should all throw what we could afford into a common kitty for meals, liquid libations and other communal needs. Mrs. Brown chipped in a little, saying she wouldn't always be joining us for meals.

After a few measly Chinese dinners--we didn't even get fortune cookies!--I'd become fed up with picking bugs out of the salad included with the entrée. The noisy place was full to capacity when I stood up and said as loud as I could, to be heard by all, "Do we have to pay extra for all these wiggling bugs in the salad?" Everyone laughed except the owner who kicked us out and said we couldn't come back. This was a bit upsetting since it was the cheapest place in town and now, if such even existed, we'd have to find another cheap place to have dinners.

We assigned "family" tasks: at night, the boys would take turns walking me the seven blocks over to the ritzier side of town where Mrs. Brown stayed; my daily task was to go to the public market place before our Radio Hour to pick up the nightly bottle of Johnnie Walker Black label because, using feminine wiles, I was able to get it for a lot less than any of them. As our "Elder", we let Mrs. Brown off the task hook.

The third morning in Las Palmas, I went to the Office of Tourism to ask for help about being swindled. The Director took a personal interest. Every morning, he had me stop at his office and then he'd drive me proudly around the banana plantations in his 1954 Chevrolet while we discussed what to do about my situation. He cabled the agent daily and after 10 days was able to get half my money back, most of which I promptly added to the family's kitty. I hated the idea of acting like the typical American student calling home collect for money even though I knew my father wouldn't have flinched at wiring whatever I needed. I just couldn't make the phone call, and hoped the Tourism Director would soon be able to get back the rest of my money so I could buy my return ticket to Barcelona. With each passing day, the cables he sent included stronger demands until finally, he was threatening to have the agent's license revoked.

When they left Barcelona, Uncle Brad thought he and David could set up a beach chair and sun umbrella rental business on the main beach in Las Palmas. They were disappointed to discover there were no tourists and no need for beach chairs. Our kitty was getting very hungry, so the next afternoon, the boys drew straws to see who had to shave off his beard, put on a clean shirt and long pants, and go with the rest of us by bus to the end of the island where we heard the U. S. had a satellite tracking station and might be hiring. Richard lost. I was elected to buy a used unclaimed starched long-sleeved white shirt from the Chinese laundry. When we got down to the far end of the island, Richard was told all hiring was done in the States. This gave us an excuse to hop on a bus back to Las Palmas to celebrate that none of us had to give up our uncomplicated lifestyle to go to work.

Next idea was to find a rich American whom we could charm (lure?) into joining our family and who would then be expected to toss some pesetas into our kitty. Where to find such a fellow? At the American Express office where American travelers always go to pick up forwarded mail and complain about stolen passports. David and Pim were elected to make the trip to American Express while Uncle Brad, Rich and I would sit on the beach, each nursing a fancy rum-fruit drink with a cute tiny umbrella stuck in a pineapple slice--we could only afford one each and had to sip slowly, acting as if we had all the time and money in the world

8

After about an hour, Uncle Brad nudged me. I looked up and strolling towards us with David and Pim was a handsome young fellow, either American or Scandinavian. We invited the three of them to sit down and enjoy a drink with us. When he said his name was "John Smith", I said, "Yeah, and I'm Pocahontas."

The newcomer told us he had finished a two-year job assignment in Germany when the Berlin Wall was going up, and then he launched into some stories of his adventures during his job there and what he had been doing since his assignment ended. I felt like we were listening to a spy-thriller on Uncle Brad's radio. One story I'll never forget was about how, before his job commitment was finished, he met a beautiful blonde at a tennis match in Vienna. She was visiting from South Africa. The next day, Smith went to the library to bone up on her homeland before their date that night. First phrase he saw in a book he pulled off the shelf was, "The darkest thing of Africa is our ignorance of it."

He decided when his job assignment was complete, he would know Africa, and the next day, began to teach himself Swahili. Once his job was finished in Germany, he spent the next two years walking alone from Cairo to Cape Town. This adventure included a dangerous trip down the flooding Nile with soldiers butting natives off the boat with rifles as they tried to climb aboard to escape the floods, a climb up and over Kilimanjaro without a guide because the guides all said the weather made it too dangerous (in those days, climbers were allowed to go up the mountain without a guide), and learning to eat locally baked goodies filled with ants and who knows what other vermin.

My favorite story was when he described coming across a woman lying in his path, alone on a dusty road in East Africa. The half-dead young Masai was trying to escape her husband. Our storyteller said he offered her water from his canteen and learned that according to tradition, if she could get back to her father's land before dark, her father wouldn't have to return the dowry the husband had paid for her (a combination of cattle, goats, cash, blankets and honey). If she didn't make it home before dark, her husband could keep it all, force her back to him, and make her life unbearable. John Smith said he carried her over his shoulder for many hours. Just as the sun was setting, they arrived at the lands of her father who turned out to be chief of the Masai. John was greeted as a hero, carried around on the shoulders of tribesmen most of the night during a wild celebration. He had to sneak away in the dark as he feared for his safety, not from brutal harm but from too much non-shamanic revelry most likely induced with the help of psychoactive plants and mushrooms like *iboga* (*Tabernanthe iboga*). After reaching South Africa (which he claimed was the most beautiful place he had ever seen), he visited the woman he met in Vienna as guest at her wealthy family's enormous estate. In less than a week, her father suggested John might like to move there and become involved in the family's business. Time to leave. He continued walking up the west coast of Africa to Morocco where he caught a small boat over to the Canaries. I was impressed with all his tales.

We invited him to our Radio and Whiskey Hour and explained about our "family". If he wished to join, he could toss some money into our family kitty. He accepted our invitation, admitting he'd spent far too much time alone in the past two years. The boys then explained since he was the newest member of the family, it would be his duty to walk me to Mrs. Brown's *pensione* each evening. We all went out to dinner together and afterwards, John and I left the others. While strolling through town, he wanted to hit every bar, one after another. Didn't take long before he was totally sloshed. A few blocks from Mrs. Brown's, we were held up by a group of thugs. I clutched my purse to my chest for they sure were not going to get anything from me! Even though he could hardly stand up, John kept shouting that he'd beat them all up. In less than five minutes, they took off running, all in different directions, with more popping out of each darkened doorway they passed. We discovered they had gotten his wallet and all his money. We spent three hours at the local police station where the only thing the Chief wanted to do was find out where I was staying so he could visit me later. Forget that! As it was very late, we went to John's hotel not far from the police station. Before passing out, he politely said I could sleep in the spare bed while he used the other one. I was quite surprised and pleased that he hadn't tried to creep into my bed or make inappropriate advances…maybe he was just too drunk. I stayed with him in his hotel room for the rest of our time together and he continued to be the perfect gentleman. This was certainly a change from the many other men I had come in contact with while living and traveling abroad alone. I had soon become adept at discouraging them. One uninvited amorous advance from a man and I'd flick him away like an unwanted fly in my soup. It was heart-warming to learn that this John Smith was different from all the rest. I instantly respected him and later thought it was probably why I fell in love with him.

The next day, when we went to Radio and Whiskey Hour, I told the family what happened. Uncle Brad's only comment was, "Great! Now we have yet another mouth to feed!"

John and I called our parents in the morning and picked up the wired money the next afternoon at the American Express office. I stopped at the Tourism Center, but no more money had come from Barcelona. The Director helped make a reservation for me on the first banana boat back to Barcelona.

John and I spent the week together, and one morning over breakfast, he said, "I have a surprise for you. If you like, I can come with you back to France and I've made a reservation on your same boat. I can cancel it if you don't like the idea."

I was amazed and thrilled. Two days later, waiting at the dock to board, he admitted he had been kidding about returning with me. Oh, well…it had been a fun idea while it lasted. To hug without the crew watching, we went and hid behind a tall stack of empty banana crates and stood there holding each other, chatting, kissing and sipping from the glasses of bubbly he managed to produce. I had no idea how much time passed when someone started pelting me with bananas. I looked past the crates and saw my boat all loaded, starting to pull away from the dock. One of the deckhands noticed me still on the pier and had been trying to get my attention. The crew on deck swung the on-board crane over the side and lowered its now empty cargo platform. Even though I was wearing a dress, I jumped up high enough to sit on it lady-like, legs crossed, a glass of Champagne in one hand, cigarette in the other, calling out "Ta-ta" à la Auntie Mame. What a fitting farewell to someone I thought I'd never see again, and off I sailed. John took a flight to Barcelona and on to his hometown outside Philadelphia where he went back to finish college.

On board, it was the same Captain, but no friendly "family"…I was the only passenger. First thing I did was write a note on the ship's stationery to John's mother, saying I had spent some time with her son and she should be very proud of him as he had beautiful manners and was a perfect gentleman. I knew when I secretly copied the address from his luggage tag that first night after we left the police station and John was passed out that it might later somehow come in handy. As soon as I got off the boat, I posted the note and then went directly to that swindling travel agent's. I wasn't about to let that bugger get away with stealing from me and managed to get all but $10 of my money back. I then caught a train to Grenoble to finish at the university. John and I wrote weekly, sometimes even daily. It was a beautiful literary romance and with each of his letters, I learned more about him and began to find out what a brilliant and seemingly caring man he was.

After I finished my degree at Grenoble, I moved south to Aix-en-Provence where I rented an 19th-century villa about 10 miles out of town with no running water, no electricity, but a fireplace in every room and 10 acres of beautiful vineyards and orchards with every fruit tree represented. First project was to buy a very long length of hose to run from the farmer's irrigation ditch up to the villa's kitchen for water. Next, was to talk the old lady owner into putting in a toilet. Once a week, I walked or bummed a ride with the villa property's farmer into town for groceries and the weekly supply of candles and Clorox tablets to purify the water. For the walk back home, I soon managed to balance a basket full of goodies on my head with a filled basket on each of my arms. I learned to cook on the villa's original wood-burning stove/oven dating back to the 1800s. It was a major accomplishment to celebrate when I used lovely ripe apples from one of my trees to create a luscious apple pie in that challenging oven! When the vineyard's vines were sprouting in springtime, I'd choose a certain plant to check out almost daily for the optimum time to pick its gorgeous leaves to make the stuffed dolmades I had learned to love when travelling in Greece. The villa sat atop a little hill with the vineyards and orchards below. Another delight was picking wild asparagus from the field right below the villa. Life in the villa was idyllic. As it was so remote with no road leading up to it, I eventually gave up wearing clothes as I didn't have to worry about anyone coming near and also, didn't want to have to waste precious water for laundering. Mornings, I'd get up, go collect a variety of wildflowers, create a pretty long necklace to wear around my neck, and that was my dress for the day. One morning, I awoke to the disturbing sound of men's voices coming from my field below the villa. I went to the edge to look below and there were three men stealing my wild asparagus. At the top of my lungs in exquisitely perfect French "street" slang, I shouted at them to get the hell off my property. I guess seeing a nude woman standing on the hill shouting like that put the fear of death in them. They ran off like scared rabbits, never to return, and leaving behind their bags of MY asparagus which I made into a delicious soup that served as my supper all week.

When I wasn't collecting flowers or fruit, cooking or baking, or chopping wood for the fireplaces, I would spend days studying all the French classics in a variety of genres, by authors like Balzac, Flaubert, Proust, Camus, Sartre, Moliere, Maupassant, Genet and Colette. I created my own French-English dictionary to include every word I came to that I didn't previously know. It was a true masterpiece of information as not only did I include a short definition, I also used the new word in a sentence and then at the end of the week, created a short essay using all my new words learned that week. Once, I sent a letter with accompanying short essay to my uncle in Germany who spoke French. He showed my letter to a friend who taught French at Heidelberg University and the guy couldn't believe it was written by a foreigner, let alone a young American "girl".

I had told my parents I moved to Aix to study French literature which implied I was enrolling at the University in Aix. I didn't feel guilty that I wasn't attending classes because I was spending a lot more time reading French literature and studying that beautiful language than I would ever have had to do if attending classes.

My mother eventually figured it out and said, "Whatever happens, don't you dare let your father know you weren't in class!"

Before blowing out all the candles and making sure the fires were safely dampened for the night, I'd sit and write a letter to John...sometimes daily, other times, weekly. It was the beginning of a true literary romance and who knew how long it would last or when it might end.

Chapter Two

Good Grief! Marriage? Babies? A New Career?

Soon the scholastic year ended and I knew it was time to say *au revoir* to the villa and the magical life I had enjoyed there. I took the train to London to pick up the 1964 MGB my dad had ordered for me. It was his gift to congratulate me for having had the courage to demand University officials to permit me to switch out of Grenoble University's "School For Foreign Students" (which was filled with mostly Americans who kept speaking English!) and into the main University with all French and European students, and then for completing my Master's Degree there.

Mother came to meet me in London and we spent the summer driving around Europe so I could show her all my past haunts. It was the first and only fun time I ever had with my mother. I remember one day that summer driving through a small French village with the top down when it began to rain. I told her I didn't want to bother stopping to put the top up as we didn't have time and I would get too wet in the process. We could just open our two umbrellas and keep driving as the view would be better anyway with the top down. Villagers smiled as we passed by, waving at them. At summer's end, I dropped her off at Heathrow Airport in London and two nights later, the phone rang in my Bloomsbury hotel room. It was 3:00 a. m. and John was inviting me to visit him in Philadelphia. Not having anything else yet planned, I booked passage for me and my car and in a month, arrived in Philadelphia to be a temporary guest at his parents' home. His mother never mentioned getting my note from Barcelona.

Didn't take long before I got a job teaching French at Buckingham Friends School, an independent Quaker school founded in 1794 and located in beautiful Bucks County, a county filled with writers, artists and other roving sojourners. When I left John's parents' home, just 21 miles away, I discovered the village of Solebury, not far from the Friends School and rented a converted barn complete with roommate…a resident white horse. Mister Ed's quarters took up about a quarter of the barn and he kept me awake all night, scratching his back on our shared walls. But I loved him, and anytime I had a party, every arriving guest was required to ride him once around the little fenced pasture. After all, horses needed exercise and loving, too.

Just a few miles down the road from Solebury was New Hope, where the creative types congregated. They soon developed a habit of showing up at my door before noon with a pitcher of chilled martinis. I fit right in with the lifestyle. After living in France for several years, I had acquired a strong passion for French wine which gradually became more than just a mere passing fancy for other such libations. Pearl S. Buck (author of The Good Earth which earned her a Pulitzer Prize, and who was the first female American Nobel laureate) owned a farm in the county and James Michener, who had been raised in Doylestown (a museum there still bears his name) returned to a farm in Bucks County to work on several books. Oher notables who lived there at one time or another included Margaret Mead, Oscar Hammerstein II, Stephen Sondheim, Charlie Parker, Moss Hart, and George S Kaufman. Paul Simon of Simon and Garfunkel and Julia Child also lived in Bucks County while I was there. It provided a very interesting and offbeat place to live which helped me return to this new life in America.

A year later, John and I were married. I'll never forget the moment when the minister finished the ceremony. I let out a piercing wail and started to cry. I was sure everyone thought I was just a nervous bride. Actually, when the minister pronounced us man and wife, I heard a loud voice in my head shout, "Oh, my God…you've just made the worst mistake of your life."

It was a one of those "Hell one day, Heaven the next" marriages. The first month he moved into the barn with me, but soon, the commute for him was too tiresome. The next few years, we lived downtown in Philadelphia's German neighborhood where I helped my new husband with the business he took over from his father. We bought a little two-story historic brick row home around the corner from the office to avoid a commute, ate almost all dinners out, and on weekends, didn't get up until noon. After six years, planned almost down to his exact birth date, our son, Ian, was born. I stopped working to become a full-time mother.

I hadn't wanted a second child – the first one, sweet as he was, often gave me panic attacks as I attempted to be the perfect mother. My husband had other ideas – he was an only child and didn't want the same lonesome childhood for his son. One night, he plied me with wine and without telling me he wasn't using the usual protection, I got pregnant and our daughter, Sandi, was born sixteen months after Ian. I felt betrayed.

When Ian was six months old, we bought a beautiful Dutch Colonial home in the suburbs. It had been built and owned by the CEO of the Reading Railroad that passed not far from the house and was the main commuter train between Philadelphia and New York. My husband had grown up in that town where his parents still lived two blocks from our new home. He bragged that when he was in high school, the girls had a fan club named after him. He also confessed that as a kid, when his mother had a list of his Saturday chores taped to the fridge and boyfriends arrived to play, he'd tell them they had to do the chores on the list before he could get out of bed and join them. And they did the chores…while he lay upstairs in bed. That was the day I finally pulled the curtain away and realized I was living with a control freak who was using me like he used his childhood friends. I couldn't imagine how I had fallen into such a trap after being so independent in my teens, travelling all over Western and Eastern Europe and Greece alone, then living by myself in France for two years. What was going on, anyway? Well, another little drink might make all this go away…. at least for tonight, I'd say to myself, pouring a nightcap before creeping into bed where I hoped he was already asleep.

When the children were old enough for school, I had time to take a night-school class, "Writing For Publication". First assignment was to write a sample query letter to an editor. I did so and on a whim, sent it off to the local newspaper editor. The next day, the editor phoned.

"I love your feature story idea and we can use it. In the meantime, I need a reporter to cover the editor of a well-known women's magazine coming from New York to our local furniture store. She's going to do a presentation on how to decorate children's rooms. Can you be there tomorrow at 5:00 p. m.? The presentation begins at 6:00 p. m. and you'll need to interview her beforehand."

"No problem," I replied and raced to the library to look up "How To Interview", "How To Write A Feature Story", and anything else close to the subject. I bought a steno-pad, stayed up half the night reading about feature-writing, and the next night, was at the furniture store by 5:00 p. m. The presenter was polished and professional. I sat down with her and began asking questions I had prepared earlier, making notes in my pad as fast as I could because I could no longer remember any high school shorthand.

When we finished and she was getting up to begin her talk, I thanked her and said, "This is very exciting for me. You're the first person I've ever interviewed."

She looked appalled and in a stilted voice said, "You mean they sent a cub reporter to cover *me*?" I was stunned and didn't know what to say, so I just smiled as she walked over to the podium.

When I got home, I sat on the kitchen floor cutting up all my notes into various categories, creating nine piles on different topics including a pile for kids' favorite colors; a pile for types of furniture best for children of specified ages; a pile for items needed in a baby's room; a pile for any other subject that came up in my notes. I carried the piles to my desk in the solarium followed by a large mug of black coffee, a glass of bourbon without ice, and my pack of Marlboros. I sat with my hands resting on the keyboard and within minutes, the keys seemed to move on their own as words began to appear on the page. It took me all night to go through all the piles and complete the story which I turned in the next morning. Including a small photo of the presenter which she had supplied, the feature took up almost two full pages in the lifestyle/women's section. About a month later, a letter came to me at the newspaper from that presenter: "Congratulations! Terrific job! Come see me when you get to New York."

Thus began my successful sixteen-year career as a journalist. I loved my work and feature stories I came up with were published every week. I especially liked finding someone out there in the community who was somewhat ignored by others but who had a hidden talent. My feature story would turn the person into a local hero or heroine. One such person, a piano tuner, would prove to be a real help to me in the not too distant future. Next, the editor was sending me out to cover various meetings for three different municipalities besides the one in which we lived. City council and county board of supervisor meetings, school board meetings, zoning hearings, planning commissions, arts councils--you name it, I covered it.

When my new career started to take off, I made my kids a promise: "Mommy will always be home for dinner." I managed what would soon become an insane schedule without ever missing a single dinner at home with them. I also promised we would always have our Wednesday afternoon "farm adventures" to the farms I had come to love in Bucks County while living there. We had our favorite egg farm where the children loved holding up a tiny pullet egg to the farm lady's candle to see if it was yolkless. She explained on our first visit that a young pullet hen's first egg is usually without a yolk and is called a "fart egg". Ian and Sandi loved that name and giggled the whole time they were holding up eggs. Next, we bought our ham, bacon, scrapple and other pork products from a farm a few miles farther along the road, our chicken from another around the bend, and apples at yet another where we also picked up a gallon of scrumptious apple cider in the fall. I let the kids each pick out one of our luscious apples to feed the farmer's horse as we were leaving. I'm sure the horses recognized our little car when we turned into the drive as one was always waiting for us at the fence as we left. They must have figured out a way to take turns for our apples. No matter how crazy my schedule was, the three of us never missed a weekly summer farm outing. After I tucked the kids into bed Wednesdays, I'd be up half the night writing to meet the next day's deadline.

Two years into all this excitement, I took up photography. The uncreative boring photos the newspaper put with my features, I believed, detracted from my stories as they were usually taken by a tired old grumpy guy slumped from the weight of too many cameras. I took out of hiding the pay-check money I had been squirreling away those two years and drove up to NYC to the avenue where, one after another, all the camera and photo equipment stores were located.

"Let me see the best enlarger you have and all the necessary equipment I'll need to set up a darkroom, and then please help me open an account," I said to the clerk.

Before the end of the week, the fanciest biggest Besler arrived with all the "trimmings". When I skimmed through the enlarger's thick manual, I learned I could even create life-size posters! It took me a week to set up the darkroom in the basement before I could even begin teaching myself how to use the equipment. After I'd complete a feature ready to deliver, I'd then go down to the basement and try to create a masterpiece photo to accompany the story. By the time the sun was coming up, there would be a huge pile of rejects on the floor and one fabulous photo ready to go. After about a year of this, there'd be three or four acceptable photos to choose from out of a roll of 36. Soon, I was being sent all over to take photos, even to all the high school ball games…a totally different type of photo gig. Half the time I didn't know what the heck was going on out there on the field or court, but I managed to please the editor with my photos. Not much time passed before "award-winning photo-journalist" was added to my resume.

Next, the editor assigned me the toughest police beat surrounding Philadelphia. Within a week of my first assignment about a warehouse full of illegally-imported exotic birds and animals, the cops were calling me at home from payphones, sharing inside info about their cases. I felt like I was starring in one of Orson Welles' film noir. Of course, I always managed to make sure a photo of the latest "wanted" person appeared on at least the first or second page of the paper.

By now, I was grateful for the good babysitter I had for times my new career conflicted with the home-front schedule. She lived three doors down the street from our house, and as a teenager and the oldest of ten, she was thrilled to get away from babysitting all her siblings without being paid. I still never missed dinner with the children or any of our Wednesday farm adventures in the summers or holidays when they were off school.

The routine of daily drinking snuck up on me. It didn't take long before there was wine with lunch, a glass or two of wine while making dinner, a cocktail before dinner, wine with dinner, brandy after dinner. It just seemed normal…it was what everyone did, wasn't it? Because of my Scottish ties from my mother, I was a member (and the youngest by about 30 years) of the Daughters of the British Empire and those polite elderly ladies seemed to drink sherry any time of the day. Soon, sherry at 11:00 a. m. was added to my drinking repertoire. If it was proper for those well-mannered old DBE ladies, surely it would be proper for me, right?

Chapter Three

Starting To Slide Downhill

The children were six and seven when I moved out of the connubial bedroom and into the guest room in our suburban house. Six months later, the need for an even more drastic change became obvious.

"I'm going to spend this summer with the children at the shore … without you," I told their father. "I need some time to think and meditate and the beach cottage will be perfect."

I had always been happy by the ocean and knew I'd be even happier there that summer…our village of Strathmere on the New Jersey seashore was more than 90 miles away from him.

He didn't even flinch at the news. Well, he'd been "working late" for months and sometimes, didn't even show up until the next day. We hardly spoke to each other. Dinner conversations around our elegant dining room table were going something like this:

"Ian, ask your father if he wants dessert."

"Daddy, Mommy wants to know if you want dessert."

"Tell her I don't want any."

"He doesn't want any, Mommy."

The day before deciding to spend summer in Strathmere, with nerves a-frazzle, I was screeching at Ian about something. Sandi, a year younger than Ian, tugging at my skirt to distract me, said in her innocent little squeaky voice, "Mommy, you look so pretty." It was a scene I'll never forget…a scene my recovery friends would later tell me to keep "green" and permanently etch in the front of my mind so I could recall it anytime I might consider picking up a drink. Friends said it was always the first drink that would get me drunk. Took a little time to figure that one out…one drink would lead to polishing off the bottle.

I stopped yelling at Ian and felt for the umpteenth time, devastated and ashamed. Trying to be the loving mother mine was always too busy to be, how could I be treating my wee boy like this? What was wrong with me? Was I going mad? I added weekly visits to a psychiatrist who didn't help by trying to tell me I hated my father. How ridiculous! I stopped seeing the psychiatrist.

In May, I gave notice to the editor that I needed to take the summer off for "health reasons". It would be three glorious months of just me and the kids making sandcastles and cookies all day. I would read bed-time stories to them, teach them card games, take them for shell-seeking strolls along the beach. Friday nights, we'd go to the drive-in movies with the top down on the car, with big bags of popcorn and them in their jammies, snuggled up in blankets. It was going to be the best summer ever. I'd make up for all the times I had been too busy writing headline stories, developing photos, and not there 100% for them. Counting each day until school was out kept me going those few weeks before we could escape.

On the last day of school, I had my MGB packed with what the three of us would need for our Grand Escape. I put the top down, the children climbed in, and off we roared, singing *"Puff The Magic Dragon"* at the top of our lungs. Two hours later, we had just arrived at the shore house and unpacked the car when their father called. He had changed his mind. The children were going to camp in Maine for the summer.

"But you agreed last month that it would be OK for them to….," I stammered, not believing what I was hearing.

"That was then. This is now. It is not OK. If you don't let them go to Maine, I'm going to make your life so miserable you'll wish you never met me."

"Is that a threat?"

"It's not a threat…it's what's going to happen if you don't agree. I'll be there in the morning to drive them to Maine." He hung up.

Sitting on the bed, I began to shiver, afraid of what he might do if I didn't agree. My thoughts brought gruesome scenarios to light. He could get rid of all my precious belongings that came from my family still back there in the house, or worse, hire someone to get rid of me. He could tell lies about me all over that damned small town or try to poison the children's minds against me. He could kidnap them off to Florida where he had gone twice already by himself that winter-- I heard you couldn't get your child back from there. The list of devastating "he coulds" continued to march through my mind for hours like an army bent on destroying me. There was no one to turn to for advice. After downing several tumblers of bourbon, I caved in and decided to let them go to Maine. All my well-laid schemes and dreams of a happy summer were washing out to sea with the low tide. The rest of the evening was spent packing up what they would need for camp.

When he arrived in the morning, I insisted on going along on the trip, with one caveat: that we stop along our route at some sort of farm my psychiatrist had been insisting I visit. He wanted me to see his former nurse who now worked there and whom he was sure could help me. The idea had been stashed away as a doubtful future possibility after I stopped seeing that useless psychiatrist who then began counseling my husband. But for some reason, visiting the nurse now seemed the right thing to do. Maybe, it was just a way to stall what would be a sad farewell at the end of the trip. The three waited outside in the car as I walked into the main building. I later learned that this picture-perfect "farm" with white picket fences was a rehab, but back then, no one ever used that word…they used "funny farm", "loony-bin" or simply, "insane asylum". Five minutes into the conversation, the nurse brought up that nasty word I didn't want to hear... alcoholism .

"I don't have a drinking problem. It's the marriage, the job, the children, the husband... it's stress city. You'd drink, too, if you were stuck with all I'm dealing with. I'm going to cut back on my drinking this summer at our beach house over in Strathmere. I won't have to deal with any of this stuff there. After we leave here, he's putting the kids in camp up in Maine."

"If you find you want to talk to someone about your drinking or any difficulties you might be having, I know a wonderful woman over there you can call," the nurse said. "Her name is Annette." She wrote the woman's number on a slip of paper which I tucked into the darkest recess of my beat-up leather wallet.

We continued on to the camp in Maine which turned out to be the same one my husband had gone to as a kid for many summers. Ian got out of the car and headed right over to the ball field where other kids were playing. Sandi, crying, clung on to me, not wanting me to leave. I gave her lots of kisses and cuddles and said we'd see each other real soon and she could send me pictures I knew she'd be drawing and I'd send some of mine back to her.

For a long time, Maine was the "M" word...it spelled "miserable". I couldn't imagine then when I had to say goodbye to my kids when I thought I'd be spending all summer with them... that four summers later, I'd be buying a $39 ticket on People Express Air to Maine, taking with me only my sleeping bag and a few essentials. I had calculated it was going to be cheaper doing that than staying home in Philly paying for air-conditioning. I rented a bicycle in Portland and spent that summer riding alone around Maine (well, pushing the bike uphill a lot) and eating lobster rolls for breakfast, lunch and dinner. At dusk, I'd pull off the road and camp in a field or in the woods. For a break from pedaling, I took my bike on the mail boat out around Casco Bay and spent a week enjoying stops at various islands, getting off on Bailey Island (2-1/2 miles long, one-half mile wide and a year-round population under 200, mostly lobstermen and their families). Writers and artists would occasionally show up on Bailey and Carl Jung is known to have visited and lectured at the Bailey Island Library Hall.

I splurged on a one-night stay in the only B&B in town so I could have the well-needed shower. The innkeeper's husband was an aged lobsterman and I had the unexpected pleasure of spending more than a month camped out in his lobster shack which was up on stilts over the water. In spite of the thick fog, very early each morning, I'd go out on his small boat with him to help bring up his lobster traps. I couldn't figure out how he found his unmarked traps in all that fog. He simply said he had been putting traps out there for more than fifty years. My job was to put rubber bands around the claws... I actually got quite good at it! When we got back, I'd find a lovely little basket of freshly-baked muffins or biscuits along with a little dish of homemade blackberry jam which his wife had slipped in and put on my sleeping bag while we were out. Before I would leave Bailey Island, she would lead me to her secret wild blackberry patch in the woods where I gorged myself on the luscious little devils while she picked them for her next batch of muffins. She also taught me how to make all things lobster, and as I was packing up my sleeping bag getting ready to head for the ferry, she tiptoed into the shack, tapped me on the shoulder, and handed me a warm hat she had crocheted, herself. Autumn had arrived along with fierce winds and cold nights. It was time to return to Philly.

My time on Bailey Island changed the "M" on my slate from "miserable" to "marvelous" but it would take a while to wipe out memories of that unhappy ride with my husband back to Philadelphia after dropping the kids off at summer camp. He stopped overnight at the same cabin we had honeymooned in 14 years before. Why he chose to stop there was beyond me. Maybe he had some insane notion that things would be like they had been way back when. Maybe he thought we could throw away the past and start all over again. Whatever his reasons, I ended up sleeping outside on the porch. In the morning, we took off without saying a word to each other. The long bitter 456-mile silent ride back to Strathmere ended when he practically shoved me out of the car onto the sand-covered steps leading up to the front door. I didn't look back as he drove off. All I could say to myself was, "Good riddance."

I loved our modest two-bedroom beach house built high up on stilts at the edge of the two-foot wide bulkhead/retaining sea wall I called our "board-walk". I no longer had to hide my morning pick-me-up in a coffee mug like before when we owned our first little one-story beach cottage several doors back down the block. Now, I no longer had to worry what the neighbors might think because they couldn't even see me. I could slosh as much as I wanted of the bourbon or wine into anything and guzzle it down any time of the night or day. Why, I could even drink straight out of the bottle if I wanted to. And I now often did, with no one around to care, nag or berate.

That last summer at the shore, I was like a rebellious renegade, removing all the curtains, keeping the windows wide open no matter the weather and never closing them. I related to Anne Morrow Lindbergh when she wrote about leaving her windows open in one of my favorite reads, Gift From The Sea. I loved this quote from her: *One cannot collect all the beautiful shells on the beach. One can collect only a few, and they are more beautiful if they are few.*

As I walked along the beach for hours every day, I'd pick up shells I didn't think I already had and upon returning to the house, line them up next to others of their kind. If the new ones were even slightly close to the size of others I had, I'd set the duplicates by the front door to return them to the sea on my next walk. When the Gulf Stream changed directions and started flowing north past Strathmere, huge hermit crabs were left stranded on the beach at low tide. It pained me to see children in the morning stabbing the crabs with sticks, kicking them, or throwing things at the helpless creatures that could live for 30 years if left undisturbed. I'd get up early and go down to the beach before anyone else could get there. I'd scramble over to each crab, gently pick it up and carry it out into the deep water beyond the waves so it could swim away to safety. Often, I wished I could swim away with my hermit crabs.

It didn't take long that summer before I had become best buddies with the sea. Poseidon was the only living thing always there for me now.

On late Sunday afternoons when the few tourists we ever saw departed and the weekend summer folks went back to their suburban lives, I'd shout my misery out the open windows and Poseidon would roar back at me. At times, when I stumbled along the beach, pleading for sympathy, he would curl up seductively around me. Other times, when I was seeking pity, he would run away like a fickle lover and hide far beyond my beloved sandbar.

After several weeks of liberation, I began to feel like flotsam floating from one direction to another. Each change of tide pushed me towards the liquor store where I bought gallon jugs of only the best rum, bourbon, and vodka. I never bought cheap stuff... only alcoholics drank that rot-gut. I wanted large bottles so I wouldn't have to hunt too soon for a different liquor store when I was running out –I was sure all the clerks kept track of how much I bought. God forbid, they might figure out I was an alcoholic. The clerk in the Sea Isle City liquor store gave me some lovely brass rockers to set the big bottles in "for ease in pouring," he said.

Paranoia began to set in when I was awakened in the middle of a stormy night by a noise coming from the open-air carport under the house. I was sure a detective was putting a wiretap on my line. And who was that man sitting out there in a dark car every night, parked across the street with no lights on? Well, maybe if I have just one more drink tonight, he'll disappear. For six weeks, hardly bothering to eat, I drank alone daily until I could pass out, hoping my pathetic life would somehow be better when I woke up. I was no longer wearing any hats...not that of wife, not of mother, not of reporter, nor society maven. I was nothing more than the hole in a donut and it felt Godawful...and frightening.

Before passing out, I would lie in bed at night, listening to the sound of high tide lapping at the bulkhead in front of the house, wondering when the ocean was going to jump in the window. I loved the fishy smell of the sea as it receded, leaving behind the sea-critters not strong enough to withstand its savagely wild embrace. At low tide during the day, I would sit at the open front window, sipping whatever was handy whether whisky or wine, watching the modest waves curl over my sandbar out there. They weren't the fierce stallions of the Pacific I had grown up with, but at least it was the salt water I knew so well. Where were they going? Wouldn't they please take me with them?

No bliss that summer. No waltzing on the beach. No nude sunbathing out on the sandbar. No swimming in the moonlight. No tracing my name in the sea sparkles that arrived with the Gulf Stream. Instead, I was stretched out on the couch, often for days, nursing a bottomless glass of Wild Turkey while trying to focus on a half-open book.Fourteen years of marriage and eight years of motherhood lay in broken pieces on the floor. That summer, I huddled under a damp blanket in a booze-induced fog, remembering the times as a kid when I would go to bed with a flashlight so I could read under the covers. Ah, those sacred childhood moments when I could hide away from everyone and feel safe, engulfed in stories of treasure-thieving pirates, of Pan and his nymphs, of islands far beyond the wind. Days passed. Nights passed. It all became one long unfocused blur.

My mind began conjuring up dangerous schemes. One afternoon, while scribbling 'Sandra was here' in the salty sand-dust on the window sill, I slurped down another swig of red wine and started to contemplate a plan. As an inveterate people-pleasing alcoholic, I couldn't figure out how to do it without creating a mess for others to clean up. Yes, I wanted to do it, but I sure as hell didn't want to be around when it happened.

I could jump off our bulkhead at high tide and start swimming to the Azores, but the next day was Sunday and some baseball-capped beer-bellied fisherman out in his little skiff would hook me and think he was pulling up a trophy blue fish. Or maybe at low tide I could walk through the surf to my sandbar, carrying my gallon jug of Chianti. I could lie down on the sandbar which I knew so well from all those years of summer days spending hours lying alone on it after saying I was just going for a little walk on the beach. In my plan, by the time high tide began slipping across the bar, dead drunk, I wouldn't know if I was being washed out to sea or just dreaming. But with my luck, my body would end up washed back up onto the beach, destroying a masterpiece sandcastle some kid had built the day before. Or what about slitting my wrists with my favorite well-honed French chef's knife, a fitting final use for it? No, I hated the sight of blood and there would surely be blue blood splattered everywhere. If only I could just sail away…. yes, sail away and end up lost forever at sea.

Not knowing where or how to begin the end, I put on an old tape a French friend had given me in France during that cold winter so long ago… Miles Davis' *Kind of Blue*… turned up the volume, and crashed on the sagging salt water-logged couch, slugging down another tumbler of warm bourbon.

Chapter Four

Barely Limping Along

When I slid off the sofa in the morning, still wearing the same shorts and t-shirt I had worn for the past week or maybe even longer, I knew it was finally time. I washed up all the dishes that had been piling up for days in the sink, made the bed, and neatly put away clothes that had been lying around for weeks. Methodically, I went around the house, tidying everything up, washing the door of the fridge, wiping off the top of the gas stove, cleaning the bathroom sink and toilet. I then slipped on a shower cap to keep my hair clean and out of the way, walked back to the kitchen where I used my hand to vaguely measure the height and width of my head. I opened the oven door, removed the top oven rack, and lowered the bottom rack to create maximum space in the oven.

I dropped to my knees in front of the oven, scooted over as close as I could to it, and slipped my head inside. It would only fit in sideways. With my head resting on the adjusted greasy lower oven rack, I reached up to the knobs on top, struggling to find the one that would turn on the oven. It would have taken too much nerve to turn the gas on first.

My fingers closed on a knob but it lit a burner instead, and I swore, "Damned drunk! You can't even do this right!"

My hand slid over to the fatter knob and I knew that was it. I twisted it. The sweet smell of gas filled the space. I knew the nightmare would soon be over. And how brilliant, I thought…not any mess left behind for them to clean up, nothing that could be used post-mortem to accuse me of being a lousy housekeeper.

My life begins to zoom past. It's 1954: there I am, age 11, going to school in Scotland and beating up the school bully for calling Bruce and me "damned Yanks". It's1958: I'm fifteen and hanging out in North Beach with Ken Kesey, Alan Ginsberg, Ferlinghetti and all the other Beat poets. Now, it's me at 16, dating Abdullah Theneyan whose father was treasurer of Saudi Arabia and whose cousin, Mohammed Faisal, was the country's Crown Prince…I'm driving Abdullah's custom-made Ferrari every day to high school because he was attending Menlo College and not allowed a car on campus. Now, I'm attending one of the many elegant dinner parties Mohammed and his beautiful wife Mona throw for Standard Oil executives and we're sitting around a table after dinner as Mohammed demonstrates levitation and other mystical things. Hey, there Abdullah and I are, a year later, skydiving up at Calistoga. Next, there I am, cutting high school classes and driving the new MGA I shared with Bruce…with me is my little poodle Robespierre, a dog I inherited from a sick old lady. The top is down and Robie and I are both wearing dark glasses and chiffon scarves à la Isadora Duncan. At the red traffic lights on El Camino Real, the main drag in Menlo Park, when there are boys sitting in the next car, Robie, exactly as I trained him, head back and looking up at the sky, is howling a long note like Pavarotti singing an aria from *Rigoletto* …great way to attract potential boyfriends! Now, it's 1961: Senator Wayne Morse in Oregon is encouraging me to transfer from U. of O. to George Washington in DC and six months later, there I am on "The Hill" in his U. S. Senate office, working part-time as his "constituent liaison"…I think he just hired me to smile and wear pretty girly dresses while parading his prize bulls in front of judges at county fairs…he probably figured we'd win first prize and we always did! Now, that same year, in between classes, I'm social secretary to the rather eccentric Grande Dame of Washington society and only if I'd take my hair out of the French bun and let it all hang down, could I play hostess at her weekly soirées for politicos like Mike Mansfield, LBJ, Averell Harriman and the embassy crowd. I could never take my eyes off Ambassador-at-Large Harriman's bushy eyebrows, wondering why he didn't at least clip them a bit. What next? It's Florida: spring break from GW, and I'm on a huge yacht as guest of a sugar daddy I met at the Ft. Lauderdale Yacht Club…someone said he made his millions with something about inventing nylon and selling the idea to DuPont…we are headed for the Bahamas with his promise of no hanky-panky (which he kept) simply, "because you're so much fun!" He's off to the Governor's Ball and I'm staying behind on the yacht, lying in bed not feeling well. A big black man wakes me up…"Not to worry," he says. "Mr. Ken sent me. I'm the Governor's butler and Mr. Ken bet the Governor five hundred pounds sterling he had the prettiest lady on the island on his yacht. I'm going to have to tell the Governor Mr. Ken won." Now, its summer 1962: I'm in Geneva, Switzerland…needed a summer job before school started at Grenoble so I talked the head of Hewlett-Packard's Sales Dept. (whom I had worked for during holiday and summer breaks from high school and college) into creating a job for me…he reminded me there was a nine-year waiting list to get a job in Geneva but somehow, for the summer, I'm the newly-appointed Assistant to the Director of HP's Geneva office. Now it's September that same year: I'm in Greece on a small cruise boat sailing around the Greek Isles, dancing in tavernas à la my role-model Melina Mercouri when she played Ilya in *Never On Sunday*. Hey, there I am, still a teenager and the only American on the final trip of the original Orient Express…got on at the northern border of Greece and am going across all those strange places--Bulgaria, Serbia, Croatia, Slovenia, over to Italy…soldiers are stopping the train, coming through the cars grabbing cameras and smashing them on the tracks, shooting men in the woods and without notice, leaving our rail car all by itself for four days somewhere in Slovenia without explanation, without food, with only one soon filthy bathroom… it's scary but I pretend I'm in an Agatha Christie movie. Now, at the university in Grenoble… Oh, dear…it's fading, fading, fading… it's dark…ah, the sweet smell of gas…not long now…

From somewhere comes a loud voice, "If you do this, you'll never see another tree, bush or flower again."

"Who's there? Who is it?" I stutter, pulling my head out of the oven and turning off the gas before the whole place will explode.

I was afraid to even think it might have been God speaking to me. Flicking on the kitchen light, I stumble to the phone, grab a phonebook and call Suicide Prevention. The volunteer on the other end of the line is the grandmother-type, kind and sympathetic. She seems to have all the time in the world to talk to me even though it's well past midnight.

We converse until I begin to feel better, and then, thanking her in my best rendition of a society matron I say, "I'll send your organization a generous donation in the morning" and hang up. Then it's back to the wine. An hour passes and I am on the phone again. Same woman. The third call, I bravely give her my phone number as she wants to have the Director of the County Health Clinic call me even though it is now almost 3:00 a. m. I no sooner put the phone down than it rings. He asks me to put the booze away, get to bed, set the alarm for 8:00 a. m., and he'll meet me at 8:45 a. m. at the clinic in Cape May Court House, 15 miles from Strathmere. He says he'll be coming from Princeton, over 100 miles away, but could leave his home at 6:30 a. m. and be at the clinic by 8:45 a. m. I am astounded. It seems preposterous that a stranger would go out of his way at that hour to help me when no one else in the world seemed to care.

I set the alarm, go to bed and when the alarm rings,, swig a quick drink of courage from the wine bottle and jump into my car, grateful I am still sober enough that morning to drive.

The Director is waiting at the door, and greets me with a hug, saying, "How can I help you? What do you need?"

Not having a clue what I need, the first thing that pops into my mind is, "I want to take an IQ test to prove there's nothing wrong with me. For 16 years, my husband has been treating me like I'm some kind of dummy and I want to prove it's not true."

"No problem. Have a seat and I'll get the test papers. When you're finished, just bring them back to my office down the hall where I'll have a hot cup of coffee waiting for you."

He was very sweet and seemed genuinely interested in wanting to help me. I answered the test questions as honestly as I could. When I was done, he looked the test over and said there was nothing wrong with my mind. Was there any other problem? I admitted I was having serious marital difficulties. He introduced me to a co-worker, Marjorie. I didn't know then, but figured out some days later that she was an angel disguised as the County's head Addiction Counselor.

I spent the entire day in her office, talking in between appointments she had with other clients. When she was busy, she had me sorting paper clips by size from one box to another. She was a loving and gentle woman…the kind I always wished my mother had been. It was like she really cared about me which made me feel safe telling her all about my drinking. She wasn't at all judgmental and everything she said made sense. I didn't even resent it when she suggested I might want to try to quit drinking. At 5:00 p. m. when she had to close her office for the day, she suggested I attend a meeting of a 12-step recovery program that night.

I grabbed onto her life-preserver suggestion like someone who, lost at sea, had been drowning for years. The 8:00 p. m. meeting was in the historic courthouse just a few miles from her office. The doors were usually open at 7:00 p. m., she said, and when I entered the building I should just tell them I was new. Before we left her office, she introduced me to her boss, an overweight man sitting in an overstuffed armchair behind an imposingly large desk.

"Do you have any booze back home?" he asked in a monotone voice while flipping through a file folder.

I lied, "Well, just a few bottles."

"You need to pour it all out as soon as you get home," he said, snapping the file shut and turning away as if I wasn't worth bothering with.

Thank goodness Marjorie took my hand and squeezed it. I felt the warmth of her caring, yet I couldn't imagine following that awful man's advice – waste all of it down the drain? Good heavens! It had cost me a fortune and some of the gallon jugs hadn't even been opened yet. I decided I would deal with this after the meeting.

Marjorie suggested rather than going home, it might be a good idea for me to stop at the hamburger joint down the street for something to eat before heading over to the meeting. For some strange reason, I trusted her and decided to follow her suggestion…to follow any of her suggestions, for that matter. She wrote her office and home phone numbers down on a slip of paper, gave me a hug and told me to call her office in the morning, adding that if I needed to, I could call her anytime at home, no matter the hour.

I didn't get something to eat – I was shaking too much. Instead, I got to the courthouse early and sat in my car until it was time to go in. Everyone I approached said he or she was new. Walking down the main aisle towards the front, I noticed all the courthouse pews were almost filled, mostly with men and just a few women scattered here and there. Towards the front where juries long ago must have sat, there was a slightly raised dais with a low wooden fence around it and a small gate standing open. Beyond the gate was a table with 12 chairs. All were taken but one. I somehow instinctively knew that 12th chair was waiting for me and stumbled through the gate and sat down.

The meeting began with preliminary recitations and then a well-dressed woman stood up to tell her "story". She spoke about travelling all over the world just like I had, of going to school in Great Britain as a kid just as I had, of the glamorous life she had lived before alcohol took her down, again, just as I had. I was amazed! I had expected to find old men with raincoats and brown paper bags and instead, I was listening to a woman telling my own story. When she finished and the meeting ended, I sat there bawling. It was the first time in my life I finally felt in a place I belonged… a misfit, an outsider no more. It was glorious but at the same time, frightening!

An older dumpy woman with stringy bleached blonde hair and a cigarette dangling out of her mouth came up and put her arms around me. She was someone I certainly would not have associated with in my Philadelphia suburban life.

"You're never going to feel alone again," she said, hugging me.

How could this stranger know I had been longing to hear those very words all my life? I cried some more and she said, "Let me give you my phone number…my name is Annette and you can call me anytime."

"I think I already have it," I said, fishing out the crumpled scrap of paper from my wallet.

She looked at it, smiled and gave me another hug.

"What should I do? I have tons of booze back in my cottage and I'm afraid it's going to do me in. I don't know how to live without it, but I'm afraid it's going to kill me."

"Joe and I will follow you and take it with us temporarily for safekeeping."

"But I live way over in Strathmere, almost a half hour away."

"No problem…we'll just follow you."

Before we left the meeting, Annette handed me a copy of a small black book entitled, <u>Twenty-Four Hours A Day</u>, saying, "Keep this handy and read it every day…it helped me and I know it will help you."

When we pulled up to the cottage, they climbed up the steep stairs and helped me haul out bottles and boxes of liquor which we stashed in Joe's trunk and the back seat of his car. As they pulled away, he leaned out the window and in a Scottish brogue said, "Now don't forget, lassie… anytime you want your booze back, just call me."

As the red tail lights were fading into the distance, I shouted, "But Joe… you didn't give me your phone number."

That first night was a nightmare. I paced up and down the living room for hours. I lay down on the floor to sleep but couldn't close my eyes…two cups of black coffee downed earlier at the meeting probably didn't help. My hands were shaking, my teeth were chattering like the castanets I learned to play once in Barcelona. I got up and wandered around the house for another hour then hit the sack, trying to sleep but started seeing bugs crawling all over the walls. Were they real? I grabbed the black book and tried to read the "Thought For The Day", July 24th. I had to read the first few words over and over before any comprehension would even begin to sink in. What language was it written in, anyway? Surely, not English.

That day's message read:

> *The program is like a dike, holding back the ocean of liquor. If we take one glass of liquor, it is like making a small hole in the dike and once such a hole has been made, the whole ocean of alcohol may rush in upon us. By practicing the program principles we keep the dike strong and in repair. We spot any weakness or crack in that dike and make the necessary repairs before any damage is done. Outside the dike is the whole ocean of alcohol, waiting to engulf us again in despair. Am I keeping the dike strong?"*

I set the book on the nightstand and years — no decades — of unshed tears began streaming down my face. It was true…alcohol had been engulfing me in despair. I couldn't stop crying. Was it a coincidence the "Thought Day" was about the ocean? No…that message was exactly what I needed. All through that first night, I read out loud the little book's July 24th message, over and over, until Apollo rose up out of the sea, giving me, for the first time ever, a feeling of peace, of hope. I didn't know then that I'd be clinging to that recovery raft for quite some time before braving to climb aboard.

"Oh, God, thank you for another day," I shouted out the window to the first passing seagull. He looked at me and smiled. Must be Jonathan Livingston, I thought.

My first morning sober, I could hardly wait until 9:00 a. m. to call Marjorie at her office.

"Guess what, Marjorie! I went to the meeting and I just know it's going to help me! Everyone was so friendly and welcoming. I've never experienced anything like it before. They didn't even know me and yet I felt they really did."

"I'm so happy for you, Sandra, and proud of you, too. It's going to be the most thrilling and most rewarding chariot ride of your life. What are your plans for today?"

"They gave me a schedule of area meetings and I'm going to go to the one at noon in Sea Isle, and then it's about an hour's drive down the Garden State Parkway to the next meeting at 5:00 p. m. over in Ocean City. Then I'll be back in time for the Cape May Courthouse meeting."

"How about you stop by my office after the noon meeting and we can chat. I want to give you a big hug for being so brave."

"Oh, Marjorie…I love you," I said, starting to cry, but they were tears of joy because I knew she wanted me to get well and be truly happy. And best of all, she was into hugs!

"Do you have anything to eat at home?" she asked.

"Yes, I think there's a somewhat stale box of cereal and some OJ"

"Well, make sure you eat something — it's important for your body's health. Maybe you can stop at the grocery before the noon meeting and grab a supply of fiber bars and some fresh fruit."

Marjorie was one of the first women in the 12 Step recovery program and had been sober then for more than 30 years. The third time I met her for a counseling session, I asked her to be my program sponsor. She would guide me through the Steps to recovery and I just knew she'd give me a leg up each time I was stumbling, about to fall. Before long, she was closer to me than my own mother had ever been. With Marjorie, I could do no wrong and if she noticed me heading in the wrong direction, she'd lovingly nudge me back to where I needed to be without guilt, shame or disgrace. I didn't quite know how to handle her caring attitude…it was unfamiliar, something I certainly wasn't used to.

"Someone was there for me when I first came into the program and now I'm here for you," she said. "That's how our program works. We help each other and we can't keep it unless we give it away."

It took several weeks of meetings before I could speak without a severe stutter — all that non-stop drinking had somehow neurologically affected my speech. Every day that summer, I drove up and down the Garden State Parkway, travelling between a morning meeting, one at noon, at 5:00 p. m. and at 8:00 p. m., sometimes crying, other times singing, and racking up one more sober day each night my head hit the pillow. I'd see Joe and Annette at meetings and they'd come over to hug me, saying, "Now don't forget…you just have to call if you want it back," and we'd all laugh. Yes, I was learning to laugh again, too!

When all the summer people were packing up to leave their beach homes and Ian and Sandi were due to return home from camp, as an unexpected surprise, their father dropped them off in Strathmere. The kids and I had two wonderful weeks together on the beach. They came with me to all the meetings most of which were held in church basements or Sunday School rooms. They'd sit in the church kitchen or a nearby room crayoning until the meeting was over. When I went to Marjorie's house or her office to work on the Steps of the program, she would have crayons, cookies and lemonade waiting for them. Marjorie had recently married a fellow in the program, years younger than herself, and an artist. He was always happy, full of enthusiasm, and had an incredible uninhibited love for life. One afternoon, she and I were upstairs in her house working on a Step while the children were downstairs with her husband. Occasionally, we'd hear squeals of delight coming up the stairs. When we were finished and went down to the living room, there the kids were, in the middle of the room where Marjorie's artist-husband had mixed up a huge batch of cement, right on the hardwood floor, and they were building a castle!

All Marjorie said was, "Honey, I don't think our landlord will appreciate the castle. You'll have to clean it up soon before it becomes a permanent fixture in our living room."

That was my Marjorie…serene, loving, and kind.

One of many stories I loved about their wonderful relationship was what happened when she was going away by herself, up to Connecticut to visit her two sisters for ten days. She made him promise not to go anywhere near the new Resorts International Casino, Atlantic City's first legal casino that had just opened two months before… she knew of his past proclivity for such places.

She had only been gone two days, when he called. "Marjorie, please don't be mad at me…please, promise?" Before waiting for her response, he said, "I know I gave you my word, but I just couldn't stay away from Atlantic City. They were advertising a huge grand opening of the city's first casino, offering lots of free giveaways. I just had to go."

"Oh, no, honey," Marjorie said. "How much did you lose?"

"Well, I didn't exactly lose, Marjorie. In fact, I won opening night's biggest jackpot and just put a check for almost a million dollars into your account. Are you angry with me, Marjorie?" How could she be? He was always so sweet, even when he blew it.

"I just hired a fancy limousine and chauffeur to drive you and your sisters all around New England to see the first leaves of autumn, Marjorie, and he'll be there tomorrow to pick you up. And when it's time for you to come home, you don't have to take the bus…he'll bring you right to our door. Oh, and there will be a dozen red roses for each of you waiting inside the limo. Have fun, Marjorie, and please, don't be mad at me."

"It's OK, honey. I can't imagine ever being angry with you. I can hardly wait to get home so we can talk about what to do with all that money!"

Ah, Marjorie...the perfect model of patience and tolerance. I wondered if I'd ever learn enough by working the recovery program's 12 Steps to come anywhere near her admirable level of those two qualities that were definitely not my strong points.

I had less than two months of sobriety when I realized the first day of school was on the horizon. I'd have to leave the security of my recovery "nest", sponsor and sober friends and head back to Philadelphia. To stay in the cottage through the winter would be nearly impossible. It wasn't heated so pipes would freeze if it wasn't winterized and I didn't have the money to set it up as a winter residence. Another factor to consider was the rural school, not one of the best. I also needed to see if staying in the marriage was even an option... to find out if I could live with him without the comforting defensive shield of alcohol. Plus, I was learning from the meetings that alcoholics often want to "throw the baby out with the bath water". I didn't want to do that with the marriage if there was any chance it could be repaired or even if he would want it to be. I also wondered if I'd be able to return to the stress of my newspaper job.

With sadness and apprehension, I packed up to leave Strathmere. The first thing I put in my suitcase was the little black book Annette had given me. It was comforting to start each morning off reading the Thought For The Day. Sometimes, I'd read it again when I was going to bed. For the rest of my days, that little book would go with me wherever I went! As soon as I got back to the suburbs with the children, I hunted up meetings, keeping in mind what my sober friends at the shore had told me the night before I left.

"It'll almost be like you're starting all over again," they said. "But hang in there. Get to 90 meetings in 90 days when you hit Philadelphia and if you decide you want to go out and do more research, come back here and we'll gladly refund your misery."

They also reminded me of the program's many useful phrases that hung framed on walls of almost every meeting place I had frequented, like, "Easy Does It" and "First Things First" and "One Day At A Time" and "Let Go And Let God". I didn't understand what they all meant, but began to have hope the Higher Power I was hearing about in the meetings might help me, too. Maybe, after all this time, God was no longer too busy with all those starving kids in Armenia.

At the meetings, I learned a lot by listening to the experience, strength and hope of others. I even did everything they told me to do like, "Take the cotton out of your ears and stick it in your mouth." If they had told me to stand in the corner on my head, I would have done so. I began to understand if I were to go back out and drink, the gift of sobriety might not pass my way again. My life depended on not picking up even one drink, they said, as it had always been that first drink that had gotten me drunk. Novel concept, I thought, and began to grasp the notion that one sip would lead to polishing off the bottle and drowning in despair, my head on the table next to the gallon jug of wine, scrawling those Godawful maudlin poems again.

When I talked to John about me and the kids returning home, he agreed it was a good idea. I then told him I'd given up drinking, been attending 12 Step recovery meetings, and would be continuing to do so if I came back with the kids.

"If you don't mind, if I do come back, it will be best for me if you don't have wine in the fridge or sherry in the crystal decanter. In fact, if it isn't too much trouble, the one condition for returning that I have is I would greatly appreciate it if you would stash all the liquor somewhere in the bedroom you're using. I can't really have it anywhere around me."

He agreed to my request. When the kids and I arrived home, the first thing I discovered was a partially full bottle of Chardonnay and two of Riesling in the kitchen fridge, a bottle of my favorite Chateauneuf-du-Pape on the counter in the pantry, and the liquor closet filled to capacity. Every day, he'd come home from the office and put ice in a glass, chink it enough for the sound to reverberate throughout the house, and then fill a glass with one of my old favorites, Wild Turkey.

A week after I returned home, I told my husband I wanted to make amends to him for anything I had done to hurt him or to make his life difficult. I explained Step Four of my 12-Step recovery program which had important suggestions, had "suggested" that I make a searching and fearless moral inventory of myself. According to the Step, "Without a willing and persistent effort to do this, there can be little sobriety or contentment for us." I explained how I had worked hard on Step Four and the following Steps. Step Eight "suggested" to "make a list of all persons we had harmed and become willing to make amends to them all". Step Nine then went on to "suggest" we "make amends to such people wherever possible, except when to do so would injure them or others."

The children were upstairs already in bed and John was sitting in the living room when I approached him and said I wanted to make amends. I had only managed to say, "I am sorry that…" when he got up and marched upstairs to bed. The next day, while he was away, I spent hours writing down things I felt bad, ashamed or guilty about that I felt had affected our relationship. When he came home, I had a cheerful fire going in the living room fireplace, the children were upstairs playing and I asked him to sit down. I handed him the neatly typed pages of my "amends" and he tossed them all into the fire and went to the pantry to make himself a drink. This is when I realized moving back into the house and marriage had been a huge mistake and I knew then that he would continue to punish me for whatever he thought I had done, real or imagined, for the rest of my life. The word, "forgiveness", was not in his vocabulary.

After many months of hurtful "you move out, no, you move out" battles, he disappeared without a word. We didn't know where he'd gone. I was grateful he left, even though I knew it was going to be difficult on my own, tougher than I even imagined. Thank God for the meetings, for my sponsor just a phone call away, and for the fellowship of other program members who gave me unconditional support and loved me, as they said, "until you can love yourself." I didn't have a clue what they meant and they just smiled, adding, "More will be revealed."

Chapter Five

Out of the Mouths of Babes...

Holding everything together as a single sober mom was a real challenge. To pay the bills, I took a full-time job managing an architect's office by day while working occasionally as Lois Lane by night. I was nurturing and caring for the children as best I could while dealing with the big house and expansive gardens. It was a delicate balance: to spend enough time with the children so they would feel loved and cared for, yet take on enough newspaper assignments to help with the bills while at the same time, advance my journalism career. Most importantly, I needed to have enough time to keep up with regular attendance at meetings,

Not very often but occasionally, Ian would say, "When is Daddy coming back home?"

I could only reply, "I'm not sure – he's on a long journey" which seemed to satisfy Ian.

After about four months, their father re-appeared and told us where he was living. He would continue paying the home mortgage (protecting his investment, of course) and would now give me $70 a week for groceries and all the other bills, hardly enough but it would help.

This was sure a new lifestyle for me. No more having our favorite nanny stay with the kids while we took two-month winter trips to exotic somewhat unknown Caribbean islands not yet plundered by hordes of noisy rude tourists. No more summer trips for me to California with the children to see Grandma. No more exquisite repasts at expensive French restaurants, nights at the symphony, the opera, the theater. And of course I had to let go of the maid and the gardener. Before long, weeds overran my prize dahlia bed while aphids and Japanese beetles set up court in my Victorian rose garden. It did make life easier in some respects and sure saved money. Plus, I no longer had to worry about what the maid slipped into her carry-all bag when she was leaving for the day, claiming it was just her soiled uniform and yesterday's newspaper. Somehow, around Christmas cookie-baking time, my supply of herbs and spices always had mysteriously diminished.

There was a positive side to all these changes. Part of my recovery was aimed at battling the degree of perfectionism of my addictive personality that had been growing out of control like the unwelcome weeds around all the graves in the cemetery behind where I had grown up. Nobody ever came to cut those ugly weeds down just like nobody ever told me perfectionism wasn't always considered a good trait. Sometimes, as was my case, it could be used to hide the truth about my drinking.

Instead of, "She keeps a beautiful home, she throws elegant dinner parties, her children are perfect angels, why, she even starches her husband's underwear!" they could be saying, "She's just a damned drunk."

Now, on my own, I could give up the obsession to be the perfect wife, perfect mother and perfect homemaker, and simply learn to survive the day-to-day traumas of this new lifestyle without the crutch of alcohol. I allowed dust balls to congregate like an army battalion under the furniture. I took delight in allowing dishes to sit in the sink for several hours after a meal before doing them. No more starching and ironing the children's clothes or even my own—just getting them washed, dried, folded and put away was enough. This was quite an about-face from the old me who, towards the end, I was now realizing, had become compulsive about almost everything.

A few months later, at their father's request, I started letting the children spend an occasional weekend with him. He was living on a gentleman farm in Bucks County where he had a big dog the kids loved, and lots of space for them to run around with the dog. Ironic that he would choose to move out to where I had always said I wished we could move back to...a place like Solebury where we could have a small farm with chickens, a goat or two, a veggie garden.

Things didn't always go well, like when he'd drop in at my friend's house across the street from school where she was taking care of the kids until I could get there after work. Without telling me in advance, he'd pick up Ian and Sandi and go off with them. I'd have to worry and wonder where they were for hours until he decided to drop them off at home. Then there was the time when seven year-old Sandi got off the school bus in tears – her father had gone to school and given her our weekly $70 check and had lost it. I couldn't fathom the folly of giving a first-grader a check to hold onto all day at school.

"Mommy, I'm so sorry," she wailed. "Now we won't have anything to eat all week and it's all my fault."

She was hysterical. I hugged her as tight as I could while wiping away her tears. "We'll find it, Sandi. Don't worry, we'll find it. I'll bet you left it on the bus."

"No, I asked the bus driver and he couldn't find it," she sobbed.

I quickly got on the phone to the place where all school buses go for the night and they said no check was found. Relying on my old childhood ability to find lost things, I could just see that check in my mind's eye, stuck under the third seat of the bus. So we drove to where the buses all were parked, climbed aboard the first one, pulled apart the third seat, and there it was.

This was a Friday about 4:00 p. m. and Ian had already taken off on an overnight trip to an Alateen conference he was attending for the weekend. I'd dropped him off earlier at the building in Glenside where Alateen met weekly and watched as the group's sponsor helped Ian climb into the old Volkswagen bus with his teddy bear and pillow while the teenaged members of the group piled in after him with their Walkman's and other teenage paraphernalia. Ian was only ten and the youngest in Alateen, but the capable leader said Ian was mature enough for the meetings. When the conference came up, the leader called and said he'd like Ian to attend along with the others of his group who were going. I was nervous at the thought of my little boy going off with a bunch of teenagers – especially since every Monday night when I picked him up after the meetings, he'd talk about pot and beer busts and other such things he certainly hadn't learned about from me.

When all the kids had climbed into the VW bus, the leader told me the last night of the Conference was devoted to a "meeting on spirituality". Everyone would share their experience of getting to know a Higher Power. That gave me hope. Other than summer camp, this would be the first time Ian would be away from home…away from me. I prayed, as the VW bus roared off, that he would have a good experience and one that might also help our relationship.

As we pulled away from the school bus yard that afternoon, I said, "Sandi, since Ian is going to be away for the weekend, how would you like to go camping, just the two of us?"

She perked up, saying, "Really, Mom, just you and me?"

"Just you and me."

"Whee!" she squealed, having already forgotten about the lost-check calamity.

We raced home. I called County Parks and was told if we got to their local office in eight minutes before it closed, we could register for a campsite at the closest park which was about an hour away. We jumped in the car and made it just in time to make the reservation. Then we drove to Sears, bought two sleeping bags (they were even on sale!), stopped at the market for a cheap frypan, some plastic knives, spoons and forks, a small ice chest and some groceries, and off we went. We had to check in to the park by 6:00 p. m. or lose our spot and it was the last one available. Everything worked in our favor. We arrived a minute before the gate closed, drove to our campsite, and in less than five minutes, had our home-away-from-home all set up. It did look a bit spartan…just two little sleeping bags side by side on Grandma's old quilt compared with the elaborate set-ups other campers had with colored electric lights strung all over the trees and bushes, televisions and radios blasting to scare away all the wildlife, and whatever else they had dragged to the woods from the suburbs for their into-the-wilds-roughing-it experience.

As we were about to climb into our sleeping bags for the night, a woman walked by and said, "You're not going to sleep out here in the open without a tent, are you?"

"Of course, why not?" I replied as she walked away, shaking her head.

"What's wrong, Mommy? Doesn't she like our campsite?"

"There's nothing wrong with our site, Sandi. We have the best little campsite this side of the Canadian Rockies. Just you wait until you hear that nice old owl hooting 'good night' to you and in the morning, the smell of bacon sizzling over our campfire… just you wait."

We snuggled into our sleeping bags watching the dying embers of our small campfire aglow as we fell asleep. On awakening and recognizing the unforgettable smell (rather, calling card) of skunks, we discovered they had eaten all the cinnamon buns we accidentally left out the night before on our picnic table. I told Sandi not to worry… they must have been hungrier than us.

Our weekend was perfect. We learned that those mischievous skunks only tiptoe past your sleeping bag after you are tucked safely inside, the mosquitoes only come out at dusk for a few minutes, trout jump for flies when the sun is setting, and the friendly Park Ranger can take a sliver out of a little girl's finger in mere seconds with the sterilized pin from his official badge. On Sunday, we spent the entire day swimming while the other weekend campers were back at their luxurious campsites dismantling all the trappings of suburbia they had hauled to the woods for a quiet peaceful weekend away from home.

Sandi and I went to pick Ian up in the mall parking lot where the Alateen leader said he would be dropping the kids off. She was already sound asleep in the backseat before we even got to the parking lot. I was nervous as we waited for the VW, wondering if Ian would have learned anything at the conference that might help us get along better.... that might stop him from running to the farthest corner of our sprawling house and as far away from me as he could get when he'd come home from school...that might stop him from camping out in his room all weekend, not wanting to be near me.

"Did you have a nice time?" I asked as we drove away from the mall.

"Yeah."

"Was the food good there?"

"Yeah."

"Did you go on any nature hikes?"

"Naw"

"Did you learn anything new, Ian?" I asked, hoping to engage him in more than a monosyllabic conversation.

"Maybe."

"Did they mention anything about a Higher Power or about God?"

"Guess so," he muttered, almost to himself.

As I was driving up the driveway to our house, I felt like crying. I had put so much stock in this conference, thinking it would help us both, but things were still just the same as before. I turned the motor off. Ian opened the car door and jumped out. I watched him run up to the front door, his hand on the door knob, ready to turn it and run inside. I sat there behind the wheel, tears coursing down my cheeks. Suddenly, he turned around and came running back to the car. He came right up to my side of the car, banging on my car door. I quickly opened it.

"Yes, Ian?"

Looking right at me, talking as fast as he could, he said, "Mom, I did learn something neat at the conference. I learned God is not way up in the sky with white hair, a messy beard and wearing a weird white nightgown... he's walking right beside me wearing dungarees!"

He turned and ran back up to the front door, opened it and went in. Sandi woke up and when we got to the door, he opened it and with his arms stretched out, gave me the hug I had so long been praying for and said, "I love you, Mom."

Little did he know I was to cherish that moment as one of the most beautiful of my life. The best part? Ian taught me that night that God was walking right beside me, too, and wearing dungarees!

At the one-year milestone of sobriety, my sponsor felt I was ready to face my mother and tell her what was going on with me. I agreed to make the trip, only wishing my father was still alive so I could share the good news with him, too. I flew out to California armed with a fistful of literature including "The Alcoholic In Your Family", "What Recovery Means", "First Signs of Alcoholism", and "The 12 Steps of Recovery". When I arrived at her house, Mother opened the door and after a welcome hug, I handed her the pamphlets. She took one look at them, then laid them on the credenza in the foyer. That evening, as we sat having coffee out on her patio, I felt it time to share with her about my new life as a recovering alcoholic.

She listened, didn't ask any questions, and when I finished, said, "Yes, your Aunt Jennie's husband was one of those. Went to some kind of meetings but it didn't last long...he died drunk."

She immediately changed the subject, telling me about the wonderful promotion my brother had just been given. She was not going to be the supportive mother I hoped she would be. It was same-old, same-old, but I was not going to harbor any resentments over this. I knew from listening to the experiences of others shared at meetings that resentments can lead to the bottle. One of the silly but so true sayings I kept hearing at meetings came right to mind: "Poor me, pour me another drink."

The next morning, I noticed the pamphlets were gone and asked if she had read them and she replied, "Oh, I burned those in the trash this morning. Couldn't have that sort of thing lying around the house."

In the afternoon she wanted to show me the prize camellias, rhododendrons and azaleas she had planted since the last time I had been there. After we were finished meandering around the garden, I made a cup of tea for us both and we went back outside to sit on her patio where she shared something absolutely astounding.

"Your father and I wanted to have children--we tried for six years but nothing was happening. When I was 40, a friend shared an old wives' tale remedy of taking a baking soda douche before intercourse which would reduce the acid that killed the sperm. It worked and I told the doctor I was going to have twins...a boy and a girl. I knew this was my one and only chance to have children. The doctor kept insisting up to the minute you were born that I would be lucky to have one baby and it was emotionally bad to keep insisting I was going to have twins."

What she said next took my breath away.

"For months before you were born, I'd spend an hour every morning walking around my lovely garden talking aloud so I could let you both know how beautiful the flowers, bushes and trees were. Every morning, I'd describe them in great detail because I wanted you and Bruce to be born with a love and appreciation of Nature."

Her words amazed me. I was humbled by what she said because what God shouted to get me out of the oven that dismal night in Strathmere was about the appreciation for Nature that my mother had taught me before I was born.

The next morning before flying back home, I invited Mother to spend Christmas with the children and me in Philadelphia. She said she'd start saving for the trip and I went home looking forward to her visit. Two weeks before Christmas, I picked her up at the airport and on the drive home, told her how happy and relieved I was to be on my own. Even though I wasn't divorced yet, I explained how healing it was to be free from what had been, for years, a miserable experience. I guess by way of warning that the house might not be in total apple-pie order, I also explained I had discharged the maid and gardener because I couldn't afford them.

We arrived home, went inside, and before even taking off her coat, she walked over to the marble-topped antique credenza in the foyer, took her white-gloved hand all along its surface. and said, "Well, maybe if you had spent more time keeping the house clean he wouldn't have left."

I was stunned…she just didn't get it. After a few days she must have realized how difficult things were for me and she backed off. During Christmas dinner, she mentioned she wanted to return home to Scotland for one last visit but was hesitant, at 76, to go alone. A flashback instantly popped up in the middle of my mashed potatoes of the time she took Bruce and me to Scotland 25 years before for a year of "good sound Scottish schooling".

"Why don't you take Ian? He's almost eleven now, old enough to help carry your bags and hail cabs. It would be good for him, too."

As soon as she got off the plane in San Francisco, she went to a pay phone, called and said, "I'd like to take them both to Scotland…just like I did for you and Bruce, and I can't make fish of one and flesh of another. I'll enroll them at Alva Academy where you two went to school. I just have to water my garden, find someone to take care of it while I'm gone, and I'll be back in a week… so get them both ready."

Ian and Sandi adored their grandma whom we nick-named "Obi", short for Official Burper, because when they were babies, after I had spent what seemed like hours trying without success, she was always able to instantly get their colic burps up. They especially loved the yummy cookies and puddings she'd have waiting for us when we'd visit her in California. More than once, Sandi said how much she liked visiting Obi because of her tidy and neat-as-a-pin house. You could literally eat off her floors. I learned later in recovery that children of alcoholics usually end up as control freaks, trying to control as much as they can amidst the alcoholic chaos surrounding them. Sandi saw how much Obi controlled her surroundings and said the picture-perfect everything-in-its-place home made her feel safe. Mother had always been a utilitarian. When I was growing up, it seemed if something wasn't used for a week, the Salvation Army truck was in our driveway to pick it up. I used to keep jiggling around from side to side, afraid if I stood still too long, I'd be sent away, too, with the Salvation Army truck.

Ian and Sandi had heard all the stories about Alva Academy and both thought it'd be fun to go there with Obi. I tracked down their father to make sure he wouldn't object and then packed up what I thought they'd need. In five days, Obi was back. Two days later, off the three of them flew to London. The whole thing happened so fast I didn't have time to think about missing them. After they were gone a few days, gratitude set in for this break from motherhood and responsibilities. What a gift Mother was giving me! Their absence would give me time to attend as many recovery meetings as possible. I could begin dealing with the peeling-onion issues cropping up and create a firm foundation for my new sober life. At the same time, a lethargic sadness also set in. I was now totally alone in the house...no giggles echoing through the place, no hugs at bedtime.

Soon, I began to feel better as I was getting to lots of meetings and working more with my sponsor long-distance. By phone wasn't the best, but I managed to slip in some weekend trips to the shore to see her. Each Sunday, on the way back home, I was singing in the car, sending up prayers of gratitude, and just plain loving life. I began to understand that the marriage problems weren't all one-sided... I had a part in all of it, too. As a peace gesture, I invited the children's father to come to a meeting where I would be sharing my recovery story for the first time...sharing, as suggested in the program's Big Book, my "experience, strength and hope".

In the parking lot before we got out of the car and went into the meeting, he handed me a small gift-wrapped box and said, "I got this as a gift for you on this auspicious occasion. Figured you could use it."

Surprised by his thoughtfulness, I opened the box. "What is that thing?"

"A vibrator," he replied with a smirk.

I tossed it onto the back seat and in silence, thanked my Higher Power for sending such an undeniable sign that my life with that man had truly come to a proper and final end.

Chapter Six

Alright, Already...I Give In! I'll 'Let Go and Let God'

During that year, living alone, I looked forward to letters from Scotland. Obi was very faithful in keeping me posted as to the children's progress in school and about their new friends. Sandi regularly wrote little notes Obi would enclose with her letter. Ian only wrote once and Obi explained that he had good intentions but just never seemed to get around to writing.

One of Sandi's notes was a little distressing. "Dear Mum: I like Scotland a lot! Are you having nice weather? We are having nice weather. I heard that you are getting a divorcement. Well, it is much better for you I think. We went to Edinburgh last week and had a nice time."

So they knew. I had a lot of time now to think things through and came to the conclusion the children shouldn't be denied a chance to spend quality time with their father. Just because he and I had differences wasn't a reason to keep them from him. He wasn't a bad person...we just weren't right for each other. My disease of alcoholism had brought out the worst in both of us and had squelched whatever chances we had, if any, of working things out.

While Ian and Sandi were still in Scotland, I started getting messages from their father that he wanted to see more of the children when they returned. I wrote to the kids and explained I was still not living with their father and asked, "What do you think about living with your dad for the next school year when you come back? I've had you both for a year; Obi has had you all this year. Maybe it's his turn now."

Sandi wrote back in her cute little scribble, saying they were both happy about the idea. I was a little miffed at their speedy decision, but understood why. When he had eventually surfaced before they went to Scotland, I would let them spend weekends with him and they'd come back home Sunday night with, "Daddy doesn't make us pick up our clothes" or "Daddy lets us eat gobs of candy" or "Daddy doesn't make us do homework" or "We got to go out and eat Hamburgers both nights" and "Daddy got us a dog". Naturally, what kid wouldn't want to live with a parent who gave them everything they wanted and seemed to have no rules.

In spite of some misgivings and even though neither of us had formally started divorce proceedings, I went ahead with the custody idea and came up with what I thought was the perfect plan: I would move out and into a small apartment in downtown Philadelphia and he could move back into our suburban house. That way, the children could stay in the familiar home and neighborhood where they had friends, and could continue at the same elementary school they had been attending before going to Scotland. According to my plan, at the end of each school year, he would move out of the house and I would move back in. We would continue trading domiciles each school year until the children graduated from high school and I would have them the first summer, he the next . If he wished, he could even move into the apartment I'd find downtown when it was my turn to live with the children in the 'burbs. He thought it a great idea. I began to put things in order for the big change.

For months, the actual road surface had been showing through much of my MGB's passenger-side floorboards, not able to hold up to salt the highway crews put on winter roads. I hadn't known to include under-coating when ordering the car in London. Putting all my pennies together now to move, I knew there wouldn't be enough left to fix the MGB. With sadness, I sold it to the teenager down the street for $300 and used that as a deposit on a used, beautifully restored VW bug, getting from the local bank the very first car loan in my own name. Probably insignificant to others, but to me, having something that tangible in my very own name was a major achievement after being so many years the unnamed invisible partner in that marriage. It took less than a week to pack up my life for the move. I couldn't afford to buy furniture but also didn't want to strip the house where the children would be living. I decided to take the no-longer-used baby bureau, the small wrought iron patio ice cream set, my Victorian wicker chaise I acquired from one of the houses I bought during the real estate days, an antique single bed and mattress from my Bucks County days and later stored for years in the garage, a pair of sheets and set of towels, a white linen tablecloth and matching napkins (had to have at least one memento of the luxurious dinner parties I threw!), the mahogany silverware box of sterling flatware inherited from my Scottish grandmother, set of antique "made-in-Bavaria" china from my German grandmother, a few other small treasures from my family, files of all the articles I had written and awards I had won for features and for my photographs, and most important of all, as many of my books as I could fit into two boxes. I then turned my back on the 'burbs to move to my new Bohemian life in center city Philly.

Two weeks before the children were due home, I was joyfully settled in the $300/month small walk-up two rooms and bath apartment I found downtown. The landlord, who lived downstairs, was a single cello-playing architect and agreed to let me pay the security deposit off in installments or I wouldn't have had any money left to stock the fridge.

Hidden behind a sliding screen was a bare-minimum Pullman kitchen. Godawful ugly chartreuse shag carpeting covered the floors and featured multiple cigarette burns from years of abuse by careless tenants. The apartment's redeeming feature was a darling bay window in the living room which overlooked the narrow one-way tree-lined Pine Street below. The ice cream set I brought fit perfectly in the bay. Well, this isn't much, I thought, but it's all mine and at least I think I'll be able to afford the rent.

Before I moved out of the house, I set up a visitation schedule with the children's father whereby the kids would stay with me downtown every weekend and with him in the suburbs during the week. The first summer, I would have them and then it would be my turn to move back into the house with them that fall. Things didn't always work out as I had hoped. Often, I'd be sitting in the Reading Terminal waiting for their suburban train to arrive only to discover they weren't on it. Panic! A call to his house. No answer. More panic! A frantic search through the station, running from one platform to another as one after another train pulled in. More unending prayers for their safety. And then they'd step off a train an hour or even two later. I felt it was part of their father's ongoing scheme of revenge for whatever he wanted to throw at me as blame for the demise of the relationship. He no longer had someone saying, "How high?" Worse, someone had escaped his controlling clutches. Refusing to play into his cruel hand, I kept turning these things over to my Higher Power. I no longer had to pick up a drink over difficult situations as I normally would have in the past. I could get rid of forever the useless attitude, "I'll show him!" Now, instead, I'd ask my HP for help to keep me in forgiveness mode rather than in anger. Sometimes this was hard, but it was important for the children to see me as the loving caring mother I was so desperately trying to be during these changing times. It was also important to my sobriety!

Ian and Sandi came home from their year in Scotland, both looking much older and much happier than before they left. Obi had treated them well. The first weekend I was to have them with me, their father put them on the suburban train to come downtown. I met them at the Reading Terminal, astounded he had sent them on the train alone. Even though it was only a ten-mile ride, it was still 19 minutes that could have presented many dangers. The three of us held hands as we skipped along the few blocks to my place. I had purchased two sleeping bags for them and could hardly wait to show them our new little nest.

The first thing Sandi said was, "How come Daddy changed all the locks at our house? Is he afraid of robbers?"

I didn't know what to say. Best not to say anything other than, "I don't know, Honey. He must have had his reasons."

The next week, a registered letter came from Philadelphia's well-known "ball-buster" divorce lawyer. He had hired this guy and claimed I had moved out and abandoned the children. I couldn't believe his treacherous betrayal and was devastated but knew if I allowed anger or resentments to take over, they could lead me back to the bottle and then he would have really won.

"I'm not going to let him occupy space in my head rent-free" became my new mantra followed by, "He who angers me controls me". I was learning in recovery that the only thing to do was to move on and try to silently wish the jerk peace and happiness. At the meetings, they said to pray for him, so I agreed and told my sponsor I would do as one woman at the meeting said, "Pray for the son-of-a-bitch." I knew living with his own conscience would be punishment enough for his deceitful actions.

"I'm going to create a beautiful bubble around me so he can't hurt me," I told my beloved Marjorie on the phone, crying after every word. "It's going to be lavender and purple and pink, and beautiful flowers will be painted all over it…petunias, pinks, roses, daphne, wisteria. If he says or does mean things, I'm just going to let it all bounce off my bubble…bounce off far into the distance." I couldn't help adding, "If he does *really* mean things, I might just bounce them right back at him. One thing fersure, I'm not going to drink over any of this."

"God loves you, Sandra, and He's going to help you get through this," soothed Marjorie. "Just keep listening for His words of wisdom and keep going to as many meetings as you can. Call me anytime, night or day. I am always here for you."

That was when I realized I felt more love from Marjorie in the short time since I first met her than I had ever felt from my own mother.

After I was able to get that lawyer's nasty letter out of my mind, I went to a meeting and a friend asked why I wasn't my usual cheery self. I explained what was going and he pulled out a business card from his wallet and handed it to me.

"That's a lawyer friend of mine. He handled my first divorce and she didn't get a damn dime."

I made an appointment to see the lawyer, but after ten minutes, knew he wasn't the right one for me. He wanted to ruin my husband financially with all kinds of schemes and tricks. My husband wasn't an evil person, and I had often suspected he, too, needed the program. I then hired a woman attorney I met in the program who was married to one of Philadelphia's most celebrated criminal lawyers; she seemed on top of things. The first hearing we went to, my husband's lawyer made mincemeat out of my attorney and we walked out without anything resolved. I decided I didn't really need to push for a divorce since I was taking care of myself now without any help from him and the children were coming downtown to see me on weekends.

It wasn't until I was eight years sober that I'd find a lawyer with a general practice who put together the plain and simple divorce papers that allowed me half of the value of the little rental houses we had bought that I had found and taken charge of restoring, and also, half the values of the home in the suburbs and of the shore house. I forgot to include the buildable lot John and I owned up at the point in Strathmere which backed up to a huge bird sanctuary, expansive beach and the ocean. I picked the appraiser for all the properties but unfortunately, my husband got ahold of him and as my lawyer pointed out, "birds of a feather stick together". As expected, the appraisals came in extremely low. I didn't have the will or energy to fight…I just wanted out and free. The divorce was final on my 43rd birthday, January 11…what a fine birthday gift as I would be heading out that year for a new life far away from Philadelphia.

A month or so before Mother returned with the children from Scotland, she had been writing about problems with her leg and even of falling occasionally. As soon as she got to Philadelphia, I had her see an orthopedic surgeon considered the best in Philly. He recommended a laminectomy, a major surgical operation to remove the back of one or more vertebrae, usually to give access to the spinal cord or to relieve pressure on nerves. She agreed to this and three days later, I was waiting in the hospital lounge for her to come back from surgery. I waited and waited… for hours, feeling sick to my stomach. By mid-afternoon, still no news, so I rode my bike back to my apartment to get something to eat. Three hours later, a nurse called to say Mother was back from surgery and in a private room. Riding my bike as fast as I could through rush-hour traffic, I got to the hospital in record time, and took the elevator up to her room. Mother looked 50 years older, lying on the white sheets. Her eyes were closed. On the bed next to her was some sort of round plastic device with tubes leading into her side. A resident came in and picked the thing up and seeing that it was empty, called in the nurse.

"Has this been functioning since the patient was brought back?" he asked.

"I don't know," said the nurse. "I doubt it – no one knew how to get it turned on."

"Well, get the damned thing started," he snarled. "It should have been draining all this time." He walked out of the room, seemingly oblivious that I was sitting in the corner. I sat by her bed until visiting hours were over – she didn't wake up once.

The next morning, when I entered Mother's room, she wasn't there. The nurse on duty said they had taken her back to surgery. No explanation. Nothing.

"But, why?" I demanded. "No one even called me."

"The surgeon will speak with you shortly," was all she said before walking away.

I sat down to wait. All kinds of terrifying thoughts flashed through my mind. What had they done to her? Was she in a coma? Would she come out of it? Was she going to die? There was no one to talk to, no one to answer the hundreds of questions racing around in my head. Several hours passed and finally the surgeon showed up. He was with another doctor, a neuro-surgeon.

"I'm sorry to report that your mother doesn't seem to have any feeling in her legs. We've done additional tests and we haven't determined exactly what the problem is," said the surgeon. "We'll keep in touch with you," he added, tossing the words over his shoulder as he walked out of the room.

I felt abandoned. I went up to the neuro-surgeon before he could slip away, and said, "When I came into her room after surgery, there was some sort of draining device lying empty on her bed. Does that have anything to do with this? I think the resident called it a hemovac drain or something like that."

The neuro-surgeon put his hand on my shoulder and said, "Quite possibly."

The room started spinning around, I felt like vomiting. He caught me just before I passed out. That night, the surgeon called in an order for medication to try and unblock the nerves or whatever was causing Mother's problem. I later found out the resident who took the call misunderstood the dosage and made a terrible mistake, writing down sixteen times the amount she was supposed to have. She was rushed off again. The next day, I found out they were admitting she was paralyzed from the waist down and if that wasn't enough, she now also had a colostomy. They had blown out her colon with the overdosed medication and she was suffering from an acute case of peritonitis. I was overwhelmed with guilt, a feeling I had never been adept at dealing with in the past without getting sloshed. One thing I did know, however, was that picking up a drink wouldn't make this all go away. I had to listen to my friends in the program who kept telling me to "turn it over" and to "let go and let God" handle this. I spent my days and nights visiting Mother. Weeks, months passed. She began to suffer from I. C. U. psychosis being in and out of that unit for almost a year. Every time I rode my bicycle over to visit her, I learned of yet another crisis. Before long, I ended up in the same hospital for three days with a near nervous breakdown over it all, unable to urinate. But I stayed sober!

When I'd arrive and approach her bed, she'd look up at me pathetically from the rotating bed they had her in to prevent bedsores and whisper in her

Scottish accent, "Sandra, please let me go home... home to my ain wee hoose in California…to my garden…to my flowers, to my trees. Please, lassie, help me, please." I vowed silently to somehow get her back home to California.

Almost a year after the nightmare began, I was wheeling Mother out of that hospital to transfer her to a rehabilitation facility a few blocks away. An I. C. U. nurse came running out the front door of the hospital, grabbed the sleeve of my coat and said, "If I were you, I'd go get me a good lawyer," and then she rushed back into the hospital. Finding a lawyer was the last thing on my mind. That was something my brother could deal with.

Mother spent three months in that rehab and every morning, I'd ride my bike over to see her. The only pleasant memory I have of those visits was one morning when the front desk told me Mother was in the gym. I walked in and saw her in her wheelchair playing basketball with a bunch of Vietnam vets. Each time she grabbed the ball, she'd toss it right into the basket. I heard one vet say to the others, "How in the heck is that old lady making all the baskets and we can't even make one!" Yep, that was my mother!

When Mother was released from the rehab, I flew with her to California and got her settled in her house. Everything was perfect in the house and on the property. Her nearest neighbor she'd hired to take care of it all while she was in Scotland had done a splendid job. A Ford Econoline 150 van with electric lift and all kinds of bells and whistles my brother had ordered for her was delivered personally by the dealer the day after we arrived home. All I had to do was have a ramp made for her to go in and out of the front door. My parents had designed the house like a fortress and all the doors in the house were wide enough for her wheelchair.

I called on a friend I knew from my recovery meetings in Santa Cruz to agree to drive Mother in the van to medical appointments, for groceries and any other such trips. Before leaving to go back home, I hired a housekeeper but when she arrived to meet Mother, she told the woman, "I can take care of my own house, thank you very much!" Mother was the most independent woman I ever knew and when my father died, she really came into her own.

He had never wanted her to wear slacks, and the day after he died, she gave all her dresses to the Salvation Army and bought a wardrobe full of slacks. Now, even though paralyzed, she seemed feistier than ever.

After spending several days getting re-acquainted with her home and gardens, the third morning when I got up, I found her sitting in her wheelchair in the middle of her sun-filled California kitchen with an apron on, ready to bake scones. She told me I could go back to Philadelphia now and said it with a commanding snap that would have sent any army private scurrying to clean the latrines. And so I returned to Philadelphia but was called back to California in less than three months for Mother's first fall-out-of-wheelchair incidents . Many other such emergencies followed when I'd have to drop whatever I was doing and dig out my one and only credit card for an airline ticket to the coast.

She never complained about her condition nor about the rigors of the colostomy…a real trooper, she was. She would go through her daily routine of exercises, trying to lift herself up off the seat of the wheelchair with her arms, up and down, up and down. When I'd come to visit her, the first thing she'd show me as soon as I came in the door was how many more "lifts" she could do since my last visit.

"Look how high I can lift myself now, Sandra," she'd say proudly. "I need to keep myself strong for the day I will walk again."

"Hey, that's great, Mom! Go for it. You're doing a terrific job!"

And then the bedsores began in spite of all the precautions she took. She would turn herself over every hour while in bed and not sit too long in one position in the wheelchair but the sores continued to appear. On one of my trips home to help, I took her to a well-known orthopedic surgeon in San Jose to check her out and also, to ask about the bedsores. First thing Mother did was show him her chair lifts.

"I don't know why you bother with those exercises…you'll never walk again," he said as he stomped off.

She looked at me as if someone had just kicked her in the stomach. That supposedly highly-acclaimed doctor had taken away the only precious thing she had left…hope. I sure knew how that felt, and for the first time in my life, I could relate to my mother. For a split second, she slumped in her chair and then immediately sat up tall and proud. I knew what she was thinking for in my early days of sobriety, I had thought the same: 'He is not going to get me. I'm going to win this battle in spite of him. I can do this.' As I looked at her, I could almost hear the little train I knew from childhood chugging up the hill saying, "I think I can. I think I can," which in Mother's case was, "I know I can, I know I can."

I took my hands off Mother's wheelchair, put my arms around her and felt her body stiffen into a pose of determination.

Loud enough for all to hear, I said, "I love you, Mother. We can do this, you and me, with the help of God. Don't give up. I know we can do this. I'll help you all I can even if that damned doctor won't."

She just stared at me without any sign of emotion as if I were speaking in a foreign tongue. Slowly, her hands began to turn the wheels of her chair and I followed as she pushed herself away from hope and into what, for others, might have been despair. Two days later, she insisted I return to Philly so I caught the next early flight home as she knew it was Thursday and the children would be coming downtown the next afternoon for their weekend with me.

My friend drove me to the San Jose Airport and promised she'd take extra special care of Mother during their jaunts in the van. I was grateful she also reminded me to be sure to keep getting to meetings and turning things over to the HP.

Chapter Seven

They Kept Saying, "First Things First"

After the initial excitement had worn off of moving to Center City and out of the suburbs where I had never felt at home — all those silk blouses and tailored linen suits had no place in the closet with my Bohemian duds — I began slipping in and out of what others might have defined as, "depression". I refused to even use the word. It reminded me of all those nasty Valium prescriptions the doctors in the past had bombarded me with. I had a separate prescription from the family doctor, the psychiatrist, the gynecologist, the pediatrician and even the dentist! I'd get the prescriptions filled because they all said these pills would help me, and then just line them all up on the little shelf under the kitchen window, keeping them handy, "just in case". When I was leaving the suburban house, I wrapped up all the little bottles of Valium and sent them to Mother with a note, "All the doctors think these are the answer to every problem, health or otherwise. Maybe they'll help you!"

I didn't know a soul downtown and had never lived in a big city other than Grenoble 20 years before as a foreign student. I was still night editor of three weekly newspapers back in the suburbs, and had to "put the papers to bed" which often took well into the wee hours of the morning. This meant a middle-of-the-night 20-mile commute from where the papers were published back to Center City, and the inevitable hunt, at that hour, for the non-existent parking place.

Driving around and around the dark narrow streets at night was scary. I was often forced to park in an "iffy" neighborhood, blocks from my apartment, then walk through the empty streets armed only with my elementary-school tetherball-champion fist. I'd slip past subway-vent bums jabbering gibberish inside their cardboard condos, past homeless red-eyed drug addicts screaming obscenities to the moon, past bag ladies huddled over trash cans playing tug-of-war with a million-dollar find, all screeching in unison, "It's mine! It's mine!"

Soon, it also became upsetting having to return to my former life. The newspapers I wrote for covered my old marital stomping grounds, once a pleasant place, now one with too many unhappy memories. Each weekend, I listened to the children report awful untruths their father was saying about me. Who knew what horrible other lies he was spreading about me around that gossipy little town. Already, several of our mutual friends were snubbing me. I sure as hell didn't want to risk a return to drinking over the stress of it all. After a month of commuting out to the 'burbs, I quit the newspaper and was instantly without an income.

Turning the mounting fear of financial insecurity over to my Higher Power (whom by now I was often calling, 'God'), I would repeat several times a day one of my favorite new mantras: "God can move mountains, but you better know how to drive the bulldozer." It would be quite a while before I was doing poppa-wheelies on my bulldozer but at least it wasn't getting stuck in the mud every time I got on it. Without a job now and no spare money for gas and insurance, I left my little VW parked in the spot I found the night I quit the newspaper. It was seven blocks from my apartment, next to a city park where kids from the Projects played basketball. I didn't go to the car for over a week.

The second Sunday unemployed, I cheered myself up with a plan to drive to the seashore to attend the first meeting I had gone to in Cape May Court House. A friend from one of the meetings downtown came over to disengage the heater fan on the VW so it wouldn't blast out heat for the 90-mile run to the shore. We got to the car and discovered someone had forced the lock and moved in. The front seat was their bedroom with a blanket thrown over the steering wheel, the backseat their kitchen with all manner of jars and boxes filled with bits of fruit and half-eaten hoagies. We threw it all out, my friend disengaged the fan, and I drove to the shore.

On the return home, the car started to smell as if it were burning up but I made it back. In the morning, I drove to a mechanic where my VW promptly died in his garage. My friend had literally "blown it" by disconnecting the wrong fan, the one which cooled the engine now blown. I didn't have enough money to pay the rent due in a week let alone an expensive engine repair. The only thing left in my larder was a half-empty box of raisins and a half-devoured can of peanuts.

"How much will you give me for the car?"

"Oh, $400?"

"Sold," I said, and walked out heading to the subway clutching four crisp $100 bills for the rent and some groceries.

I wouldn't have to worry anymore about finding parking places and I'd save not having to pay for gas or insurance. Why later, maybe I could even enjoy the luxury of an occasional cab ride to the big supermarket just outside town! I was trying to stay in a positive mood even though, not counting the student year in France, I was now without wheels for the first time in over 20 years. It was time to get on that bulldozer and look for a job but I wasn't used to driving one, and had no idea where to start plowing up job leads. The whole emotional experience of leaving the marriage, giving up my full-time role as mother, leaving my home, quitting my job, moving into what seemed a foreign land, not having any money and even being turned down for food stamps made me feel helpless, hopeless and a total loser. I kept telling myself that as they said in the meetings, "Feelings aren't facts." I knew taking a drink wouldn't help and would just make everything worse…then I'd rush to a meeting!

I started walking aimlessly through the noon-time streets filled with professionals on lunch hour rushing in and out of cafés and boutiques. Without warning, right in the middle of 22nd Street between Pine and Spruce and just a few steps from ritzy Rittenhouse Square, a sign reached out and grabbed me: "Help Wanted. Apply Within". It was the bakery I had often passed, longing to go in to buy real bagels and challah but knowing my budget wouldn't allow such frivolous spending.

I pushed open the glass door, stepped up to the counter and said, "I'd like to apply for the position you have advertised in the window."

A swarthy man behind the counter reached below it, pulled out a grease-smeared application and muttered, "Just fill in your name, address, phone number, social security number… don't bother with education and work experience," he said gruffly with an Eastern European accent, tossing the application across the countertop. I filled it out and handed it back.

He briefly looked it over then said, "When can you start?"

"Well, I guess soon. What are the hours and what do you pay?"

"Sundays, six in the morning until three, no lunch break; Tuesdays, Wednesdays, Thursdays and Fridays, eight until five, 30 minutes for lunch. A student works on Mondays and Saturdays. You get $4 an hour and we don't take out taxes…you're contract labor and you take care of all that yourself, right?"

It could be worse…starving and no money at all for rent. I wondered if he'd sell me the day-old goodies at an employee discount.

"I'll take it and I can start tomorrow, Tuesday."

"Fine. 8:00 a. m. and that doesn't mean 8:05", he added, not once looking up. "I'll meet you tomorrow morning with the key."

I worked at the bakery into the winter, and to appease my ego, wore a short skirt and cutsie little frilly apron, summoned up my best Betty Boop voice, and pretended I was playing a part in a Broadway comedy. I learned early that the poorer folks coming in for day-old goodies treated me nicer than the highfalutin heifers, society dames and professionals who didn't know I spoke five languages and had a master's degree from a French university.

A favorite bakery-related activity was on Thursdays, when I was closing up the bakery, I'd buy four day-old croissants and on my way home, as I passed them, pop one croissant into each of the cardboard condos a homeless person had built over a subway vent in the sidewalk. I thought it ingenious how they used the air from the subway below to heat their winter digs, and figured everyone, no matter their circumstances, should be able to enjoy a morning croissant. In a small way, it was a gesture to let the HP know I was thankful I didn't have to live in one of those sad little "condos". What I didn't know at the time was that the recipients of this weekly "gratitude habit" would later help me in an unexpected way.

When Ian and Sandi came down to visit on weekends, they loved spending Sundays at the bakery. Sandi would stand on the stool and use both her index fingers to push the keys down on the antique cash register. Ian would sit on the other stool, double-checking her and chatting with the customers while ogling the chocolate chip cookies. I told them if they were friendly and polite to the customers, I would treat them with my own money to one cookie every two hours. When no one was in the store, the three of us would make up stories about what we would do if I didn't have to go to the bakery and they didn't have to go to school. Our favorite was the idea of riding trains all over the country. I soon found out we could do it for 90 days and my fare would be $90, theirs half-price on a special deal Amtrak was running ... a lot cheaper than staying cramped up in my apartment all summer paying for air-conditioning, and definitely more fun than working in a bakery. As this would be my summer to have the children, I signed us up to leave the day school got out. My credit card loved the idea and after paying for the tickets, I began putting aside weekly as much as I could spare to pay for our dream trip. I figured thoughts of the adventure would help get me through the approaching cold and dismal winter.

I never saw the baker after the day he hired me…the goodies were in big trays on the counter when I arrived, waiting to be put out in the cases. My check was always in the till on Fridays. One Sunday several months later, he came storming into the bakery just as I was about to close.

"Alright. That's it. You're through," he snarled.

"What? Are you firing me?"

"Yes. The till was short again and I'm not going to put up with you stealing from me."

Flabbergasted, I said, "I've never stolen a thing in my life! Maybe your Monday/Saturday girl is stealing, but it certainly wasn't me."

"I've taken $38 dollars out of your check to make up for the shortfall and you can grab your things and get out of here."

I was mortified but grateful it was one of the Sundays the children were spending with their father as we had made a trade earlier so he could go to some weeknight party. It would have been terrible if they had witnessed this humiliating moment. Walking through the dismal streets, I felt lower than a one-legged cockroach. It was raining. My only good pair of shoes was getting soaked. I had no raincoat. When I left my dingy little apartment early that morning, it wasn't raining and I had only grabbed the umbrella. Now the rain was blowing up around my legs about to ruin my only suitable-for-work outfit. All I had to my name was a pair of dungarees, a couple of tops, a sweatshirt and pants, my "Lois Lane" suit, a pretty summer frock, one pair of heels, a pair of sneakers, and the shoes and dress I was now wearing which were getting hopelessly soaked.

Aeolus made fun of the umbrella I had picked up for a buck the week before at Woolworth's. Each gust turned it inside out, ripping ribs away from the flimsy material. It didn't matter if I got drenched… it didn't even matter anymore about the shoes and dress. I tossed the umbrella into a trash receptacle and started walking through downtown with rain dripping all over my face and down my long hair. It felt cool and wonderful…cleansing, healing, refreshing. I stepped right into the mud puddles at the curbs making the water splash into the air. I was a child again with all the inhibitions and restrictions of the adult slithering off to hide in some dark corner. I had one of the best times of my new sober life that Sunday afternoon, finally set free from the bondage of my mother's Victorian principles and her inflexible rules of proper behavior.

I felt lonely in the apartment. It was still raining which made it even more dark and dreary. The walk had lifted my spirits, but they were now quickly sinking back into the quagmire. I refused to put a name to these miserable feelings. Change attitude, change attitude, I kept hearing from the meetings. Think positive, think positive. Sitting in the bay window at the ice cream set table, I gazed out into the street and resurrected memories of the previous weekend when I had the children. That Saturday afternoon, I was in the bathroom doing our laundry in the bathtub because I didn't have money for the coin laundry three blocks away. Ian and Sandi were giggling in the living room.

"It's my turn now, Ian," said Sandi in her high-pitched little voice.

"OK, Sandi, here. What's going on?"

"The man with the white hat is riding on his horse and those two men with the black hats are chasing him," she reported. "Now, he's getting off his horse and it looks like he has a rope in his hand."

"It's my turn, Sandi. Hand it over."

"OK, Ian, here. Now what are they doing?"

"Let's see… the man with the white hat has tied his horse to a fence and now he's pulled out a gun and it looks like he is going to shoot those two bad men!"

"Oh, no, really, Ian? Did they fall down?"

"Nope, they're still standing."

What on Earth were the kids doing? I peeked around the corner into the kitchen-living room where they were seated at the bay window. Ian was holding my grandmother's mother-of-pearl opera glasses given to her in

Scotland when she was ten years old by two old dowagers who had just returned from Paris. The opera glasses were over 100 years old and one of the few family treasures I grabbed when I left the suburbs. It took me a few seconds to figure out the children were using the opera glasses to watch the neighbor's television across the street where the man on the third floor had his TV near his front window. They had come up with a very creative use of time while I was occupied. I slipped back to the bathroom to hurry and finish the laundry before having to put them on the train back to the suburbs. Hide-and-go-seek in the tiny apartment, Monopoly games, cooking "lessons", making fudge and cookies, and lots of giggles… it was always more fun on weekends when Ian and Sandi came to visit rather than when I was alone weekdays, often feeling like I was stuck in solitary confinement.

When they came to stay, we pretended we were on a camping trip. One weekend, we'd set up "camp" in the west corner of the living room… that corner was Greenwich Village and their sleeping bags were next to Le Figaro Café where, when I first came back from France, I'd race to in my MGB from Solebury alone every Sunday afternoon in 1963 and '64. I'd hang out all day drinking thick espressos while playing chess and eavesdropping on Bob Dylan, Lenny Bruce or Jack Kerouac spinning esoteric tales. The next weekend, it was the east corner which was North Beach and "camp" was next to the hungry i club where I attended the Kingston Trio's first gig there in 1958 and drooled over "Tom Dooley". Another weekend, our south corner was the left bank of Paris next to the Café Des Deux Magots where I spent so many nights eating fresh escargots slathered with garlic. The kids would always say, "Snails? Yuck!" When it was time to camp out in our north corner, the sleeping bags were smack-dab in the center of Trafalgar Square right under the statue of Admiral Horatio Nelson where I used to sit glued to C. S. Forester's biography of Lord Nelson. We never seemed to run out of fascinating places to call our "campground".

A week after The Firing, alone and jobless, I sat Sunday evening at the table looking out into the silent narrow one-way street, counting the silver rain drops sliding down the window in a whimsical pattern. My eyes went beyond the raindrops to Grandfather Sycamore right outside, almost touching my window. He was the only tree on the block. Aeolus, in his angry winter mood, had stolen all Grandpa's leaves. I tried to relate to the tree. Maybe I was one of the big branches stretching skyward, but I felt too insignificant. Maybe I was the smaller branch going off at an artsy angle. No, it looked stronger than me. What about the tiny limb coming off that shorter branch? No, it had a firm grasp of the branch and looked healthier and more vibrant than I was.

A whirlwind of utter desperation filled the room. What's wrong with me? My life was supposed to be getting better--I wasn't drinking, was going to two and three meetings daily—and yet I was miserable and couldn't even relate to a tree limb! Then I espied a tiny leaf clinging to the end of the smallest twig. The rain was blowing through the tree and Aeolus was trying his hardest to blow that leaf off the twig, but she hung in there, steadfast and determined to cling on. I watched the leaf as she battled into the night. She gave me hope…. I just had to cling on like that little leaf and if she could make it through the cold night, so could I…and without drinking, too. The next morning, I got up and sure enough, she was still there, dangling and dancing timidly with her manic waltz partner, Aeolus.

"Hang in there," I called, cheering for her. "We're in this together! I won't give up if you don't!"

When I'd come back home from a meeting or from wandering through Center City trying to figure out what to do next with my life, I'd run to the window to see if my leaf was still there. She hung in through the winter rains, she hung in through the snows…and so did I. And then came the first hint of spring and when I went to the window one morning, I saw fresh shoots on the tree. New leaves were appearing. Would my pal still be there? Sure enough…still hanging in there. She clung on until the tree was completely covered with shiny new green leaves. Then one day, I couldn't see her anymore. All her new friends had gathered around her, just like I was discovering new friends around me at meetings. I knew she was in there, hiding among the new leaves smiling and cheering me on. I wanted to change my name to "Leaf" so

I would always remember to think about her valiant struggle and be inspired by it when times might get tough.

"What do you think if I change my name to Leaf?" I asked the kids on their next weekend visit.

"Leaf? That sounds way too silly, Mom," said Sandi. Ian agreed.

So instead, it became my secret name I didn't share with anyone but Marjorie and my Higher Power. Sometimes, on rare occasions when I was in one of my past-life elegant moods, it became *Feuille*.

My piggybank was empty now, my financial situation bleaker than a moonless winter night on the Scottish moors. I was steadily losing weight because of the meager diet. One night I felt so bad in spite of my leaf, in my mind, still rooting for me, that I lay down to meditate on the only piece of furniture in the living room. It was the Victorian wicker chaise-lounge I had hauled out of one of the small houses I bought at a sheriff sale when I was working with my husband in our real estate office before the children were born. I usually bought houses when someone had died and the sale included everything... furnishings, dishes, corsets, rats and all. I had assembled a team of not-always-sober paperhangers, painters and carpenters and learned early on to tell them they would not get paid until the job was totally done. It was fun fixing these houses up and restoring any interesting furniture I acquired with the sale. This Victorian chaise was one of those acquired treasures. I had cleaned up the wicker and then covered its long cushion and back-rest pillow with floral chintz. It was now the centerpiece in my humble apartment. I flicked off the lights and lay on it for some time, meditating to try to chase away the fears that were hounding me like a hungry stray mongrel.

"Are You up there? I'm sorry to bother You, but I need Your advice now, God. What should I do? I have no money for the rent due next week, I'm on a steady diet of raisins and peanuts, and I feel lost and alone. Going back to drinking will just make things worse, but I don't know how to get out of this black hole. Please, God, help me!" I pleaded out loud for the first time in my new sober life, and lay in silence, hoping for an answer.

As I was drifting off to sleep, I heard softly spoken into my left ear, "Don't worry, Sandra. Everything is going to be alright." I opened my eyes to see who had snuck into my apartment. A warm glow filled the room and I saw a specter standing by my bare feet at the end of the chaise. It was all in white and although I didn't see its face, it must have been God. Who else could it have been? And then it was gone, leaving behind the greatest sense of peace. I no longer felt abandoned, hopeless. In an instant, outlook on my situation changed from negative to positive…and I felt sure I was going to make it through these hard times.

There were lessons everywhere that would help me and all I had to do was put one foot in front of another as I worked the program's Twelve Steps. I didn't have to solve all my problems overnight. In fact, now they weren't problems anymore…they were challenges. My life wasn't going to be one hardship after another…it was going to be a series of interesting challenges, all, I hoped with successful solutions. And the best part? I had a funny feeling that wonderful things were waiting for me out there.

"Keep paddling, girl, you're going to make it! Open yourself up and get ready to accept the gifts," I'd hear, whispered in my left ear. "You're worthy and you deserve to be happy, joyous and free."

I'd go to sleep whispering my new mantra, "Hey girl, learn to be grateful, then just go for it. Everything is going to be alright."

Chapter Eight

"One Day At A Time"

With this new positive outlook came a higher level of courage, confidence and motivation. A series of interesting job possibilities started creeping into my head. Certainly not as a barmaid for that would be around the "people, places and things" I needed to avoid and which program friends said could lead to a drink. Not as a waitress, either. I tried that when I was ten days sober and had heard hotels and restaurants in Ocean City needed help because the summer-help college students were going back to school. The resort city was only eight miles north of Strathmere, just a 21-minute drive across the free bridge. So, off I went to The Flanders, a grand hotel built in 1923 on the boardwalk and known then, with all its Victorian architectural adornments, as "The Queen of the Jersey Shore". It was named in memory of the fallen Allied troops of World War I's dreadful Battle of Flanders fought in Belgium in 1914, and walls of its sumptuous ballrooms were covered with hand-painted images of poppies to symbolize the Battlefields of Flanders. In the "old days", my husband and I enjoyed many Sunday brunches at The Flanders. Greeted at the entrance to the exquisite dining room by a trio of accomplished musicians, we'd listen during our lavish meals to the strains of Chopin, Haydn, Brahms and others. When I applied for the job, I was told I had to wear tennis sneakers.

So, taken out of my slim wallet came the price of that luxury. Three days later, first day on the job, I followed the "trainer" around the huge dining room for hours and quit when the shift was over, as all day, I hadn't even been able to keep track of which table had ordered what. Not totally a useless exercise—at least, I now owned a nice spanking new pair of sneaks!

Now, a year later down the road, I was once again attempting to find a job. I waited a week after being fired by the baker before trying again. This time while meditating, I got a weird "message" suggesting I muster up some chutzpah, walk into one of the city's well-known art schools, claim I was an experienced artist model, and ask if there were any openings for models. Two days later, I was running to the library to look up how to be an artist's model for my first gig that night…a course in Fashion Design. I wore the one pretty dress I brought with me when I moved downtown…an all-white sleeveless, low-cut full-skirted summer frock with lace around the neckline. To the ensemble, I added a white feather boa from my beatnik wardrobe, string of pearls and a lovely wide-brimmed summertime straw hat I found on sale at Woolworth's the same day I bought the umbrella.

I was a nervous wreck that night, entering the class just before it began at 6:00 p. m., so I pretended it was just another role I was playing in a theatrical production. The class was filled with drafting tables and a student sat at each one. In the center was a raised platform with a spotlight hanging from a pole.

"When you're ready," said the instructor, "you can get up on that platform and start by doing 20 croquis in 20 minutes and when the buzzer rings, take a five-minute break before doing 20 more."

I had no clue what a croquis was. Wracking my befuddled brain, I guessed that since he wanted twenty in twenty minutes, a croquis must be a one-minute pose. Every minute, I turned a different way, set my head at various angles, moved my arms one way, my legs another and got into as many different contortions I could think of without breaking my neck. He didn't stop me and nobody threw paint brushes at me, so what I was doing must have been in the ballpark. When I got down for my break, an older gentleman at a nearby table motioned me over.

"How long have you been doing this?"

Oh, dear…the jig's up, I thought, but looked him straight in the eye and said, "This is my first time modeling. Why, didn't you like what I was doing?"

"*Au contraire*," he said. "You're the best model we've ever had and I've been attending these classes around town for years."

That night began a new career that would provide not only the long-missed bacon and maybe even sausages with my eggs, but also give me a reason to get up in the morning, get dressed, and go out and enjoy facing the world. Before long, I had a full schedule of gigs at the three major art schools downtown.

Second week of modeling, I arrived at a class to hear two art instructors arguing that one had reserved me while the other argued back that he had reserved me first. Another time, when I did an especially difficult pose which I could only hold a minute or two without stopping for air, the instructor broke out of his normal stiff demeanor.

"My goodness, students…I've never seen any pose like this. Take full advantage of it as you'll never see another as difficult and interesting." During my first break, two students went downstairs to the café and came back up with a cup of coffee and a Hershey bar for me as they said they had noticed I enjoyed these before during other breaks. At the end of that class, the students all stood up and gave me a standing ovation.

Modeling was turning out to bring me more pleasure and gratitude than I had ever expected. Before long, I was modeling in unheated rooms above bars with artists pooling their pocket-change to pay me for modeling sessions, at well-known artists' private studios, at the prestigious Philadelphia Sketch Club and other arts locations. I wasn't making a fortune at $7/hour, but it was paying the bills. I heard one day that the models at art schools in San Francisco were striking outside the schools for a raise…nude! This would definitely not go over well in conservative Philadelphia! So we all were satisfied with $7/hour.

I modeled under an alias: at one school, I was Laura Langsdorf, at another, Laura Lippincott, names used when I was hanging out in Stanford's Student Union during high school days. I was afraid if the children's father found out about the modeling, he might claim I wasn't a responsible mother and I could lose my visitation rights. When someone phoned for "Laura", I knew it was another modeling gig.

One afternoon in a coffeehouse off Rittenhouse Square, I ran into a Black artist who was also a Temple University art professor. I had interviewed and written a complimentary feature article about him and his art the year before I left the newspaper. He invited me to join him at his table for coffee and before the second cup of cappuccino, I would be starting the next week as his "artist assistant" at a very good hourly rate. Between my art school modeling commitments, I set up promotional interviews for him, wrote and submitted press releases of his coming exhibitions, organized new show openings of his works in Philadelphia and New York City, and even helped him with his printmaking when he was behind for a show deadline. We had fun together and I even had the courage to share with him some of the poetry I had been writing. When he'd go away for a short break or even long vacations with his girlfriend, I'd stay in his high-ceilinged home/studio which took up the entire third floor of a warehouse downtown. He needed me to keep refilling and checking the water level of a large humidifier set up to protect his antique Steinway grand piano. When a friend from my recovery meetings (whom I suspected was with the FBI) found out where I was staying, he asked if he could put "just a little thing" in the front window. Turns out the small Italian restaurant downstairs across the street was rumored to be a frequent haunt of the local Mafia. After careful consideration, I told him although I'd love to help the FBI, I couldn't allow it because I was there on a job and he would have to get permission from the artist.

After working on printmaking one afternoon, my artist friend intro-duced me to some fabulous Black jazz musicians, mostly older men in their 60s and 70s who always wore dark blue suits and starched white shirts. My mother would have approved – they were polite, gracious and extremely talented. I was honored when the leader of one group invited me to be a regular on a jazz radio show to recite some of my poetry in between pieces they performed. After the programs, they'd take me to their favorite soul-food hangouts where I was usually the only White person in the place. I was in my element after having spent most of my teen years hanging out with Beat poets and frequenting jazz clubs in San Francisco…with a fake ID, of course. No need for one at these homey eateries where booze wasn't even on the menu.

As I began to feel more comfortable in my sobriety, one day I worked up the courage to apply for a job as director of the Women's Committee Office, the fundraising/special events arm of The Academy of Natural Sciences. On the way to the interview, panic hit and I stepped into a phone booth to call and cancel the appointment. When the woman I was to meet answered, for some weird reason, all I said was that I would be a few minutes late. I got the job and a week later, was sitting in my private office, setting my own hours, and soon organizing gala fundraisers, creating new Academy-sponsored events like the Philadelphia Wildfowl Exposition, running The Academy's esteemed Philadelphia Wildlife Art Expo, and the city's largest festival, Super Sunday, an Academy benefit. The New York Times featured the event for the three years I ran it, calling it, "the world's largest block party". When I took it over, it had drifted down into more of a carnival. I brought it back up to a highly respected Arts event with every type of music and dance going non-stop from 10:00 a. m. to 7:00 p. m. on seven different stages along the Benjamin Franklin Parkway that led from The Academy's location on Logan Square up to the Art Museum. The Parkway was converted from busy boulevard to bustling bazaar.

According to an article one year in the New York Times, "There was music from strolling minstrels and the choral concert at a nearby cathe-dral and special exhibits at the Philadelphia Art. Museum and the Franklin Institute and the book sale at the Free Library and men riding old-fashioned bicycles and gushing fountains and a giant, paint-it-yourself mural and sheep and goats from the Philadelphia zoo — but the biggest show was the people. There were well-dressed lawyers from Bryn Mawr and young Black men in broad-brimmed hats and old white women in aging furs and babies in carriages and babies in carts and babies in papoose frames and teen-agers with long hair and bankers with no hair and young girls in short skirts and middle-aged matrons in long ones and children by the hundreds —screaming, laughing, eating, drinking, spilling, running, falling, pulling the tails of dogs and patting the tails of policemen's horses and getting lost."

It was important to me that the event be open and free to all…a way to share all kinds of music and dance with some who might never have had a chance to attend a performance at *The Academy of Music*, Philadelphia's cornerstone of the Arts and the oldest opera house in the United States. It first opened its doors in 1857 and was still hosting celebrated musicians and performers from around the world. My husband and I had enjoyed many concerts and operas there where I would later be appearing on stage in operas, myself.

Since profits from Super Sunday came from the booth fees of over 300 vendors selling all kinds of wonderful things, I was also able to set up an entire plaza of free booths for non-profits to showcase their services. I got the best fireworks from Japan to end each festival – they were amazing! The second year, for fun, I helped a friend of mine who each year brought a large truckload of ceramics, pottery and art items up from Mexico for the event. I couldn't believe how fast he was selling things. In fact, he could hardly get something out of a big box under his sales counter before it was sold and someone else wanted two or three of the same. He told me he made more at Super Sunday than he made in a year anywhere. What a fanatical frenzy of shopping! At the end of the day, I was exhausted and could hardly wait for the fireworks to finish so I could get home to my comfy little bed. The <u>NY Times</u> estimated that more than 500,000 attended the one-day event each year. Every festival brought in more than $100,000 clear for The Academy, and the other non-profits added a tidy sum to their coffers as well.

While at the same time working at The Academy, I was also learning the ropes to be a lobbyist for the Arts in Pennsylvania under the tutelage of Philadelphia's toughest and most successful woman. She had served as right-hand woman to the city's mayor for years (everyone said it was Natalie who was really running the city). The Academy Women's Committee members were so happy with all I was doing for them that they didn't mind when I took a few days off occasionally to travel with Natalie to the State Capitol to charm Budget Appropriations Committee members into allocating more funding to our clients which included The Academy of Natural Sciences, Philadelphia Museum of Art, Carnegie Institution of Science, the Franklin Institute, Lincoln University and others.

Juggling my schedule became my forte, aided by the 'I-can-do-this' outlook which landed me in the most interesting and creative situations. My new surgeon beau introduced me to his friend who was Philadelphia's biggest wheeler-dealer developer. The three of us started playing tennis weekly at a private club. After royally beating the developer on more than one of these tennis bouts, what a surprise when he asked me to curate and manage his world famous art collection. I managed to squeeze in time to work for him while still helping the artist, keeping my job at The Academy, working with the lobbyist, and occasionally modeling. I think the developer admired that I wouldn't cow-tow to him like all the others around him. He respected the cheekiness he saw peeking out from behind my smile as I gained confidence with each success, small or grand, that I was tucking under my new wings.

All these enterprises coming together made it financially possible for me to move out of the apartment and rent an adorable historic cottage on Philadelphia's smallest official square, Lantern Square. It was a three-story "father-son-holy ghost" house with one room on each floor. The children loved visiting because they could eat their lunch outside sitting in the little square under its solitary beech tree, sit out there playing cards, or chat with the neighbors whose houses looked into the square. The cottage had a small den on the second floor and I bought a used sofa-bed for the room and a third sleeping bag so they could take turns bringing a friend from the suburbs with them for their weekend visits.

At a recovery Step meeting one night, I mentioned to a friend how much I missed my piano that I had to leave behind in the suburbs. He shared that he'd had a rather illustrious career as a violinist and one night, in a drunken frenzy, had smashed his priceless violin into smithereens ending his career and bringing him to our program. He just happened to know a fellow a few blocks from Rittenhouse Square with a store selling antique and used instruments.

"The last time I was in Vintage Instruments, I saw an antique petite square grand piano for sale. I think it was made in 1838 and needs some work, so you might be able to bargain for it."

I went to the store which was up a long flight of stairs on the second floor of a row of elegant shops and just a few blocks from my cottage. There it was, the only piano in the place, standing bright but lonely in a corner. The price was $1,000 including delivery which was way above anything I could even think of affording and I walked out. A week later, I returned to ask if the storekeeper would sell it to me on credit…a little down, a little a month. He wouldn't and didn't take credit cards. I walked out. The next visit, I asked if he would reduce it and he said, "800." Still too much. Another visit and I got him down to $600 but that was yet too much. One last try, five weeks later, on my way to Vintage Instruments just before noon when I was sure they'd be up, I stopped at two of the side-by-side cardboard condos. Three of the residents were sitting out catching some rays.

"Remember me? I'm the one who used to drop off croissants each week. I was wondering if you'd do me a favor. I need three strong handsome fellows like you guys to help me carry a piece of furniture from a store a few blocks over to my house four blocks away. When we get to my house, I'll give each of you $10 and a big bag of delicious croissants and pastries to share. What do ya say?"

They stood up and practically saluted me and without uttering a word, turned, ready to follow me to the store.

"Listen, I'm grateful you're willing to help me, boys, and I'm not fussy, but before we get going, you've all gotta zip up your pants."

When we got to the store, I told the boys to wait downstairs while I went up to make final arrangements.

"Not you again," grumbled the storekeeper.

"Well, I see you haven't sold that old piano over there in the corner and my final offer is $400 and I'll take it right off your hands today, with no need for delivering it."

"OK, but only if you get it out of here before I close at 3:00 p. m."

"Not to worry – start unscrewing her legs and my movers will be right up."

The legs were off, a rope was tied around to hold them to the top of the piano, and with me at the right flank, the four of us started to carry my beloved new piano through the streets of Philadelphia's swankiest shopping district.

"Hey, listen…if you sing *St. James Infirmary* with me as we walk through town, I'll toss in an extra couple of bucks, each." They just smiled and off we went to Lantern Square.

As soon as I had paid and thanked them, I sat down at the piano which fit just by inches into the corner of my living room, and without music, played my favorite piece I'd been playing since I was a child…Chopin's Nocturne Op 9, No 2. In the morning, I looked up the number of the nice gentleman I had written a feature about three years before. Merrill Jackson had been the renowned piano tuner for the Philadelphia Orchestra for countless years (never used anything mechanical, just a tuning fork!) and my feature showed what a kind person he was, teaching others at a very nominal fee how to tune pianos in the basement of his modest home.

"Merrill…it's me, Sandra Smith. I was wondering if you're still tuning pianos and if so, could you tune mine?"

"Sandra! What a delight to hear from you. Most certainly...when shall I come over?

"Well, it's not the piano you knew as I'm not living out there in the suburbs anymore, I'm living downtown and it's a petite square grand piano with organ, built in 1838."

In a week, Merrill was seated at my piano and when he finished his first attempt at fixing things, he wouldn't take a penny, saying how much he had appreciated the kind words I had for him in my feature article. I arranged a trade –each time he would come to my piano, I would have the name and phone number of someone else downtown who needed a piano tuned. It took several months which included ordering an entire set of new strings from Kentucky. I didn't mind the cost...it would just be one less steak on my plate, one more Hamburger. He apologized for not being able to work on the organ part of the instrument. I assured him I was thrilled with what he had already done to make my piano sing again.

It wasn't long before I was hosting free Sunday Afternoon Musicales in my home, playing with a number of program friends who had been classical musicians before getting sober and were grateful to get back to their music. One of them, another violinist, showed up three times just to listen and the fourth time, walked in with a violin which he didn't even take out of its case. On the fifth Sunday, he arrived with a pile of music he had checked out from the library and his violin, all dusted off and ready to be played. It was kind of sad when, after many musicales, he announced he was taking up jazz and wouldn't be playing with us anymore. The musicales faded into the distance and other activities came into my life.

Three months after moving in, I turned the cottage into Philadelphia's first bed and breakfast in Center City, taking reservations through a service but only at times when the children wouldn't be coming down and when I needed extra bucks. Of course, I only had one bedroom, one pair of sheets and two decent towels. If I got a reservation, I'd race to the nearby laundromat to have clean linens for the guests and then stash all my personal things downstairs that normally were in the bedroom upstairs.

If I had taken a reservation for a night when I had a date with my beau to go to a fundraising ball or something else as glamorous, I would simply leave the key under the big rock by the front door, an envelope pinned to the front door with the guest's name on it and a welcoming note inside, saying to follow the walking directions provided in the note which also stated that the key location would be provided in a recorded phone message at the end of the short walk. The message was: "Go out the square's gate, turn right, walk 52 steps along the wooden cobblestoned lane to the corner, take another right to the next corner. Walk across the street to the phone booth in front of the pizza parlor and call 215-732-4019" which was my beau's phone number, hooked up to an answering machine. The recorded message would say, " Now, to finish the treasure hunt…retrace your steps back to Lantern Square where you'll find the key under the big rock lying to the left of the front door."

Once inside, greeting them on the entry counter was another note: "Freshly-roasted coffee from the Reading Terminal and a French-press coffeemaker are by the kitchen sink next to a plate of my homemade scones; butter, fig jam and cream for the coffee are in the fridge with a plate of fresh fruit and a pitcher of freshly-squeezed OJ. Some homemade fudge and yummy cookies are by your bed in the bedroom upstairs on the third floor (no crumbs in the bed, please!). The bathroom is on the second floor and your towels are sitting on the little table outside the bathroom. Help yourself to anything you'd like, play the piano as loud and long as you wish (no one can hear!), and have a wonderful time. Just lock up and leave the key back under the rock when you check out and thanks for staying in my cottage. Love, Sandra."

When I'd return home after spending the weekend at my beau's, I'd often find a vase with three roses on the piano, or a bottle of French perfume, or a box of Lady Godiva chocolates on the entry counter with a note telling me what a wonderful time the guest had.

Reservations included fascinating guests such as a Harvard professor who had published tomes on the isolated tribes living in New Guinea, and several of The Academy's visiting scientists including, from Paraguay, the world's expert on legless lizards, and from Florida, an ornithologist renowned for his extensive studies of sea birds. I ended up with an arrangement with The Academy to house their visiting scientists on a longer-term basis at a very modest amount, thereby saving The Academy money on rent which they could put to inviting more scientists to study their collections. This resulted in going off on long weekends with the ornithologist to study the scientific collections of the Field Museum in Chicago and the American Museum of Natural History in New York, helping him count feathers for his research on the molting patterns of sea birds and how this affects their feeding habits. I found it entertaining to wander around the hallowed halls of these august institutions carrying in my arms a huge stuffed Royal Albatross, Northern Gannet or a Solan Goose, then setting the old boy on a table and counting, one by one, his feathers to see which ones he had already molted.

I also had as guest, an Ivy League university librarian who at the end of her week's stay literally let her hair down. She'd sat in on the nightly rehearsals held all week downstairs in the living room of a six-member activist playwriting group I helped found called, *Popular Neurotics*. We wrote social-justice skits based on current news items which we then performed monthly on City Hall steps and other appropriate places around town. The night before checking out, with some mild encouragement, the middle-aged librarian took her hair out of the bun it had been tied up in all week (and probably her entire life!), put on some of my Bohemian duds I had dug out and put on her bed to choose from for her costume, and looking 20 years younger than when she arrived, came shyly down the stairs to the living room where we were all waiting to leave for the bar where we would perform. She played to perfection the small part we added for her in the skit we had been rehearsing all week. That opening night debut performance would change her life.

The piece was about the controversial and highly condemned MOVE police action and house bombing which killed six MOVE members and five of their children and destroyed an entire block and 61 houses in West Philly where the Black liberation group members lived in a communal setting, abiding by philosophies of "anarcho-primitivism". We performed this skit first (with the librarian) on a small stage in a somewhat seamy and slightly sleazy bar near where the bombing incident occurred and the next week, performed it, with much trepidation, in a community center there in West Philly where we were the only White folks in a filled-to-capacity auditorium. When we arrived, we were met with suspicion and mistrusting looks; when we finished the skit, it was to a standing ovation with the loudest cheers and applause we had ever received.

Two weeks after she returned home, the librarian sent me the sweetest note thanking me for everything and telling me that in the one week spent on Lantern Square, her entire life had changed and she was now ready for new adventures and exciting experiences. She had already moved out of the boring stifling relationship she had been in for fifteen years and found herself a cute little apartment downtown. I wrote back, "You go, girl!"

I had other favorite guests including two gay guys who were reuniting after a year apart when one had been severely injured in an accident. His entire face had to be reconstructed and this would be the first time his partner would see him after all the surgery. Ahead of arrival, he called to express anxiety over the upcoming reunion.

"Everything is going to be alright," I assured him, remembering how helpful those words had been to me not too long before.

A week after they checked out, he called to say he had lost his wallet and could I please look around the house for it. I searched everywhere with no success.

When I called to express my sorrow at not finding the wallet, he said, "Sandra, I'm so sorry. I lied. I didn't lose my wallet. I just had to talk to you because you were so kind to me and so sympathetic about my situation. I returned to NYC, my friend went back to Atlanta and I haven't heard from him since."

"Don't worry, Sweetie. Just keep on keeping on and everything is going to be alright."

He started to cry and I said, "I am here for you, Hon. Call me anytime, night or day."

My favorite guest was a professor at the Sorbonne who flew over from Paris regularly for academic meetings. It was a joy speaking French and then receiving little gifties later from Paris like tapes of French café music or of works by Eric Satie. If he was staying on a weekend when the children weren't with me due to a switch with their father, we'd often go out to dinner to a small bistro down the street or to the symphony and he always obeyed "house rules"...no hanky-panky!

Aspects of my life were definitely beginning to look better as was my checking account. I was able to open an American Funds account to buy shares with spare cash at the end of the month. Imagine...all these warm fuzzies and without drinking! It was hard to believe. Every night before going to sleep, I offered up a prayer of gratitude for these unexpected blessings, never dreaming that living sober could be so rewarding and so much fun!

Without explanation or advance notice, 13 year-old Sandi called me one Friday night and said, "Mom, I want to live with you. Can I, please? I'll help with the dishes and keep my space clean. I'll be really and truly good! You won't have to worry a thing about me."

"Oh, Sandi...it's an answer to prayers. I would love to have you with me...I think I'm going to cry...for joy!"

"I already have everything I'll need packed and can be on the train arriving at 8:05 a. m. tomorrow morning."

"Yay, I'll be at the station waiting for you. Yippee! I love you, Sandi, and I won't be able to sleep all night. This is just too too cool." I didn't dare ask if she had told this plan to her father.

To celebrate, I grabbed some change out of my "food-money" peanut butter jar and skipped down the sidewalk for a huge hot fudge sundae at the corner ice cream shop where I had become good friends with the woman owner. She knew Sandi from the weekends she would come stay with me. With no children of her own, the owner adored Sandi who was becoming a very mature, responsible young lady and looked a lot older than 13. In less than a month, Sandi was working in her ice cream store three days a week after school and before long, almost running the place by herself while the owner took cooking classes somewhere.

Rather than enrolling her in one of the private schools downtown, I got Sandi into 8th grade at the local school five blocks from our house, McCall Elementary, which had the highest rating of elementary schools in the Philadelphia School District. After living in the suburbs, I figured she needed some steel in her ass and this school was perfect: the student body included kids from the Projects, from Chinatown, the "English As A Second Language" students, and a few White kids living in our neighborhood whose parents were mostly writers, musicians or artists. Sandi was going to be in the minority for the first time in her life!

The first few days when I walked to school to meet her at the end of the day, she was brushing away tears. I panicked thinking I should try to get her into the mostly all-White Catholic School a few blocks away. I called her school first to talk to a counselor who said because Sandi had arrived mid-term, she'd assign a "buddy" for her. The counselor felt this would help Sandi adjust and she'd make sure the buddy would be one of the more outgoing girls.

"We don't want to lose Sandi," confessed the counselor who was African-American. "We're trying to maintain an even balance here and your daughter will sure help us boost our White minority figures. It's very important to us," she added. "We'll take good care of her for you."

I was touched, remembering how open-minded our parents were when Bruce and I were in high school and invited Black, Japanese and other foreign kids to parties in the big room my Dad had added on to the back of the house so we could have friends over. Yes, this would be a win-win...good for Sandi and good for the school. Three days later, as we walked to school in the morning, Sandi told me I didn't have to meet her after school. She told me she had a neat buddy and that afternoon, came home on her own with a scrap of paper crumpled up in her pocket.

"Look, Mom! I got something really cool from my new girlfriend who lives in Chinatown. She handed me this note at lunchtime."

Sandi passed me the note but I couldn't decipher the strange writing and said, "What does that mean, Sandi?"

"It's Chinese for 'I love you'. Wasn't that nice, Mommy? And I just love my new school."

I shed a little hidden tear as I then knew everything was going to be just fine. I was also grateful for her after-school ice cream shop job as I wouldn't have to worry about her between the time her school got out and when I got home from work. The owner let her eat as much ice cream as she wanted and told me Sandi was the best scooper she ever had.

"Your Sandi could sell ice cream to a snowman in Alaska," she said. "She's so friendly and capable and best of all, completely reliable and trust-worthy. Plus, the cash drawer is always right, down to a penny. You must be very proud of her."

Her words were engraved on my heart and for the rest of my life I'd remember those words every time I ate an ice cream cone.

For the two weekdays she wasn't doling out ice cream, she also got a volunteer after-school job as a docent in the children's area of The Academy of Natural Sciences. She loved it and so did I as she'd come upstairs to my office to visit on her breaks.

In my spare time, before Sandi came to live with me, I had decided to return to an interrupted acting career which in the past before getting sober had been very important to me. I wanted to see if I could learn lines and even get up on the stage, sober. The acting began when I was at the University of Oregon and resumed again in the early 1970s when I was still living in the suburbs after a bad car accident about five years before I got sober. My life had come to an abrupt halt when my husband and I were hit head-on returning one night from our shore house. Luckily, our toddlers weren't with us as we had hired our regular nanny to take care of them for the weekend.

The car was totaled and the State Trooper told my husband that the guy was going at least 100 mph when he crossed over the center line and hit us. We were only alive because we were in what the trooper called "that Sherman tank", my father's Mercury Marquis Brougham which I had inherited when he died. My husband only had a scratch on his arm. I suffered head injuries. I don't remember how John got home. I don't remember the ambulance dropping me off at the nearest medical facility, a rural nursing home filled with old people and one man who kept getting out of his straitjacket at night and waking me up to ask what I had done with his wife. I still don't remember anything about the accident. I don't even remember to this day exactly where it happened. I just know it was out in the middle of nowhere, far from any towns.

The nursing home administrator didn't know what to do with me and just left me in a room with rotating roommates. After a week when two old ladies had died a day apart in the bed next to me, I knew I had to get out of there. I walked into the administrator's office, put on a terrible scene, yelling and screaming nonsense as if I had gone bonkers, then called my husband to come pick me up. If he wouldn't, I told him I'd walk the 80 miles home! He came and got me the next morning. A month or so later, when we went back to a small one-room New Jersey court house for a hearing on the accident for which we had received a Notice to Appear, they knew nothing of the accident...the records had all been purged but somehow they hadn't managed to snag the notice before it went out. We went home. I never knew if my husband received money from our own auto insurance for my injuries and my car. If he did, he had pocketed it.

This memory-loss situation was difficult for me. I had been very active in our suburban community and after the accident, I'd go out and see people on the street or in the shops who would say, "Didn't we have fun last night?" I couldn't remember where I had been with them. Or someone would call and say, "Why didn't you bring the casserole you promised yesterday?" and I couldn't remember where I was supposed to have been with a casserole. I started hiding out in the house and soon, not even answering the phone. My husband had me seeing his friend, a tennis-playing chiropractor whose only solution was to have me down more of his free-sample tranquilizers. I began to think my husband knew something serious about my injuries and just wouldn't tell me what was wrong.

When I'd ask him to describe the accident, he'd say, "I don't want to talk about it. Every night when I go to bed, all I see are those headlights coming at us. For Christ's sake…stop asking."

One afternoon, I secretly went to the County Health Department and when the woman in charge heard my story, she said, "When you feel distressed, why don't you have a little drink. That will make you feel better." It was all I needed…an official license to drink and that was when my drinking started getting worse. I knew I had to do something about the miserable reclusive life I was leading and secretly again, made an appointment with a brain surgeon in downtown Philadelphia who had many tests done on me.

When I went back for the results a week later, he took my hands in his and in a fatherly way said, "Sandra, I am pleased to tell you it is nothing serious and I'm giving you a written report that explains everything I'm about to tell you so you can read it over later. You have short-term retrograde amnesia which results from a traumatic injury like your car accident. It's a loss of memory-access to events that occurred or information learned in the immediate past and is caused by damage to the memory-storage areas of the brain in various brain regions. Sandra, don't be alarmed when you experience sudden, temporary episodes of memory loss that can't be attributed to a more common neurological condition, such as epilepsy or stroke. During an episode your recall of recent events simply vanishes, so you can't remember where you are or how you got there. All you need is rest and tranquility and your memory will soon return, but little by little, you must try to venture out of the house. You can't keep hiding away if you want to get better and conquer this." I was relieved at his findings, and the first thing I did was to sign up for private tennis lessons with the pro at the nearby tennis club. This got me out three mornings a week and I didn't have to speak to anyone. The pro was way over there on the other side of the net and I left the club as soon as the lesson was over. Next, after reading a notice in the paper about a mime class starting at a theater about 20 minutes from the house, I signed up for it, figuring I could attend the classes and not have to speak to anyone. The director was very savvy and after three workshops, gave us an assignment to bring something to recite at the next class that would show the others something about ourselves.

I picked a haiku poem I had written in high school, got up on the stage and in a booming voice said, "The wild waves crashed against the rock and the bird, screaming, fell from his perch."

"I knew you had something in there somewhere," said the director and then asked me to audition for the next play she was directing and to read for the part of the grandmother in Federico Garcia-Lorca's, *House of Bernarda Alba*. I got the part which launched me onto the stage in every play she directed including Lorca's *Blood Wedding* and his *Yerma*, John Synge's *Playboy of the Western World*, and many others. My favorite role was that of the ingénue, Irma, in Jean Giraudoux's *Madwoman of Chaillot*. I ended up getting so enmeshed with the character that I was soon "taking her home with me" when I left rehearsals and performances. Irma was a happy young girl, blissfully in love. I went home every night after rehearsals feeling happy and blissful. We did that play in repertoire with two other plays for three months and the whole time, I was Irma, both on stage and off. It didn't matter if life at home was unbearable---I was seeing everything through the rosy-colored glasses of Irma. The theater had become, along with an increasing affection for booze, my great escape.

After my husband walked out, I kept up with the acting and would take the children with me to rehearsals, setting up their sleeping bags at the bottom of the stage. Ian usually fell asleep before the first act was over, but Sandi stayed awake to the end, mesmerized by it all.

When we were leaving the theater, Sandi would always say, "Mommy, when I grow up, can I do what you are doing? I want to be on the stage just like you."

When she was 13 and had moved in with me, I was performing again. Now it was supernumerary parts with the Philadelphia Opera Company, the Pennsylvania Opera and dramatic roles with another theater company downtown. I managed to get Sandi "super" parts in the operas with me. We had such fun sharing a dressing room and especially when my latest beau, a gentleman tobacco farmer from Virginia, had ten dozen long-stemmed red roses delivered to our dressing room for opening night. There were so many roses everywhere that we could hardly step over them to see the mirror as we put on our elaborate costumes and make-up.

"Oh, Mom," exclaimed Sandi, twirling around in circles while tossing roses in the air. "This is just too awesome!"

My tobacco farmer travelled from Virginia to Philly for our opening night and during intermission, I showed him how to climb the catwalks above the stage where he perched and watched us performing below. Sandi thought this was the cat's meow. I found it rather amusing when she told me her father was sitting out in the audience. At the end of the school year, Sandi's father lured her back to the suburbs with the call of the mall, use of his credit cards, and the promise of her own car when she turned 16. I couldn't compete… my lifestyle was still chicken one day, feathers the next. The night before the last day of school, I helped her pack up all her little treasures and souvenirs of our life together.

I could see tears in her eyes as she said, "Mommy, I love the ice cream shop job and volunteering at The Academy, but Daddy keeps telling me I shouldn't be working after school…that a girl my age should be shopping at the mall or out having fun."

I didn't respond for I was doggedly learning that it is sometimes better just to remain silent rather than try to argue or fight a war that couldn't be won.

"Pick your battles carefully," my sober friends would tell me.

When I got in from work the next day, Sandi had a surprise. On her way home from school, she had stopped at the local pet store and bought me two goldfish in a bowl which we named Rigoletto and Sparafucile, two characters in the opera we had just been in.

She wrapped her arms around my neck, and in her sweet voice whispered, "I got the fish because I don't want you to be lonely when I'm not here anymore, Mom."

I would remember for a long time her comment that afternoon in the living room of my little house on Camac Street that I had bought to make a nest for the two of us. For many years later, any time I bought goldfish to replace those a cat or raccoon had grabbed out of the pond in my garden, I always named two of the fish, Rigoletto and Sparafucile.

Chapter Nine

Go Buy A Sailboat?... God, Are You Crazy?

As Ian and Sandi progressed from elementary to high school, their weekend visits were less frequent and more disappointing. Although I had my wonderful job at The Academy and money coming in from the other part-time jobs, I still couldn't afford to make ultra-lavish plans to entertain the children. There were also now mortgage payments to come up with for my Camac Street row house.

I hadn't seen the children for three weeks because of their hectic suburban schedule and was looking forward to time with them this particular weekend. Friday morning, I checked out the Weekend section of the newspaper to make plans, desperately wanting us to enjoy this weekend together. They were growing up so fast and I was losing touch with them — they were almost becoming like strangers. Dragging themselves downtown to see me was getting less and less appealing and even though I understood their need to be connected with school and friends, it made me feel unloved, unwanted and alone.

The Philadelphia Museum of Art was having an exhibition of the Impressionists and if we got there by 1:00 p. m. on Sunday we could get in free. That would work ideally with my slim budget. Plus, it would follow my plan to keep introducing as much culture as possible into their pedestrian suburban lives. I figured out where I could afford to take them each night for dinner and what other fun things we could do including a splurge on tickets to Philadelphia Opera's *Cinderella* for Saturday night. They didn't arrive on the 5:20. I sat in the noisy Reading Terminal as I had so many times before waiting for the next commuter from the northern suburbs, hoping they would be on that one. This Friday night, waiting yet again without a phone call to alert me of their delay and no answers to my repeated phone calls to their father's, I tried to silence the voices of the committee arguing in my head: "Stay in Philadelphia near your children," said the one. "No, move to California to care for your mother," retorted the other.

The children finally showed up on a much later train that Friday, said their father had already taken them out to dinner, and they just wanted to go to the house. We walked the few blocks home, almost in silence, and when we went inside, they plopped down in the living room talking to each other about their school friends as if I wasn't even in the room. I finally gave up and went to bed. Saturday afternoon, we walked over to South Street to watch the break-dancers. They didn't want to go to the opera, so there went that splurge. On Sunday, my plans to enjoy a day with them at the Art Museum started off badly when the two of them marched off together, arms linked, down Benjamin Franklin Parkway in the direction of the Art Museum leaving me far behind in their wake as if I didn't even exist. I wanted to shout out, "Screw you two brats!" but didn't.

As I walked along several paces behind them trying to keep up, my mind wrestled again with the idea of moving to California, not to take care of my mother who was now 82, but rather to improve the quality of her life. I recalled all the times she had fallen out of her wheelchair, the times she had burned herself taking scones out of the oven, and began realizing I would be more useful in California than in Philadelphia. Would the children think I had abandoned them? Would they understand how she needed me more than they did? Would I look like an irresponsible selfish mother? Would moving west just be what those in the meetings referred to as a 'geographical cure', carrying all the old baggage out there with me? The way things were going, or rather not going with the children, maybe it would be best to decamp. I could move to California and start a new life.

With help from my Higher Power whom I now had no problem calling "God" when I had really serious questions, plus regular attendance at meetings, working with my sponsor and helping others in recovery, I began to experience a slow but miraculous daily reprieve from the addiction that had so long plagued me. I was learning there was more to life than merely tempting the Fates.

One of my heroes, Robert Louis Stevenson, wrote, *You cannot run away from a weakness. You must sometimes fight it out or perish.* Although I had refused to think of myself as burdened with weaknesses, I did not know exactly how to identify the true adversary. I hadn't yet discovered along my new foggy path that the enemy was me.

Shortly after the disappointing weekend with the kids, I flew out to California for a week of sorting Mother's medical bills, receipts and other papers for tax time. One evening, Bruce called from North Carolina to tell me after almost two years of battling, the case against the surgeon and hospital had been settled and Mother would get around $80,000 after lawyer fees. I wondered how they had come up with that amount, but didn't ask, just glad they were going to pay her something. He also mentioned it was our high school class's 25th reunion. He couldn't fly out to attend but thought I might enjoy going since I was already out there. Why he thought that, I couldn't fathom, for surely he must have remembered how much I had hated high school. The only thing that got me through those horrendous years was masquerading as a Stanford student. I was one of a few high school students selected to participate in a special experimental gifted program where I attended English and History classes at Stanford instead of the boring ones at high school. With a legitimate Stanford library card, I spent most of my free time on campus, either in those special classes, in the library, or the Student Union. It was a glorious escape from the constraints of Godawful high school where, in my beatnik duds, never felt I fit in and didn't even want to. I went to the reunion just to see if the classmates were still ensnared in the same old boring cliques or if they had finally grown up and improved with age. Jimmy Johnson, our neighborhood friend, was the only other classmate there without a spouse or partner. Over dinner, I was enthralled with his stories about adventures on an old schooner he had bought years before and was still sailing solo on in the South Pacific, looking for sunken ships and pirate treasures. He hadn't found any pirate's gold yet but had come across old shipwrecks from which he collected "interesting trophies". In talking with Jimmy, my mind began to race, wondering wistfully if I, too, could ever sail the oceans blue and better yet, do it alone.

"Sure you could, Sandra. You just stuff your fears in your back pocket and go do it. Do you want to spend the rest of your life in myopic suburbia with all these poor suckers? I don't think so. C'mon, let's get outta here. I smell rotten fish and I'm suffocating!"

On my way back to Mother's, I pondered the possibility of going out in the "Big Blue" alone and realized I just had to step off the dime like Jimmy said. Maybe it was time now to take the advice of my childhood hero, Henry David Thoreau, who once said, "You have built your castles in the sky and it's now time to put foundations under them".

The morning after the reunion, I found Mother wheeling herself around her garden dragging a long hose. Even paralyzed, she was as indomitable as ever. Did I really want to come back home to her subtle comments implying I was never good enough, to the feelings of inferiority I had always felt growing up? Did I really want to have to listen to her touting everything my twin brother was doing 3,000 miles away with no mention of my accomplishments, no hint of even the slightest appreciation for things I was doing for her?

Even though she constantly insisted I shouldn't move back to California for her sake, why was she so often falling out of her wheelchair? Were these unconscious pleas for help? Could she not give in and for once, say she needed me or even just needed someone? One thing was for sure: I was learning how to swallow that brand of ego-driven stubborn pride ever since the day I got sober and I was not going to put my sobriety at risk for anyone, not even for my mother! I returned to Philadelphia without telling her I was seriously contemplating a move back to California.

A year later, Mother was still insisting on living alone in her beautiful world surrounded inside by books, art and music and outside by amazing gardens she continued to create and nurture. Before my father died of cancer years before I got sober and was married, the two had designed their dream retirement home and built it on their own private plateau in Scotts Valley, seven miles from Santa Cruz. The property was surrounded by towering redwoods and looked down on what was years later to become Silicon Beach.

I'd already flown to California six times for Mother's emergencies. This seventh disaster, while trying to dig a hole to plant a rhododendron in, she'd fallen out of her wheelchair and broken a leg again. Each visit, she'd greet me with a cursory "Thank-you for coming" and then as I was leaving to go back to Philly, it was always, "Don't move here on my account." This time, I finally said, "If you say that once more, I'm going to have it engraved on your tombstone!"

My children were now 16 and 15 and more frequently, didn't show up for their weekend with me. It was painful when I finally realized I was no longer a significant piece of their puzzle…in fact, I wasn't even on their board!

On this "rescue visit" to Mother's, I went outside one morning to sit under my old friend, the now giant redwood I planted 15 years before to watch over my then newly-widowed Mother. For the six prior broken-leg crises, I would sit under it to meditate and hope to end the perennial debate: kids or Mother, Mother or kids. Previously, there'd never been an answer, not a peep from my Higher Power. So, when no answer came, I did nothing and without guilt, would fly back home.

This time, without warning, I heard a loud voice, almost a roar, shouting, "It's time."

"But I don't want to move here."

"Sorry, kid, you asked."

"You know I can't live with Mother... she pushes all my buttons. Any brilliant ideas?"

"Go buy a sailboat," came the command.

"You gotta be kidding. I have no clue about sailing."

"I'll help you," said the voice firmly and with a bit of impatience.

The next morning, I splashed on some perfume, tossed my hair up into a rebellious ponytail over my right ear, donned dungarees, a sweatshirt, artsy earrings, and drove to the nearby Santa Cruz Yacht Harbor. I walked into the first yacht brokerage.

"Hi, I'd like to buy a sailboat," I said, trying to appear nonchalant.

"What kind you like?" said the broker with a Greek accent.

"Why don't you show me what you have available? I want one big enough so I won't get all soaked every time I take her out."

He rowed me around the harbor in a rubber dinghy, pointing to various yachts which all looked alike. While he spouted incomprehensible nautical lingo, I was giggling inside, feeling like this was some kind of cartoon. Any minute, the Looney Tunes melody would blast across the harbor and Porky Pig would chant, "That's all folks." Then, I saw it...a sailboat that seemed to be calling to me. It looked how I felt about my new sober self: sleek and elegant, but determined and tough as nails when necessary.

"What about that one over there?"

"We have one like it for sale in Moss Landing."

"Is that a good boat? Could I sail it around the world?"

"Lady, it's a 35-foot Ericson designed by Bruce King, one of the finest naval architects. You could sail it anywhere...it's a very comfortable live-aboard coastal cruiser."

"Excellent. I think you might have just sold it."

He looked at me quizzically as we returned to his office where he called the owner.

"They just took the boat north for a cruise. How serious are you?"

I knew this meant money. I had about 53 cents in my checking account, but as this was pre-online banking, I calculated I'd have about ten days to cover a check.

"That's how serious I am," I said, flipping a $500 check across his desk. He called the owner on his ship-to-shore radio.

"They're still out to sea but can meet you at the Alameda Marina across from San Francisco in three days, about 9:30 a. m.

"I'll be there," I said, and walked out of his office, not even daring to imagine what wild and perilous adventures I might soon be embarking on. There were a zillion things to worry about but I turned them over to my Higher Power. After all, it had been His wacky idea to buy a boat!

Days later, I arrived at the Alameda Marina wondering how I would find the owner in this vast sea of ships all looking alike. Not to worry. An older man came swaggering across the parking lot, a beer in one hand, cigar in the other. At his boat, we stepped below deck to the main salon. It was a mess: the dining table was lowered, sheets and blankets draped helter-skelter over it; pajamas strewn in the aisle; dirty dishes piled high in the sink; something yucky spilled on the greasy stove. If I were selling a boat, I would have a posy in a vase on the table, bread baking in the oven, charts of exotic destinations on the chart table, and a tape of sea chanties playing.

"If the little lady hadn't gone and gotten a heart attack, we would already be sailing this little honey to Mexico," he said with seemingly more regret for his aborted voyage than for his wife's declining health.

"Would you mind stepping off for a few minutes so I can sit below here by myself and meditate about all this?"

"Meditate?" he bellowed.

"Yes, this is an important decision."

He climbed the ladder, muttering, "Now, I've heard everything. I'll be back in five."

I sat down on the settee, trying to clear my mind. "O. K., Big Guy," I said, envisioning Him wearing a Greek fishing cap, dungarees, sandals, and jiggling worry beads. "Is this what You really want me to do or is this another one of Your jokes? This really feels terrifying."

"I told you I'd help. Besides, you're 43 and eight years sober…you can handle it and anyway, it's about time you trusted me more. This is all about faith."

The tide was changing and the dock lines began pulling rhythmically against their cleats, singing a lullaby as the boat gently swayed with the surge. I felt safe and at peace. The boat seemed to enfold me in a loving embrace. It was like the first time I stepped into that recovery meeting so long ago…I knew I had finally come "home" and his was the right thing to do.

"OK, I'll take it," I said to the Greek when I returned to his office in Santa Cruz.

"How much you offering?"

I had no idea what sailboats were worth… $20,000? $100,000? With the Greek staring at me, my mother's lucky number 13 started dancing on the table and I mentally reduced the $61,000 asking price by $13,000.

"$48,000, and not a penny more, not a penny less…that's my only and final offer," I said, walking out of his office.

Four days later, he called and began trying to haggle over the price.

"I told you…not a penny more," and I hung up.

Two days later, he phoned. "It's yours!" and hung up.

It wasn't long before we became best of friends, spending days together at a big table in his office where he had charts all spread out to teach me dead-reckoning navigation. I learned that this is the process of calculating one's current position by using a previously determined position, or "fix", with estimations of speed and course over elapsed time. The system is based on the mathematical calculations of time, speed, distance and direction and was used by mariners from as early as the Middle Ages, including Christopher Columbus. They were seeking new sea routes to transport spices as many wouldn't go near the equator, fearing hot waters and sea monsters lurked near it. Some wouldn't even use the compass, believing it operated by black magic.

Later, in my own seafaring experiences, I would find it boring having to continuously stare at the compass, and especially at night when its light would blind me on those very dark moonless nights. So I started following constellations. A fellow sailor would later tell me the constellations moved which explained why it took me so long to get to that destination. Even though I hated math, I had neither affection nor affinity for the complex electronic navigational devices, radar equipment and other such gadgets men always buy that my Ericson 35 had come equipped with and which I would get rid of as soon as I owned the boat. I knew that maybe someday, my life would depend on knowing dead-reckoning so I could figure out where I was and how to get to my next destination. If the system was good enough for old Chris, it was good enough for me.

Next, how to tell Mother my plan to move back to California, then, how to pay for the boat. The following week, on a crisp afternoon with the fog just beginning to saunter in, I took Mother to her favorite restaurant, Stagnaro's, on the Santa Cruz wharf, for a scrumptious sand dab dinner. Just before that local fish we both so loved arrived, I mustered up some courage.

"Mother, I've decided to move back... not to take care of you but to improve the quality of your life. When was the last time you went to the ballet, to a play, or for a picnic on the beach? When were you last to a fancy restaurant with white tablecloths?"

Mother sat motionless, reflecting, and then to my amazement, admitted she hadn't done any of those things since before she was paralyzed. She chirped her usual stern litany, "Don't move here on my account."

"I'm not. I've decided I miss you and California. Neither of us is getting any younger. Plus, we're both always eating dinner alone and I sure don't like going to nice restaurants by myself."

"Well, where are you going to live, then?"

Here came the hard part. If I said I wanted to move in with her, she'd say, 'Don't you think I can take care of myself?' If I said I'd rent an apartment, she'd say, 'Don't you like your own rooms up at the house? So you have money to throw away on rent?' Damned if I did, damned if I didn't.

"I've been working on a book and I'm stuck. Maybe if there was an interesting place, a kind of secret hideaway, I'd feel more inspired. How about I buy a sailboat to live on in the harbor? I can get a phone. We can call each other anytime, have dinner together occasionally, go on picnics, attend plays up in San Francisco. I could even take you sailing! What do you think?"

My heart was thumping so hard I was afraid the waiter might call 911. In her best clipped Scottish accent, she said, "Why, my dear, I think that's a splendid idea… but how do you expect to pay for it?"

"My credit is good and I'm pretty sure I can get a boat loan."

She reached across the table, put her hand atop mine and said, "You know, when I go across the herring pond for my final voyage, you're going to inherit a few pounds sterling. Appears you could use some now, eh?" Her lively eyes were twinkling like they often did so long ago, when as a child, I'd watch her re-create on local stages some of her past roles as a leading lady on Broadway.

I told the owner he could keep his boat until noon on Thanksgiving Day but at 12. 01p. m., I would be taking possession. Promising Mother I'd be back before she had the turkey in the oven, I returned to Philadelphia to end that chapter of my life and get ready for the next one as a live-aboard on a big sailboat. God, it sounded exciting but terrifying!

Chapter Ten

Adventuring Was Definitely In My DNA

As expected, the kids were happy to remain with their father and stay there to finish high school with their friends. They said they understood Obi's need for me and promised to visit in the summer. It took about two months to wrap up all my various jobs and responsibilities and arrange for my lawyer to get my little house sold. Two days before I left Philadelphia, Sandi came downtown and we upheld the Philadelphia tradition of meeting at the huge eagle statue on the first floor of the John Wanamaker department store. It was her favorite store to visit when we were together.

We hit the cosmetic counter and I treated her to a small fortune in creams and goos — it would be a long time before we would be doing this again. As we were leaving the store, a sign announcing a sale upstairs in the Antiques Department jumped out at us.

"Oh, Sandi — one last rummage through the Antiques Department."

I saw it as soon as we got off the escalator. "I've got to have that," I said, pointing to an antique Italian accordion with green mother-of-pearl inlay. Sandi just stood there grinning, then tried to pull me away from the temptation.

"Hold on…think of this," I said to her. "I can't bring my piano onto the boat and this will sort of be a substitute. And look, Sandi, it's 50% off! A real bargain!"

I carried my new treasure home and then hunted in the phonebook for an accordion teacher and found one right across the river in Camden.

"Can you give me about three hours of lessons on an accordion I just bought?" I asked.

"I'm pretty busy. How about next week?"

"No, I mean today. I'm moving to California in the morning."

He agreed and Sandi and I made a bee-line for Camden. As soon as he saw my antique accordion, he said it was too good to take on a boat and sold me a newer one that was only about 30 years old. I madly tried to learn how to play the accordion in four hours and he included a lot of music in the bargain, including a book, Chopin for the Accordion.

That last night in the sweet little historic house I had scraped and saved so hard to buy, trying to figure out what I needed for this newest adventure, I scrambled around the house like the madwoman of Chaillot, the title character in a play by Jean Giraudoux . It was written the year I was born and ironically, about an eccentric woman living in Paris struggling against the straight-laced corrupt authority figures in her life. A few years earlier, I had played the young girl, Irma, in that same play and some 20 years later, as the Madwoman, I would bring to the stage the same leading role I had been playing all my life.

I ended up throwing into my biggest suitcase some dungarees, a bunch of t-shirts and sweatshirts, a pair of leather sandals, black flats and sneakers, two snazzy dresses, my purple hooded slicker, two bras and a pile of undies. Into the car trunk went the suitcase with the newer accordion and all the music. Tucked under the music went the rough draft and notes for the book I had started what seemed eons ago when I formally left the living-separately-marriage and moved downtown. There was still space in the trunk for a sturdy box of my favorite French perfumes, another of all my prized earrings and bracelets, for my big well-worn Oxford dictionary, my thesaurus, <u>Brewer's Book of Phrase and Fable</u>, a dog-eared copy of <u>Treasure Island,</u> a book of Poe's stories, and a prized book of world poetry I had been carrying around since 1960, used for a class my freshman year at the University of Oregon. The bowl with the two goldfish Sandi had given me two years before would have to balance on the back seat. Rigoletto and Sparafucile smiled at me as I nestled their bowl into a small pile of my favorite videos: *Around the World in 80 Days, Auntie Mame, Zorba The Greek, Never On Sunday* and *Breakfast At Tiffany's.*

At the last minute, Sandi decided since it was the first day of her Thanksgiving break, she could drive across country with me if I paid for her flight back home.

"No problem, Sandi. We'll just put the ticket on my trusty credit card and I can pay it off one day at a time."

Off we zoomed in Mother's Oldsmobile Cutlass Supreme which she gave me when she got the van, taking with us our old CB radio and radio handles from some of our other past adventures... Thunder Thighs and Little Miss Whistle Britches, on the road again.

I felt a little sad as I watched Philadelphia disappearing in the rear view mirror. I hadn't realized how much I'd come to love that city where I had spent my first eight sober years and learned there so many of life's lessons. If I was going to move on, this was as good a year as any to make the Big Move.

Driving west across the country with Sandi, I was still reeling from the unexpected direct intervention into my life from that Man Upstairs. I couldn't quite get around the idea that for some odd but miraculous reason, He had suddenly decided to grace me with His presence again and especially, to proffer that totally wild suggestion (almost command!) to buy a sailboat.

My formal introduction to Him had ended abruptly when I was six years old. That Sunday morning, my twin brother Bruce and I were sitting on the steps outside the Palo Alto Methodist church Sunday School classroom waiting for Mother and Dad to get out of church. After watching clouds flying by and then counting 23 snails and two slimy slugs in the grass and seven chubby robins digging for worms, I was glad to see our parents finally coming through the big church doors.

Just before reaching us, I heard my father say to Mother, "Well, I'm not going to get up early anymore to come over here and listen to that man up in the pulpit spouting about the imminent end of the world while at the same time, pleading for more money."

I jumped up and with hands on hips, chimed in with my squeaky six-year old voice that could probably have been heard a block away, "Yay! I won't have to get all dressed up in these stupid dresses to come over here to color-crayon silly pictures. I can color my own pictures at home wearing shorts and a t-shirt!"

My father grabbed my hand and with great defiance, the two of us marched down the rest of the steps to the street as the faithful moved away from us as if I were contagious with chicken pox and Dad was a known criminal. As soon as we got home, I yanked off that darned dress and stuffed it under the toy chest where hopefully it would permanently reside since I wasn't going to have to go back to Sunday School anymore. I kicked off the spit-shined Mary Janes, pulled off the white socks, threw on my play clothes and raced outside barefoot to continue working on a nifty fort I had begun the day before in the tall pungent mustard weeds.

After that, Sundays were a lot more fun. Mother got up early and made a picnic of our favorite chopped egg sandwiches on her fresh-out-of-the oven rolls, slipping some of her yummy peanut butter cookies into little paper bags, one bag for each of us. In our kitchen, there was always a cake, cookies or bread either going into the oven or coming out of it. The neighborhood kids liked to hang out at our house because they knew there would always be warm cookies to snack on.

Before the Sunday picnic basket was complete, Mother put in a liver-wurst sandwich on pumpernickel for Father. He was German through and through and liverwurst was the only kind of sandwich I ever saw him eat. I don't think he really liked sandwiches as he ate them with a knife and fork. In

Germany where he grew up, I guess it was impolite to eat with your fingers. He'd even strip the kernels meticulously off a cob of corn with a knife before he'd eat the corn.

While Mother was assembling the picnic basket, Bruce and I'd gather a pile of the empty sacks stored in the garage and previously filled with feed for Mother's chickens. We needed the sacks for filling up with the dark rich leaf mold we were going to find up in the woods. Mother loved to scatter it in her garden which always had more beautiful flowers than I ever saw in the neighborhood, and around our orchard which always had more fruit on the trees than anyone else's. We'd then pile into the station wagon and head for the hills.

Dad knew all the abandoned logging roads. He had worked as a logger in the late 1930s after the doctors told Mother her earaches wouldn't go away unless they moved from New York City to Florida or California. She wouldn't hear of going to Florida as she said they had huge horrid bugs there. So when he headed west, Dad left Mother in NYC with the family she was still working for as executive-chef and where, when Dad left, she had moved back into her own quarters they provided. He knew she would be safe because she had a good job and lots of friends and, after all, she had come to America alone across the "herring pond" from Scotland when she was only 17.

Although my father could easily have gotten funds for the trip from his wealthy parents in Germany, he relished the idea of creating the new adventure on his own. He made his way to California by hitch-hiking with trucks and jumping off and on boxcars to find a new life for him and his wee Scottish lassie. This was quite a feat for a fellow who had grown up in luxury wearing starched lacy shirts and fancy short linen pants later traded for lederhosen when he took up climbing the Alps, whose father had palled around and travelled with Kaiser Wilhelm (they were the first occidentals to visit Eastern China), and whose parents owned exquisite estates all over Germany. My grand-father started an import-export business between Hamburg and NYC after the Kaiser abdicated, fleeing to the Netherlands. Opa, short for "grandpa", became an American citizen for business reasons in the 1920s. In 1932 on a business trip, he whisked my father out of Germany and over to America. From the moment he passed the Statue of Liberty, Father gave up his life in Germany and the first thing he did was to become a U. S. citizen. He loved his new homeland and waited more than 20 years before making a trip back to Germany when he was needed to tend to his widowed mother.

After arriving in America, Mother had a success-story string of fabulous jobs beginning as governess to the children of a wheeler-dealer real estate tycoon in Akron where she first ended up. Then she got a job as companion and chauffeurette to the elderly Mrs. Firestone (the rubber baron's mother) and went everywhere with her. After some years of adventures with the Firestones, Mother returned to NYC where she worked as live-in chef to a wealthy Jewish family living on Park Avenue. She was always proud to tell us she even learned to cook kosher.

Mother was also balancing a career as light opera singer on the stages of New York when she began to date a very interesting fellow. My father only once told the story how he stole her away from that beau. As the story goes, Mother was sitting with the fellow in a snazzy restaurant on the 65th floor of a swanky building on Rockefeller Center. Her beau was doodling on a cocktail napkin which he passed over to her.

"What do you think of this one, Anne?" he asked.

"No one will like a mouse. Come up with something else, Walt."

The next day, her girlfriend took her to a tea dance at the German Club where she met my brilliant and elegant father. Less than a year later, they were married.

My grandfather, whom I never met, came over from Germany for the wedding and the only advice he gave my father was, "I want you to promise you will take this lovely lady out at least once a month to a restaurant with white tablecloths."

All through growing up and even when we were still using high chairs, my brother and I got to enjoy those white-tablecloth dinners out to restaurants that always had relish trays (I loved the black olives!). My honorable father kept that promise until he was bedridden some 30 years later, dying of cancer.

Dad jumped off a box car in Northern California and landed a job as a lumberjack in a logging camp in Scotia up near Fort Bragg. Later, when I was a kid, he'd tell me stories about those coast redwoods known as Giant Sequoias, and how they were taller than any other living thing and could live for over 2,000 years. He explained they could withstand fires, floods and insects, and many species of plants, animals and insects lived almost exclusively in a world 300 feet above the ground at the treetop level of those amazing trees. In 1927, John D. Rockefeller, enchanted with the redwoods, donated a million bucks to preserve them and another million again in 1929. In 1970, loggers started disregarding and outright disobeying the unwritten agreement that they should at least leave a swath of trees along both sides of highways.

Hundreds of people, the Sierra Club and other such organizations rose up in arms and the tree-huggers revolution began, dedicated to preserving some 189,000 acres of California's redwood forest for future generations. I donated money to the cause and somewhere, there's a redwood with my name engraved on a plaque attached to it.

Before recent forest fires, there were 17,000 acres of ancient Coast Redwoods and Douglas fir trees still protected in California's Humboldt Redwoods State Park. The 2003 Canoe Creek fire started by dry lightning rampaged through nearly 14,000 acres of that park. The old-growth redwoods survived and have since thrived, with the forest floor cleared of brush and the forest canopy opened to more sunlight. Sadly, only 4% of the original redwood population remains. According to a local botanist, some of the trees still standing are over 2,000 years old – the redwoods first appeared in California some 20-million years ago and 240-million years ago elsewhere.

The man who managed that branch of the lumber operation where my father worked soon found out his German logger was good at accounting. At night, when my father had nothing else to do, he'd work in the office on the company's books. One day, the owner of the lumber company showed up from the company's headquarters in Palo Alto. He took one look at the books and knew from their perfect balanced condition that it certainly wasn't the work of the manager. My father was called into the office and told to pack his bags. He was surprised to find out he wasn't being fired, but rather going with the owner to Palo Alto where he was put in charge of the company's entire financial operation. That was the beginning of my father's long illustrious career in the financial aspect of the California building industry, wheeling and dealing while providing us with a very good life.

On these Sunday leaf-mold jaunts, Dad would maneuver the car around fallen tree limbs while Bruce and I'd scamper ahead to push rocks out of the way that were trying to block us from reaching our favorite place next to a stream. I loved that spot. The trees were so huge and tall that some Sundays, we couldn't even see the sun. It smelled musty and damp, fresh and clean, all at the same time. Under the canopies of the redwoods, many different types of ferns grew along with rare sorrel, which years later, I would go hunting for in those same woods to make a delicious sorrel soup or some herby spiked-sorrel butter to lather over a salmon I had just caught. Coast oaks, bay laurels, red alders, and big-leaf maple trees also joined the leaf-mold party. I loved to toss handfuls of their fronds and leaves up in the air and watch them pirouette down all around me. It took us about two hours to fill up the bags. While Mother spread out the picnic on a quilt she laid next to the bubbling stream, we'd wash our hands in the ice-cold water which was so clear you could count the fish going by. After lunch, Dad took a nap while Mother leaned against a redwood tree with Bruce snuggled next to her on one side and me on the other while she read to us from a thick book called, Stories From The Bible For Children . I especially liked the neat colored pictures of Jesus doing strange things like walking on water, changing water to wine and making a zillion loaves of bread out of just a few loaves, but I sure didn't like the picture of him dragging a big cross along a dusty road. Mother said I would understand all that a lot better when I got a little older. I never did quite get it.

Sundays in the redwoods went on for a number of years until Bruce and I got our grown-up matching bicycles. Instead of the Sunday leaf-mold adventures, he and I rode around town taking turns each week going from one church's Sunday School to another, depending on what they were offering. In the spring, I liked to go to the Menlo Park Presbyterian Church – they had a fun Wednesday night dinner. In the warmer months, I'd arrive early for their Sunday School as I loved crawling under the huge fig tree at the church entrance to grab luscious gooey sweet figs to snack on during the lessons. I enjoyed singing so joined the choir which provided the extra bonus of attending summer Choir Camp on the shores of Lake Tahoe. I think I mainly went because I could water ski during free time. The first summer, I learned to ski behind a small sailboat. The two fellows who owned it were at war with the woman who owned the marina next to our camp. They said she was ripping people off with the high rates she charged to rent boats. When they overheard me asking about learning to water ski, they borrowed a tow rope and pair of skis from a friend, invited me to follow them to their sailboat, and into the drink I went. I was pulled along behind their boat, basically submerged, because it didn't have enough power to get me up on top of the water. But I eventually made it up at least three times each afternoon, usually just a few minutes before free-time was over. In eighth grade, I discovered the Lutheran Sunday School and liked riding my bike the extra mile to it because two Saturdays a month in the winter, I could go with the class in the church bus up to Dodge Ridge Ski Resort in the Stanislaus National Forest where I learned to snow ski. The first time, the boys helped me rent skis, poles and boots and then told me snow was softer on the trail that started up at the very top where we would get off the chair lift. I hopped on the lift, not thinking how hard it might be getting down the slope, and mostly fell all the way down the mountain. But that wouldn't stop me from later becoming a champion skier. I guess I'd always been a born dare-devil ever since fighting my way out of the womb almost two months too early and twelve minutes ahead of my brother. When people asked which of us was older, he always piped up and said, "Sandra is…ladies first, you know."

The two of us together weighed slightly more than seven pounds and spent the first six months of our lives in the hospital in a shared incubator.

Mother told us later she insisted on a single incubator as she didn't want us to feel alone and afraid when she wasn't sitting beside the incubator to comfort us. The nurses joked saying that because she was Scottish, she just wanted to save money on incubators. We weren't home a month when Bruce came down with whooping cough and was back into the hospital. When he was four, his appendix burst and back into the hospital he went again. I can see now why Mother was always more concerned and attentive to my brother than to me… why she fussed over him a lot more than over me. But as a kid, it always made me feel less-than, inferior. Once, I fell off my new bicycle and badly skinned my knees. Blood was flying everywhere. I wanted to go into the house to get bandaged up and seek a little comfort from my mother, but I didn't go in. I knew, even if my legs had broken completely off at the knees, she would probably have said, "Oh, just brush them off and go get back on your bike."

I did a lot of daring things as a kid besides careening down the snowy slopes of the Sierra Nevadas which beckoned just a five-hour drive from home. On many Saturdays, I'd ride my bicycle for miles up the steep roads in the Santa Cruz Mountains all day (often on the way up, hailing a passing beer truck which always had room in the back for my bike) just so I could enjoy the long downhill coast back home. Many summer days were spent hiking in those mountains alone to track the San Andreas fault which often woke me up at night with its mini-quakes. As a teenager, if I wasn't hiking or biking, I was water-skiing, scuba-diving, or sky-diving.

Maybe I was trying to impress my adventurous father who, besides his mountain climbing prowess, had also been the iceboat champion of the North Sea, and had once canoed alone down the Amazon, batting his paddle at the hungry piranhas he passed. I didn't know then when I was being mesmerized by his stories, that many years later in my mid-fifties, I would be weaving my own Kon-Tiki raft from balsam limbs I hacked off trees in the Amazon jungle and then be racing aboard it down the fast-moving Amazon, and to do my dad one even better, jumping overboard for the scariest swim of my life!

I always wished, if I could only share some of my own stories someday with my father, he'd be saying with the thick German accent he never lost, "Now that's my girl, Sandra!" and giving me a thumbs up. Well, perhaps, he was watching me from Above during some of these escapades.

Maybe I had always been trying to measure up to my father in a desperate plea for his attention since I could never count on any sympathy or real comfort from my mother. But my father never had much time for Bruce and me. He would come home late from work, have dinner and then become engrossed in his stamp collection or reading one of the many leather-bound tomes from his expansive library. On weekends, he listened non-stop to classical music and opera. Occasionally, he'd take me to book sales and auctions at the large Atherton estates that surrounded us and even as far as San Francisco. I'd clutch the quarters from my piggybank and maybe a dollar bill he'd given me that morning as spending money and come home with odd books I still have in my own library…History of Metal-making in the Middle Ages, Principles of Thermodynamics and others. I loved those book-buying excursions because while driving from one sale or auction to another, Dad would tell stories of his past wild adventures.

Whatever rhetoric each of my childhood Sunday Schools was putting out, none ever made a lasting impression on me. I'd sit in the class thinking about how I would improve my fort in the mustard weeds if I could ever get out of that boring classroom. But I'd always remember when Bruce and I were little, sitting at the dinner table with Mother trying to encourage us to eat up our vegetables. In her Scottish brogue she'd say, "Think of all those poor wee starving children in Armenia…eat those vegetables up now!" I'd wonder what those starving children ate and where was Armenia, anyway? Because of images I conjured up of those poor skinny kids, it took years before I could even think of asking God for any help. My problems were far too insignificant and He was too busy to help me when he had all those starving children somewhere over there to take care of.

Back then, books were my only salvation from the demands of that strict German father and perfectionist Scottish mother, neither of whom I could ever please. I wasn't like my twin brother who could do no wrong. Growing up, everyone, even old ladies and dogs, seemed to love him. I was the dark twin, lurking way back in the shadows, while he, by eight a child actor in plays with our mother, was out front waving to all his fans.

"Treated you both even-Steven," Mother always used to chant, whoever Steven was. As a kid, I didn't understand that her words weren't matching what was really going on. Most of my growing up years were spent burrowing into books as an acceptable way to hide from those sorrowful feelings of never being good enough, of always feeling less than, of never doing anything quite right. When I wasn't reading, I was outside making forts in the tall weeds where I could hide and no one could find me. Not wanting to be called a wimp like they called my brother, I'd out-do all the neighborhood boys by climbing higher than they could to the top of the tallest tree in our neighborhood, or by scampering up an oak to bring down a handful of mistletoe to sell from my milk-crate stand at the street corner, donating all the nickels and dimes to the March of Dimes.

For some odd reason, I never resented Bruce. Ever since I can remember, it was my job to watch out for him, to take care of him while we were at school even though he'd often hiss, "Stop mothering me!" I'd fight off the bullies teasing him in grammar school, then later admire his successes in high school when he was playing the lead in all the school plays or serving as class president each year. He was charming and talented...who wouldn't like him?

We had a special closeness I wasn't even aware of until one incident when we were sixteen. Bruce was off somewhere and I had gone to bed. I woke up in the middle of the night from a nightmare where I saw him and his boyfriend flying over a cliff in our shared sports car, a 1960 MGA. I watched him being thrown out of the car just before awakening. I went back to sleep and some hours later, he was shaking me.

"Wake up, Sandra. Shhhhhh – we don't want to wake up the folks but you'll never believe what happened. I was driving the MG down that windy mountain road near Memorial Park and missed a turn. Jerry was with me and we flew over the cliff and were both thrown from the car. Thank goodness the top was down. We weren't hurt and the car's OK…just some pin-point gravel dings on the fenders, but the windshield was smashed to smithereens and came completely out. I got a tow truck to haul the car back up the cliff and was even able to drive it home. It's parked outside almost hidden in the lower limbs of Mother's big Deodar cedar tree. Can you lend me the money to get the windshield replaced before Dad sees it? The tow truck guy said it would probably cost about $80 for a new shield."

"What time did this happen?" I asked.

"About two hours ago," he replied, exactly the time I was seeing it happening in my dream.

"Yeah, I have a little over $100 saved in my peanut butter jar from my last paycheck, but you'll have to pay me back as soon as you can. I'll still be lifeguarding at the city pool for another month but won't get my next check for three weeks."

He gave me a huge hug. I couldn't help smile at the mischievous sparkle in his eyes in spite of nearly being killed. I guess he thought he was invincible.

When I graduated from high school, I was able to get 500 miles away from home by attending the University of Oregon. Free from them all at last, I was ready to be my own person! That was when I met Senator Wayne Morse who came to Eugene from D. C. to speak at a student gathering. I chatted with him and when he found out I was studying Political Science and International Economics, he encouraged me to transfer to George Washington in DC (3,000 glorious miles away!) and offered me a summer job in his DC office as his constituent liaison. I didn't go home that whole year at GW and it was wonderful--my low self-esteem started to crawl out of the darkness and glow a little, even in the dark. Mother and I did write back and forth and Dad always added a little note of encouragement at the bottom of her letters. She even sent me a box of her scrumptious shortbread at Christmas with a check for $100 tucked inside the box. In the spring, a shoebox arrived of freshly-picked daphne wrapped in wet paper towels. The lavender blooms came from a flowering bush in her garden that I always loved for its beautiful perfume. As a kid, I would use ribbons to tie up sprigs of daphne to sell for the March of Dimes.

While away at school, it was nice to hear from Mom and Dad, but I was glad to be on my own, away from Mother's put-downs, away from having to watch out for my brother and cover for his screw-ups. And those years away from them were the years I gradually figured out that a little booze kept those bad "less-than" feelings hidden away in the back of the closet. I would drink when I was nervous or when I was excited, when I was sad or when I was happy …but I always drank like a lady, and was never a falling-down drunk. To take a bottle in a brown paper bag to a BYOB party was unthinkable. I brought my booze in an antique teapot with 10-karat gold flowers designed on its sides with a matching gold-rimmed cup and saucer. The year after DC, I transferred to Grenoble University, an entire continent away from them!

It wasn't until my late forties that I was finally able to accept that Mother had always favored and always would favor my twin brother and there was absolutely nothing I could do about it but to just get over it and move on. That was a battle I'd never win and a war I no longer even wanted to fight!

Chapter Eleven

All Aboard?

Author J. M. Synge, one of my most admired scribes, warned more than 100 years ago in his classic, <u>The Aran Islands--A Journal Of Life On The Irish Coast</u>: *A man who is not afraid of the sea will soon be drowned.*

Growing up an hour's drive from Pacific beaches, I was always thrilled when Mother announced we were taking a chopped-egg-sandwich picnic to the beach. Those early childhood picnics were entrées to years of glorious times spent hunting for shells, of staring into tidal pools at strange critters scurrying about, listening to the calls of gulls, peering out to sea for sail boats heading for exotic ports. Early on, I developed a fascination for the sea, coupled with a healthy respect for it. Later, when I was in high school, anytime there was a bad winter storm, I would cut classes and drive the 32 miles over the hills to Pescadero Beach. Often, I had to zoom my little MGA through mini-landslides of mud to get there, but it was worth it. I was the only person in sight for miles of beach and usually, no one had even been there for days. I'd walk for hours along the seaweed-strewn beach, collecting all kinds of treasures including unusual shells I had never seen before.

My favorite find was always the Japanese glass float balls that decided they no longer wanted to be tied to a fisherman's net and would escape all the way across the sea to California. By the time I graduated from high school, I had a collection of 14 of these beauties in various sizes from 2-1/2 inches to five inches, and in many colors. Some even still had the rope ties the fisherman had wrapped around them to make sure they didn't get loose from his nets, but they were determined to be free, and managed to break away despite his efforts. Sometimes, I dreamed of being a floating ball, myself, escaping to some deserted beach far from whatever always seemed to be anchoring me just below the surface of what could have been a happy life. Yet, here I was, years later, thinking to return to California, the scene of so much of that adolescent angst.

I decided if I were to move back, I would call my new life not an adventure, but rather a "spiritual odyssey". I needed to find out if I was truly a survivor, but also to learn, once and for all, that God loved me and would protect me as long as I kept turning to Him for guidance and help. I also needed to acquire more willingness to trust and follow His directions, to learn how to be grateful, and above all, to thank Him when He helped me. This was not going to be easy for an independent, stubborn and often defiant get-outta-my-face, I-can-do-it-myself kinda gal.

No wonder I was like that. I came from a long line of strong-willed women who, for the last four generations had been leading ladies in an ongoing Greek tragedy.

On Mother's side, my Scottish great-great-grandmother broke her neck when she fell off her horse racing alone across the heather-covered moors. My great-aunt was blinded at youth but didn't let that stop her daily walk around her village outside Glasgow - she died in her seventies from a fall after tripping over her cat. Mother's mother, my granny, was burned to death in a freak rubbish-burning accident when her clothes caught fire. Mother's sister was blinded in one eye as a girl in Scotland when a youth threw lye at her, and she later died in her early forties when the galley stove on the sailboat she and her husband owned exploded in her face. Mother survived three mastoid operations as a child, with the last a hair-breadth from the brain, and then she was paralyzed in her late seventies.

The curse was on both sides of my family. On my German father's side, my aristocratic grandmother (who seemed to enjoy a little too much red wine before we went to the Bremerhaven Symphony when I visited her as a teenager) reportedly died of alcoholism. My father's sister died at fifteen of leukemia. This curse even crossed family lines. In Philadelphia, I cared for my bedridden mother-in-law for more than a year until cancer stole her away. During that year, I also had the duty of taking groceries and supplies every week to my husband's old-maid great aunt and discovered her dead on her kitchen floor the very day Kennedy was killed. With all of them gone and me next in line, I began to wonder then what tragedy might be looming over my own head.

Throughout my life, the thought of dying, at times, seemed appealing, at others hideous. I envisioned Death as a powerful Drama Queen riding down from her mountaintop hideaway on a black stallion, wielding either her jewel-encrusted sword or her razor-honed scythe over my head, determined to cut my life-line as she had done to all the other women in my family. As one of the last of our women, I refused to be cast in the same Aeschylean show-stopper, but nevertheless, this familial proclivity for tragic endings kept trying to get me. At four and one-half months pregnant and a week after the death of my mother-in-law, while alone at home, I lost my first child, a daughter, in a painful miscarriage. While married to John, after our son was born, I had Sandi. Now, there were just three of us women left… my mother, my daughter Sandi, and me.

After decades of challenging Death, I would continue hell-bent on trying to shake off the curse. If I could just discover the right charm to break the sinister spell or at least rip to shreds Dracula's black cape which had been trying to smother me all my life. I needed something that would destroy the death-wish libation I kept reaching for, trying to satisfy my unquench-able thirst for life-threatening adventures. But where would I find it…on a psychiatrist's couch? at the foot of a guru? on a year-long retreat studying Edgar Cayce's secrets to Enlightenment? taking umpteen geographic cures? booze? pills? suicide? I tried all, none worked. Instead, I discovered during the never-ending search that opportunities were being missed or avoided to fix or even try to begin a relationship with my mother. Chances to truly bond or just get closer to my teenaged son and daughter weren't anywhere near the horizon. And here was I, about to buy a sailboat which might just be a way to get out of the auditions and decline a role in The Tragedy…a chance to learn I was, instead, a true survivor. The prospect was mind-blowing.

Sandi and I had a great time on our road trip west and arrived just in time to see Mother sliding the Thanksgiving turkey into the oven. Needing to get back to Philadelphia and school, Sandi could only stay a few days before she had to fly back home. It was hard to see her go as I knew I'd miss her. Even though she was only 15, Sandi seemed so much older that afternoon as she hugged me in the San Jose airport.

"I'll write a lot, Mom, and we can call each other all the time. Don't worry -- summer will be here in no time and I'll come out to stay with you for three whole months!"

The first thing I did after signing all the papers and handing over a check for the boat, was to have it hauled out, inspected and the bottom painted. Chris, the Greek yacht broker, agreed to sail with me from the Moss Landing Harbor (where I took possession of the boat) over to the boatyard in Monterey. He said it would take about three hours. I still couldn't believe, at age 43, I had actually bought this 35-foot Ericson and might someday be sailing the ocean blue, plowing through the big swells that seldom merely sauntered but more often came careening down the Moss Landing channel to the marina.

I was adamant the name, *Gourmet Lady*, which the former owner had given her, had to go even though some said it was unlucky to change a boat's name. For the three days on board before heading from Moss Landing over to Monterey, I spent hours trying to come up with a new name so the boatyard could paint it on the hull at haul-out. But what name to choose? In the 12-Step meetings I found around Santa Cruz from the moment I arrived and was faithfully now attending, the groups, like at every other meeting I ever attended, often closed with the Serenity Prayer: *God, grant me the serenity to accept the things I cannot change, the courage to change the things I can, and the wisdom to know the difference.* That prayer had given me great solace from day-one eight years before when I would lie in bed, not able to sleep, reciting the prayer over and over until finally drifting off. For my new boat name, I wanted something to do with "serenity" but too many boats were already named that. I finally settled on *Sérenta* with the French accent over the first "e" to add a foreign ring to what I thought was the perfect moniker for this elegant craft. Plus, it would help remind me to be grateful for sobriety and my blossoming new relationship with my Higher Power.

When the yacht broker arrived for our sail to Monterey, that December morning was the kind North Central California was noted for.… a few white wispy clouds and a glorious sun streaming down to chase away the fog and warm the chilly morning. A gentle breeze was playing with the directional tell-tales on the boat's rigging.

"Let's just motor-sail over," said Chris. "We'll put up the mainsail to steady the boat but we'll have the motor on, too."

"Isn't there enough wind to just sail over?" I asked.

"Well, maybe, but I don't want to scare you on your maiden voyage!"

Chris was such a sweet fellow. In his charming Greek accent, he spent the three-hour trip explaining about wind angles on sails, how to read the wind indicator on the top of the mast, the purpose of the tell-tales on the rigging and how to read them, and other nautical things I had no clue about. The best part…he was very patient with all my questions.

The haul-out was quite an operation as the marina workers pulled my new "home" out of the water on straps with a huge crane that slowly moved the boat through the air about 20 feet above me. I watched with one eye closed. It was awesome to see, hanging in the air, the full size of the object that was possibly going to be my salvation from terrifying storms and life-threatening battles with waves, and goodness…maybe even drug-dealing pirates! I hadn't realized how large the fin keel was, and liked the idea of all that weight under there to steady the old girl.

For the rest of my nautical days, I would be participating in the never-ending debates over which was safer…a mono-hull like *Sérenta* or a multi-hull catamaran or trimaran. Mono-hulls, with all those pounds of leaded keel, were pretty difficult to turn totally upside down and sink, whereas multi-hulls, with no such similar keels had a reputation for capsizing in bad conditions. Multi-hullers would argue back that they could easily crawl back into their boats even if they were upside down, and live for months in the twin hulls until help arrived, whereas once a mono-hull turned over, you and the boat were gonners. Sailors would spend entire evenings in debate without ever giving up their opinion – you were either a mono-huller or a multi-huller and that was that! So I'm a mono-huller, I mused to myself one evening walking back to my slip after an evening in the Elkhorn Yacht Club's clubhouse. A few days before, I hadn't even heard of the term I was to use to describe myself for maybe years to come.

Moss Landing Harbor is a small harbor at the southernmost end of the Monterey Bay, with one half of the harbor devoted to sailboats and pleasure craft and the other side of the channel to the commercial fishing fleet some of which boats dated back to the old heydays of Cannery Row. There were only about a dozen boats on our side of the channel that had live-aboards due to the limited number of permits, so our section of the harbor was pretty quiet.

The Elkhorn Yacht Club, on our side, had been formed some 50 years before and the clubhouse back then had been an old barge dragged up onto the beach. It definitely was not a posh yacht club like the hoity-toity high-fa-lutin St. Francis up in San Francisco which wouldn't even consider giving reciprocity rights to the hoi polloi Moss Landing members. I looked on most of the Moss Landing boaters on our side of the channel as "Salinas cowboy sailors" because many of them showed up at their boats at 7 a. m. wearing cowboy boots and cowboy hats, with a can of beer in one hand and a cigar in the other. If open-carry had been allowed back then, they would probably have also had a gun strapped to their belts. It was a time-warp smack dab in the center of Steinbeck country surrounded by miles of Brussels sprouts and broccoli on the one side of the road and huge luscious Driscoll strawberries on the other. I got to know those fields intimately from the day the farmers put in the seeds to the day the little plants sprung up in the fog and finally to when the pickers came through and harvested. When Ian and Sandi would come to visit me on school breaks or holidays, I'd rave about the fields as we drove past them on our way to and from fun trips to Santa Cruz and visits to Obi.

"Oh, look kids... the tiny shoots have just appeared," or "Wow, will you look at the size of those strawberries in that field?" until Ian would finally say to Sandi, "Oh, no, she's not going to get off about the fields again, is she?"

They just didn't understand what joy those eternal nourishing fields gave me, the hope and comfort I found in them, because for that moment at least, everything was right with the world. Maybe my love for those fields came from memories of all those nights I had gone to bed hungry when I first moved to downtown Philly and often had no food in the cupboard. I took great delight in buying an entire "arm" of sprouts and hanging it from my boat's boom, picking them off as needed. Often when I'd be gone from my boat for the day, I'd return at dusk to find a big bag of fresh broccoli tucked into my cockpit from a fellow boater who owned the largest vegetable operation in the valley and who knew how much I loved those fields and especially, his broccoli.

I'll never forget the first night I slept aboard *Sérenta* that December after I brought her back from the haul-out. It was a misty night in Moss Landing and I was wandering around below deck, sorting things and trying to figure out what would go where. I unpacked my little can't-live-without treasures – the elegant bottles of French perfume I took with me everywhere, box of jewelry, the Anthology of World Poetry I always had with the tattered piece of paper stuck between pages with quotes from my favorite writers and philosophers--Thoreau, e. e. cummings, Tennyson, Nietzsche, Gibran, Rumi, Jung, Stevenson, Synge, Poe--and the small Bible safely wrapped up in a plastic baggy with all our Scottish family history, one of the few treasures my mother had brought with her from Scotland when she came to America in 1921.

By the time my own few prized possessions were ensconced in their new resting places, a feeling of homesickness for Philadelphia wafted through the salon. I began to wonder if my Higher Power had managed to pull off the worst joke of the century on me with this sailboat. For starters, I didn't know the first thing about sailing, and worse, nothing about engines let alone diesels. I didn't even know how a battery worked or what it did except start the car (or not) when I wanted to go somewhere! Now I was going to be living on a 12-volt system, whatever that meant. In the past, during stressful situations, when all else failed, my standby solution since an early age, was to run to the piano and play a Chopin Nocturne, and as a teenager, when filled with anger or anxiety, after finishing the Chopin, continue to muddle through a Mozart Sonata. For the first time, I was really glad I had bought the accordion now tucked under my bunk to be pulled out for solace when needed.

"This is that moment the accordion needs to come out of hiding," I whisper to the moon peeking through my starboard port light. *Sérenta* is softly rocking from side to side, her hanging brass oil lamp putting out warm flickers below it on the beautiful teak chart table. Taking the accordion out of its case, I begin a valiant attempt at my favorite Chopin's Nocturne, Op. 9 No. 2 in E-flat major. After struggling through the piece for almost two hours, about midnight, feeling a lot better about my life and everything connected with it, I climb into the forward V-berth for the night. As I attempt to get comfortable in this weird-shaped "bed" I'd be using as my nest for some time to come, from across the harbor somewhere, floating on the fog, comes the clear strains of Chopin's Nocturne being played on a trumpet!

I never did find out who it was but always had a vague notion it was the reclusive single-hander from Denmark whose story was remarkable. He had been into soaring engineless gliders until one late afternoon the year before, when he crashed into a box canyon in the Mojave Desert. With almost every bone in his body broken, he crawled painfully to civilization which took more than a week. Frostbite had set in, then gangrene. He ended up losing both legs. Undaunted, now he was teaching himself to sail in preparation for a global circumnavigation. Yes, only a survivor aboard a sailboat could play Chopin's Nocturne faultlessly on a trumpet.

Maybe someday, stuck for days or even weeks on the windless waters in the doldrums or drifting along on calm waters beyond the Horse Latitudes, I'd be sitting on my sailboat playing Chopin faultlessly on my accordion. What was it Thoreau said... something about putting foundations under dreams?

Chapter Twelve

Here I Go, Ready Or Not!

It took several weeks before I could finally get up the nerve to maneuver *Sérenta* out of her slip. I'd come up with all sorts of tasks and reasons why I couldn't pull away from the dock and instead, would spend hours studying <u>Royce's Sailing Illustrated: The Sailor's Bible</u> which the yacht broker had given me as a boat-warming gift. But all that technical jargon confused me more than it helped. I am one of those hands-on learners and would just have to go out there and do it.

I promised *Sérenta* when I bought her she wouldn't be another one of those "dock birds" tied up at the dock for weeks, months, sometimes years. No, she wouldn't ever be one of those boats the "White Pants" only used for plying various mistresses with martinis. I solemnly promised *Sérenta* I would take her out every day, no matter the weather. It was imperative I begin to act on my promise and figure out how to get her out of that narrow slip. If I broke my promise, she might not be there for me when I needed her.

The first time out of the harbor alone was frightening. I had spent about ten days sitting in my cockpit watching nearby boaters going in and out of their slips. It seemed a matter of timing. Our side of the harbor was built in a "U" and there wasn't a lot of room in the middle…maybe about 50 feet at most between the stern of my boat in her slip over to the stern of the boat in the slip on the other side of the "U". That Thursday morning the day before my birthday, I knew it was to be the Big Day as I'd have to get going before the wild and wooly weekend boaters might show up. I had been stewing about this long enough. It felt like when I was working my 12- Step lessons and found myself sitting too long on the same Step. Without any other known reason, I would suddenly become uncomfortable and restless until realizing I was lazily sliding into complacency and it was high time to move on to study and work the next Step.

That nautical mile-marking Thursday, I waited until late afternoon when the wind usually dropped, then watched the water in the harbor to check for any current that might pull my boat in the wrong direction when backing her out. I tried to visualize the exact turning spot mid-channel between my dock and the one behind me. I'd have to start turning the wheel at that spot to avoid crashing into the boats behind and still have enough space to clear the ones on either side of me as I brought the bow through the turn. I calculated the time I would have once I let loose the lines from the dock before *Sérenta* would start drifting into my neighbor's boat. It seemed there'd be less than a second!

My throat felt tight as if it was either going to close up completely or I was going to throw up. My heart was pounding like a jackhammer. My mind was filling up with ideas of all kinds of crazy things that could go wrong and I hoped my insurance would cover them. I was petrified, but began warming up the 27hp inboard Yanmar diesel. It must have been ten minutes before I felt brave enough to get off to untie the bow and stern lines. I asked for help from my HP, then jumped off, grabbed each of the lines, tossed them aboard, hopped back into the cockpit and slowly eased the gearshift into reverse, giving it a little throttle to get the boat moving. She was heavy and I knew if I waited too long without giving her some juice, she'd just coast into the pleasure fishing boat next to me. Thank goodness no one was around to watch. If those "cowboy sailors" were watching with their arms crossed arrogantly on their chests, I'd feel so nervous I'd surely mess it up. Slowly, *Sérenta* eased out of the slip into the zone of no return. I turned the wheel slightly and her bow gracefully cleared the end of my dock. It was a miracle! I slipped the gearshift into forward. All I had to do now was keep her in the center of the channel leading to the entrance buoy, then hang a right into the main channel leading out to the bay. I prayed there wouldn't be any incoming boats to contend with. Not a boat in sight as no one seemed to sail weekdays in winter. Water was crashing up on the rocks on either side of the channel and out there, the blue Pacific was beckoning, daring me, luring me to come out and challenge her.

Once out of the channel, I headed out to the one-mile buoy marker where sea lions were piled on top of each other around the small above-water ledge of the buoy. They were all looking so relaxed, sunning themselves and didn't even bat an eye as I glided past. I felt sorry for these huge innocent mammals because I had heard that often, fishermen would illegally shoot them, claiming they stole fish off their lines. I shot up a little prayer for their well-being as I passed them.

I didn't feel ready yet to leave the safety of the cockpit to go up to the bow to hoist the jib sail. It was enough just getting used to maneuvering the boat around in the water under power of the engine. Then out of nowhere came a huge wave lifting *Sérenta's* bow up in the air. I was sure she was going to do a backflip. I held on to the wheel like a python strangling its prey, feeling the power of the water moving underneath my boat which seemed totally at its mercy. And then the wave passed. *Sérenta* rested back down in the water as she had been before the wave dared to disturb our tranquility. I was able to breathe normally again. Going around in circles for about an hour was enough for the first trial. A few gulls had the nerve to laugh at me as I entered the jaws of the harbor. Now came the ordeal of getting the boat back into that thread-the-needle slip and jumping off to tie her up before we either crashed bow-first into the dock or sideways into one of the boats on either side.

I rounded the corner into the final channel and headed down the narrow passage towards my slip on the right, halfway down the dock. I steered the boat as far to the left as possible, slowed to a crawl and then threw the gearshift into neutral, easing the steering wheel to the right. *Sérenta* gently headed into the slip. I completed the turn, jumped off midair onto the dock in time to grab the stern dock line, whipped it around the cleat at the stern and then ran up to the bow to secure the other dock line to the bow cleat. She had come to a gentle stop right where she belonged. It was another miracle!

Looking at my beloved *Sérenta*, sitting there so proudly in her slip, I quietly whispered, "Cheated Death again. Thank you, Lord." That was to become my mantra every time I managed to get *Sérenta* safely tucked in, whether in the Moss Landing slip or one of the many strange and faraway anchorages I might come to know before this odyssey was over.

Indeed, there would be many times when *Sérenta* and I cheated Death, with God's help, of course. On some of the first sojourns out beyond the safety of the harbor when the wind came up and the waves started to do their thing, I just had to close my eyes and pray. I learned when you don't use your eyes, your ears become more attuned to what is going on around you. I could hear the waves heading in and could calculate how close I was to the beach just by the shhhhhhsh sound of the water rolling up on the sand. If I was close, it was loud, farther out softer. This early-experience knowledge, gleaned out of fear, was to hold me later in good stead.

I settled into my new lifestyle without too much stress and began to meet other live-aboards in the harbor. George, unofficial mayor of Moss Landing Harbor, lived on an old catamaran he had single-handed back from Hawaii some years before. He was a husky guy who had played football for Santa Clara University, became an arc welder when he graduated, and then switched to selling fertilizer to the local farmers. He knew a lot about many things and best of all knew just about everything about sailboats. He never seemed to tire of my persistent questions. One morning, he took my side when all the other men were gabbing about me. I was lying up in my V-berth with the hatch open a crack to let in fresh air. The men were standing on the dock in front of my boat, not aware I was "home".

"She's doing real well," George was saying. "Five days ago, she took it out for the first time alone. You should have seen how she eased it out of the slip as if she had been born behind a wheel. You guys oughtta cut her some slack and give credit where credit's due. How many 43 year-old women--or women any age, for that matter--do you know who would buy a 35-footer and then teach herself how to sail it? My cap is off to her. She's had it out every day this week, just going around in circles out there, but at least she's doing it, not like some of you guys who own dock birds rotting in the harbor."

It was reassuring to know I had at least one fan amongst the group of old salts who thought women were only good for making sure there was plenty of cold beer aboard, frying the fish they caught, swabbing the decks, and satisfying them in the bunk.

I hadn't taken a job yet, and while waiting for my next dividend check, was living off some cash I had squirreled away back in Philadelphia. Thank goodness I bought stock anytime I had spare moola back when I was working at The Academy and as a lobbyist! In my new life aboard *Sérenta*, I was free of nine-to-five responsibilities and able to spend mornings investigating all the different parts of the boat, figuring out which lines pulled up which sails, which pulleys were geared to which blocks. I had never known an engine so intimately before having been raised on antiques and embroidery, and was going to have to learn everything about that dang little Yanmar. One false move on my part, I was sure, would either blow us up or sink us.

When my buddy George arrived back at the harbor after work, he'd sit on *Sérenta*'s deck and slowly and methodically explain one thing after another. I don't know what I would have done without George. It was a horrible tragedy when he died suddenly a few months later. One day he was sitting in my cockpit drawing pictures of sail trimmings, the next day he was dead amidst rumors there had been some change in his blood pressure medicine. He had no relatives so we live-aboards and "harbor rats" gave him a royal burial at sea. I read a beautiful poem I had written for him... I would miss George.

Chapter Thirteen

Out There In One Of The Worst Storms Of The Century

Shortly after I bought the boat, I met Darryl. He was 13 years younger than me, also, a twin, and was a shipwright working at the time on various boats in the Moss Landing Harbor while living in an old camper. I wanted to replace the ugly blue shag rug glued down throughout *Sérenta*'s cabin with a wooden sole. Occasionally, I'd see the former owner wandering about as he was still the yacht club's Commodore. No matter the project, he always insisted Darryl was the only person for the job.

"But don't get romantically involved with him," cautioned the old guy. "He's a former rock musician and he's fried his brains on LSD. Nevertheless, he's still the best shipwright in California."

I learned Darryl, also, a guitarist, had often played at The Fillmore Auditorium in San Francisco which hosted performances by the most memorable acts and counterculture icons of the last century, even launching some of their careers… the Grateful Dead, Santana, Jimi Hendrix, Otis Redding, Muddy Waters, and The Who, just to name a few. He did act a little odd from time to time, but mostly, he was very helpful and very friendly in a shy sort of way. One afternoon after he had finished for the day working on another yacht, we started to design *Sérenta*'s sole. I wanted all exotic hardwoods which seemed to please him. I soon figured out this was no ordinary carpenter. We spent days driving around lumberyards throughout the San Francisco Bay area and even farther afield, looking for hardwoods... picking up some purple heart and black cherry here, some cornelian and Pacific coast mahogany there. The sole was going to be gorgeous.

My cash stash was dwindling and dividends weren't coming in as high as expected so I got a job at West Marine in Santa Cruz answering phones for catalogue sales. It was perfect! I was getting paid to learn about boats including my own, plus getting a hefty employee discount on everything I bought. Hired on as seasonal help, I had days off to practice sailing around Monterey Bay. From about December 1st to mid-March, *Sérenta* was almost always the only sailboat gracing the horizon.

The new sole project took months. I soon figured out Darrell was not only the West Coast's best shipwright but also a gifted artist with wood and a perfectionist as well. At the same time he was helping me, he was also working on restoring a classic wooden trawler in the Moss Landing harbor for a fellow who had developed the idea for wooden pallets…nothing but the best for Dick and his trawler. When Darryl was finished for the day working on the trawler, he'd come and work on my boat, usually in the late afternoons just before the sun was going down. That was when he started sailing with me and I discovered what a fabulous sailor he was, having sailed some years back all over the South Pacific on a multi-hull with his twin brother.

Every afternoon that spring of '87, when I got back to my boat from West Marine about 5:00 p. m., we would take *Sérenta* out to watch the sun dipping into the sea. We'd try to catch a glimpse of the magical green flash just as the sun sank below the horizon but never managed to see it. The wind wasn't as strong in the late afternoon, making early attempts at dealing with the sails easier. Darryl usually did most of the sail-tweaking and I soon realized this was his way of keeping me dependent on him.

One day, when we were ready to take *Sérenta* out, I announced, "I'm going to do the sails myself this trip and I won't need you to do a thing. You can just sit back and enjoy the ride." It felt very empowering to say that and I even surprised myself, feeling like a brazen hussy.

Darryl seemed a little miffed sitting up on the bow like a stern schoolmaster, rod in hand, watching every move I made as we headed out into the bay. It was the first time I'd have to get the mainsail tuned properly to carry the boat on a steady course long enough for me to leave the wheel, run up to the bow, and hoist the jib. The wind picked up several notches just as I was running forward. The boat climbed high on a wave and when she headed back down the other side, I was sure we'd tumble stern over bow or as sailors call it, pitch-pole. I was in a panic but I knew I had to hoist the jib myself. To ask Darryl for help would put me always under his thumb out there and I had already spent too many years under another man's thumb. I grabbed the jib sail's line and pulled with all my strength. Up she went, resisting me like a headstrong filly until I could winch her into shape.

"Just think of *Sérenta* as a cork," he shouted above the din of the sea. "A cork will bounce around a little but it will always rise to the top and never sink."

That was the best piece of sailing advice anyone ever gave me. *Sérenta* went waltzing over the tops of the waves just as she was designed to do. There might be other life challenges difficult to overcome, but I had mastered this one and gained a great respect for *Sérenta* and an even greater faith in God's willingness to just "be there" for me. Thanks to Captain God, I was no longer going to be living daily under the fear of sinking and drowning at sea…maybe, occasionally, doubts would plague me, but at least not every day.

Late April that year, Darryl announced one afternoon when we were sailing *Sérenta* back into the harbor that it was time for me to get a feel of what it was like to voyage out on the high seas. He had been asked by a retired oil tanker captain to deliver the man's 55-foot Grand Banks trawler from where it had been worked on in a San Pedro shipyard just north of San Francisco back to its permanent slip in Moss Landing. The old captain didn't want to bring the boat back himself and later confessed to me that even though he had gone around the world many times skippering huge tankers, he was not comfortable out there in his small 55-footer.

Darryl invited me to go along as crew. I had a few days off work for Easter and my little duffle bag was packed in less than five minutes, ready to set off on the Big Adventure. The yacht-owner drove us up to San Pedro and as he waved goodbye, shouted, "God speed". Darryl knew the boat well as he had worked on it for years. We spent the rest of the afternoon going over systems and checking fluid levels so we could take off early the next morning.

Once outside San Francisco Bay, we made our way south. A few miles past Half Moon Bay, we met up with three Pacific gray whales heading to the warm Baja calving lagoons.

Darryl said they had gotten a head-start as they usually aren't seen until early fall. They were gigantic, breaching and blowing bubbles in the air. I was thrilled as it was the first time I had ever seen these behemoths in the flesh. They followed us all day on the starboard out-to-sea side of our boat, playing with us, coming up close and then taking off again.

When we turned into Monterey Bay, I watched two of them take off down the coast. Where was the third? It was the biggest, too. I was nervous. Was it right underneath us and any minute might poke its head through the hull? Without warning, it appeared just about ten feet from our starboard side shooting straight out of the water like a gigantic ballistic missile. It performed as if in some slow motion ballet, soaring towards the heavens until I could see the whole whale from its nose to its toes, its white belly facing me. It was about 50 feet long, almost as long as our boat and so close I could count all the crabs and crustaceans hitchhiking on its belly. And then it slowly fell backwards and gracefully sank below the surface. As it disappeared into the sea I thought I saw a grin and was sure I heard it say, "Love you, girl." It had come up close just to say goodbye and now it was heading back out to sea to join its companions frolicking in the distance. We made it safely to Moss Landing and I was happy to see my *Sérenta* safe and sound, waiting for me in her slip.

When I had owned the boat six months, to celebrate the occasion, Darryl agreed to join me over Memorial Weekend for a voyage south to San Simeon, the little cove in the shadow of Hearst's magnificent castle. Mother was flying to Spokane, wheelchair and all, for a week to visit my brother who had just been transferred there. It was the ideal chance for my very first cruise. Darryl and I studied the charts and figured we could do the roundtrip in five days and be back in plenty of time to pick Mother back up at the San Francisco Airport. This was a near-fatal error I learned never to make again. To take off sailing with a time constraint and to assume you've calculated correctly how long that voyage might take is absolute madness. There are too many variables such as ever-changing weather conditions, unexpected mechanical failures, and not least of all, hardiness of the crew to maintain rigorous and exhausting stints on the helm.

We sailed out early in the morning, headed towards Monterey then along the coast past Pacific Grove to our first anchorage in Carmel Bay's Stillwater Cove. It's a beautiful little natural harbor in view of the famous Pebble Beach Golf Course above. There would be no familiar dock slip to greet me -- this would be the first time I would anchor *Sérenta*. I was a nervous wreck as I handled the sail and helm duties in the small cove, leaving only the actual dropping of the anchor to Darryl. Watching him deftly as he positioned the 45 pound CQR, I determined to try the anchor-drop procedure myself, at our next anchorage. I did not want to be dependent on anyone (except my HP, of course) for anything to do with my *Sérenta*…especially if I were ever going to sail away to exotic places. All went well. We enjoyed a delicious dinner of warmed up Chinese food I had picked up before leaving Moss Landing, followed by a peaceful night of sound sleep.

We weighed anchor just after 6:00 a. m. when the boat had started to swing around on her anchor. Aeolus must have let the violent Storm Winds out of his cave as they had already started to act up, a harbinger of what was soon to come. Bad weather hit as we rounded Point Sur, a notorious nemesis for sailors heading in either direction. We sailed night and day with monstrous waves climbing up our stern threatening to slam into the cockpit. They were humungous walls of water and I was certain we were going to know Davy Jones on a first-name basis. The merciless powerhouse waves pushed my boat forward and side to side as if they were playing with a little plastic boat in a kid's bathtub. *Sérenta* would doggedly cut her way through the water and finally, the wave would pass under us. It felt like we were surfing. I had been one of the first girls in Santa Cruz to ride a surfboard back in the early '50s and now I was surfing again, but this time on a 35-foot surfboard.

When we got beyond sight of Point Sur lighthouse and its comforting beacon, I felt a fear I hadn't known for some time. It was so dark out there, especially with no moon, making the water black and unwelcoming. Before we left, we had charted our course and I put to use principles the yacht broker had taught me about dead-reckoning navigation techniques. Darryl agreed to share helm duties... four hours on, four hours off.

It is odd what one thinks about when fearing a possible imminent ending. Out in that darkness, I chanted aloud lines from a poem by Wordsworth I learned three decades before when in school in Scotland as a kid. We were battling *wind that sang of trees uptorn and vessels tost*. I quickly changed thoughts to something less fateful. *Sérenta* was speeding along on the *wings of the wind*. While glued to the helm, I couldn't hear the yacht broker's kind words, "Oh, you'll be just fine out there... Darryl's a good sailor." I couldn't hear Darryl shouting comforting words to me above the lion-roar of the sea. I couldn't hear God saying, "Everything is going to be all right." All I could hear was the wild whoosh of the waves passing us, the hiss of the white water on their tops as they crested behind the boat. I was too afraid to turn around to look at the monsters chasing us.

"Are you sure you're still OK?" Darryl shouted from the cabin. At the end of his watch he had gone below to replace his wet-water jacket that had totally been soaked when a rogue wave came crashing over the side of the boat and swirled around in the cockpit.

"Want me to take back the helm?"

"No, I'm fine, thank you."

I wasn't about to give up the helm nor let him see how scared I was. That would have been admitting defeat. Come hell or higher water, I would stick it out until midnight when my watch was up. After the second hour, I started to feel a certain rhythm to it all. Turning the wheel almost 50% to port towards shore each time a wave grazed us kept us on course when the bow of the boat wanted to pull to starboard. It soon became a steady pattern. First the stern would rise up, then the boat moved faster as the wave ran along under the boat, then the wave seemed to crest and the boat would slide downhill plunging to the right so much that you had to yank the wheel real hard left to keep the boat going straight on her course. After an hour of this, my arms were aching and I was totally exhausted but refused to give in. The wind was rising now. Every wave that passed left a salty spray of water that blew back into the cockpit like the blast of a fireman's hose. I was now soaking wet and freezing, but kept on. This was a night from Hell. Thank God I didn't know then that the trip back would be even worse!

Darryl took the helm at midnight. I hadn't eaten anything since noon and went below to make a cup of instant soup. The boat was pitching and rolling so much, I started to feel seasick. Couldn't afford to get sick so chased that thought away, grabbed an apple, and rushed back up to the cockpit. It would be better to sit out there in the fresh air keeping Darryl company than be thrown from side to side below deck.

It hardly seemed an hour had passed when the ship's clock bell below clanged out signaling 4:00 a. m. and my turn at the helm again. The worst of the storm had passed and the wind was lighter now. We were on a new heading, one that would take us into the San Simeon anchorage. Our charting was right on the money and we cruised in shortly after 5:00 a. m., surprised to see lights ahead at that hour and so close to shore.

"I don't remember them building a new pier out here, but then again, I haven't been by for a couple of years," said Darryl. "Oh, well... we'll just drop anchor over there," he directed, beckoning to an area to the right of what we thought was a pier.

As we approached, we saw it was not a pier at all but rather a huge ship lying off the shore. I decided this wasn't a good time for my first stab at solo-anchoring. Darryl went right into gear to handle the anchor as I managed the helm. Just as we had everything tied up and were ready to go below for some long-overdue sleep, I noticed crew aboard the big ship lowering a smaller craft over the side and into the water with two aboard. Next, they were heading our way.

"Oh, good grief, it's the Coast Guard," said Darryl. "I think they are going to make an inspection of us. Anything on board that shouldn't be?"

"Well, you know I don't drink, do drugs, or shoot guns, but there's something else that could bring us grief. I don't think the former owner ever hooked up the holding tank for the head. Not sure, but I think it flushes directly into the sea which is probably illegal. I don't ever use it since we have such nice bathrooms at the yacht club and was planning to have it checked out next week. What should we do?"

"Pray they don't notice."

Their boat was now at our stern and one of the men aboard said, "Permission to come aboard, Sir."

Sir, indeed, I thought, hopping quickly to the stern, smiling at the two and saying, "Do you think you could come back tomorrow? We've been sailing all night and we're exhausted."

Apparently you don't say that to the Coast Guard. The two half-smiled as they climbed aboard. The sailing community had been putting out some very bad press about the Coast Guard's practice of boarding and inspecting vessels claiming they were "Safety Inspections" while boaters called them "Drug Raids". Thank goodness I wouldn't have to worry with nothing stronger than aspirin and Tums in the medicine cabinet.

I decided the best way to handle the situation was to immediately disarm them of their titles and said, "Hi, my name is Sandra and this is my friend, Darryl. And you are…..?"

"Lieutenant David Strauss and Lieutenant Francis Morris."

"Sure glad to meet you, Dave and Frank. What can I do for you? Like some coffee?"

They seemed to soften a little and proceeded to ask me for all the usual things -- fire extinguishers, bells, lifejackets, flares which they said were out of date but they wouldn't put it on the report if I promised to replace them when I got back to my home port. Then Frank headed towards the bathroom. I watched him poke his head around the commode and check all the through-hull handles.

"This all installed according to Hoyle?" he asked.

"Frankly, I wouldn't know a thing about the plumbing. I just bought the boat from the commodore of the Elkhorn Yacht Club and I'm sure he'd have everything in order."

"Well, you've got the handle turned so that it dumps overboard. I've switched it for you. When you're in an anchorage you need to use your holding tank."

"Aye, Aye. Sir," I said, wondering if he really knew and was just being a nice guy.

They handed me their report and written in big letters across the top was, OWNER VERY COOPERATIVE. That was my first experience with the Coast Guard and it wouldn't be the last. Quite a few times while sailing alone in Monterey Bay, I had to call them when the engine died or something else disastrous was about to happen.

"Coast Guard, Coast Guard…it's me again…*Sérenta*," I'd say on channel 16, the hailing channel.

"*Sérenta*, we told you the last time… we don't come out unless it's life-threatening."

"But Sir, this time it really is. The cabin is filling with black smoke and if you don't get here soon, the whole boat may explode and sink and you'd be looking for bits and pieces of my body all over the bay. Then they'd wash up on the beach and spoil someone's sandcastle. Please, just this once?"

They'd show up in a half hour to help. Another time, I took some friends for a sail and made the mistake of putting one of the guys on the bow to direct me into the harbor and we ended up aground. Another call to the Coast Guard.

"Sir, I've got the boat stuck on the sandbar and I don't know how to get off."

"Where are you located *this* time, *Sérenta*?" came the voice over the radio on channel 16 which everyone in the boating world and even landlubbers tuned in to.

"I'm actually almost in the Moss Landing harbor, Sir. I made it down the channel but then got stuck in front of the café."

"Where are you exactly, *Sérenta*?"

"Right in front of the restaurant in the Moss Landing Harbor."

"What is your latitudinal position, *Sérenta*?"

"Listen, I don't know latitudes from longitudes as I haven't learned about all that yet, but I'm close enough to this Moss Landing greasy spoon to see the guy at the window table putting peas on his fork. Now do you know where I am?"

I felt humiliated. It was bad enough being stuck on a sandbar but to be grilled like this with the whole harbor listening was mortifying…especially when it hadn't been my fault in the first place.

"We'll be sending a vessel your way, *Sérenta*. Just stand by."

Did he expect me to somehow move? They sent a cutter which stood approximately 20 feet off with about eight men aboard who just stood on board, taking turns watching me. When high tide came four hours later, I was able to power myself off. Well, at least it was comforting that they were there just in case something terrible happened. After these incidents, I would thank them profusely on Channel 16 for being so wonderful. When everyone else was saying bad things about the Coast Guard because of their "safety inspections", I thought they might like to hear something nice. They never acknowledged my remarks, of course, but I knew they were listening.

After the Coast Guard inspectors left, Darryl and I were so exhausted from the voyage we stayed on board trying to get caught up with our sleep although we could hardly keep our eyes closed for the tossing and turning of the boat. At dawn, the wind was already howling so we hauled anchor and headed out. It would be a long voyage back. The storm was raging and getting worse as we chalked off each nautical mile. Making things worse, we were heading north, against the wind and against the tides. *Sérenta* was a real champ. She'd ride up on mammoth waves coming at us and then careen straight down on the other steep side. From the crest of one wave to the trough of the next looked more than the length of the boat and sometimes I wondered if we would pitch-pole and not ever come back up.

We took turns on four-hour watches and finally, I gave up and decided to try and find a place to tuck in for safety. I was reading the <u>Coastal Pilot</u>, a thick book which gives a play-by-play description of the entire coast. I read aloud about a little cove where they filmed much of the movie, T*he Sandpiper*, right below Pfeiffer State Park. According to the book, this tiny cove was supposed to be "a haven in bad storms, but very small and not offering much protection". I decided to try for it.

"I don't know how you expect to find that dinky little cove in this fog," growled Darryl, as we plowed through one mountain of water after another. He was starting to get grumpy which was natural under the stress.

"Darryl, I think we just passed it about five minutes back. The book describes it as *'a cove with a dark brown promontory reaching out in a southerly direction with cliffs light to dark brown and three rocks standing off the northern end.'* I'm sure that's what we just passed."

Darryl argued saying we hadn't come to it yet but I was sure we had. Besides, ever since I was a kid, I had an uncanny knack of finding lost things and was hoping that old power was at work, now.

"I hate to pull rank, but I am the skipper of this ship so we are turning around and heading back there. I'm sure that was the cove at Pfeiffer."

We came about in silence and as we did so, a small fishing boat that had been following us was turning around, too. Sure enough, there the cove was, right where I thought it would be.

The fisherman came up on the radio saying, "Figured when I saw a big sailboat like you turning around to go back to the cove, thought I better do so as well. Let's hope we can get some sleep in there."

It was reassuring to hear another human voice. We weren't in this alone. Darryl and I anchored and tried to sleep, but everything was crashing to the floor as the boat tossed from side to side. It felt like Leviathan was trying to dislodge the anchor and attempting to pull the boat over. I lay there listening to glasses breaking, pots and pans hitting the floor, shelves being ripped out. Even my brand new solid brass barometer screwed into the interior hull was dashed to the floor, gouging the beautiful new sole, its first battle scar. After an hour of this, I suggested we weigh anchor and keep going... out there couldn't be as bad as lying there listening to everything I owned being smashed to smithereens. Darryl agreed. The little fishing boat followed us out.

I learned an important lesson that first trip.... to never have a set deadline when going out sailing. Normally, you would just sit it out in a safe anchorage until the storm passed. We, however, couldn't leave my mother sitting in her wheelchair at the San Francisco Airport and even if we could get ahold of someone via the ship-to-shore radio, I didn't know anyone I could ask to do the 95-mile drive up to the airport to get her... we simply had to sail back. After that trip, if I invited someone to go with me for a sail, I'd tell them I didn't know when we would be back. If they had a deadline, I had an envelope full of rain checks. If a storm comes up, you just wait, that's all... wait, watch and listen. Pacific storms can be treacherous...and deadly as I was soon to find out!

The second day of the return voyage, I went below to make lunch and almost overcome with the stink of diesel, started to feel seasick. Sick or not,

I had to make lunch -- we hadn't had any breakfast and no dinner the night before. I simply told myself, "You're not allowed to get sick" and that was the last time in my entire sailing career I would ever feel seasick. I became convinced seasickness is a manifestation of fear and you just have to con yourself out of it like so many other fear-creating situations.

The last leg of the journey found us in pea-soup fog. For an instant, it would lift and we could pick out the Point Sur lighthouse beacon scanning the horizon for lost or weary sailors. I learned to love and respect lighthouses during that trip. We followed the sound of the surf pounding the beach all the way back to Moss Landing. Those early days of "blind" sailing were now coming in handy. I was able to follow the sound of the waves on the sand to keep us from beaching and at a safe distance off the shore all the way into the harbor. I eased the boat into my slip, stepped onto the dock, into the cockpit, and fell into a pool of tears. Darryl jumped off the boat, reached down and picked me up in his arms, saying, "Sandra, I didn't want to tell you this out there, but first, you're a terrific sailor, second, that was the worst storm I have ever come through in all my sailing, even in the South Pacific, and third, there were times when I honestly didn't think we'd make it."

I just looked at him. I couldn't speak…I was too busy thanking God for His help.

Later, we heard a fishing boat with seven men had disappeared that same weekend near the Farallon Islands some 28 miles off San Francisco, outside the "Gate" (sailors' affectionate term for the Golden Gate Bridge). Native Americans called these the "Islands of the Dead". The wives of the fishermen were adamant about finding out what happened and were certain the little yellow fishing boat had been rammed and sunk by a freighter. It took up a lot of the news because a freighter had been in the area when the fishing boat disappeared although the owners steadfastly stuck to the story their freighter hadn't been anywhere near any fishing boats.

A year and a half later, when *Sérenta* and I were hanging out in San Diego for the hurricane season, the very same freighter was hauled out for repairs at a San Diego shipyard. The wives of the deceased fishermen who persisted in following the freighter's trail, arrived at the shipyard and discovered yellow paint all over its bow. I never did hear what the widows did, but I hoped they got themselves a good Admiralty attorney to prove negligence on the part of that freighter. It made me shiver remembering my own nightmare voyage with Darryl in what was officially hailed as, "One of the worst storms of the century".

Chapter Fourteen

Ahoy, It's The Titty-Pink Boat

After that mind-blowing cruise to San Simeon and first winter spent sailing in and out of Moss Landing, I wanted to see if I could move my boat to Santa Cruz for the summer. Moss Landing had been perfect for winter when all the fog was up in Santa Cruz, but for some climatic reason, the fog reverses its favorite haunts and comes to Moss Landing for the summer. It would be chilly. Everyone said I would never get a slip in Santa Cruz -- there was a 12-year waiting list.

"A little waiting list ain't gonna stop me," I thought, and marched boldly up to the fishermen's dock in the Santa Cruz harbor.

The fishermen were readying their boats to head north for three months of fishing for herring. In minutes, I charmed one of them into sub-letting his slip while he was up north, showing how it would save him a summer's worth of slip fees. I actually managed to acquire the choice of four different fishermen's slips! If there was one thing I continued to enjoy throughout my life, it was in accomplishing something everyone said couldn't be done.

All this sailing business was starting to improve self-confidence in other aspects of my sober life, especially in dealing with people. I was never good at confrontations, but now sober, I was learning to stand up for what I believed in, and back down when I saw I was wrong. It wasn't embarrassing anymore to say, "Whoops, I made a mistake" or "Gosh, I'm sorry…I was wrong." While I had been drinking, if I admitted my shortcomings, good grief… they might figure out I was an alcoholic! In my new life, I no longer had to struggle to be perfect which gave me license to try just about anything. If it didn't work out, I could apologize or make amends if it involved or hurt someone, and then head right back to the dime to step off in another direction.

I picked a calm day and for the first time, motor-sailed *Sérenta* north to Santa Cruz alone and without a single problem. Mine was the only sailboat on the Santa Cruz fishermen's dock. I was much happier there than being on one of the yachties' docks where I knew I wouldn't fit in with those beer-sloshing fellows with perfectly creased white trousers and $195 white boat shoes. After I had been there a few weeks, one boater who almost always won the Wednesday night beer-can races, asked me to crew the next race. I was totally amazed and honored he felt I was good enough for what was mostly an all-male event. I showed up on time and the race began. On board, they were all taking it much too seriously, shouting at each other if someone made a slightly wrong shift of sails that would "cost us the race, you damned fool." That was the one and only race I crewed. Not a good place for a sober woman, and besides, no fun at all.

The Santa Cruz Harbor fishermen were a bit leery of me at first when I moved in to their turf -- they thought I was just another one of those fancy yachties. After a few weeks watching me scrub my decks, climb the mast to attach masthead lights, sail out there every day even when it was pouring down rain, and avoid Wednesday night races like a tsunami, they seemed to have collectively concluded I wasn't that bad after all. On days I had to work or drive Mother somewhere and couldn't go out fishing, they would take turns secretly tossing a salmon into my cockpit when they passed the stern of my boat returning from their morning fishing. It was always just the right size to fit on my barbecue. When I got back to my boat and found the giftie, while they were away getting ice or something to eat, I would quickly nip over and tuck a little split of Champagne into the ice in the nearest fisherman's deck-side ice box.

Those Monterey Bay fishermen taught me a lot about cleaning and cooking fish. Many times it would be a mackerel I'd find in the cockpit. Most people turn their noses up at mackerel, calling it the "garbage fish of the sea". If I wanted the salmon they might give me, I knew I would have to take the mackerel as well since I couldn't go out and fish for salmon every day until my part-time job at West Marine was over for the season. I ended up really liking mackerel, especially since, as an oily fish, it was a rich source of omega-3 fatty acids and I was trying to stay healthy in this new lifestyle. Learning to appreciate the mackerel worked in my favor when I talked the manager of the harbor's snazzy fish restaurant above the fishermen's icehouse into hiring me. I told him he was losing a lot of bucks by only serving lunch and dinner. As an experienced breakfast chef with all the fabulous breakfasts I had become known for at my B&B in Philadelphia, I said I could bring him in a lot of money by opening the restaurant for Sunday brunch and weekday breakfast. I was hired to start the day after my seasonal job ended. My first day as chef, the manager announced the owner had bought 50 pounds of mackerel.

"Whose gonna order mackerel?" the manager wailed. "Nobody eats that garbage fish."

"I know a great way to fix it," I volunteered, having eaten many a gifted mackerel.

He didn't have all the spices and ingredients I liked to use. In fact, there were few herbs or spices in the restaurant's kitchen supplies, so I ran down to my boat and got what I needed. This was to be my culinary trial by fire. I was the new gal and now was to prepare this dish for the other chefs (all surfer dudes) to sample. I slipped the mackerel into some raspberry balsamic vinegar, added a hefty splash of brandy, threw in some fresh garlic and dill, a dash of Tabasco, a few chopped green jalapeños and quickly grilled it. They gave it a five-star rating, and for the rest of the week, the blackboard special read, "Sandra's Mackerel". Pretty soon, patrons were coming in and specifically asking for it long after we'd sold the last filet.

I soon learned that the fishermen were having a major fight with the restaurant owners who were reputed to be associated with the local Mafia. According to the fishermen, the building had been built mostly with Fishermen Association funds so they could have an icehouse. Then the restaurant all of a sudden appeared on the second floor and the owners started telling fishermen they could only buy ice if they sold fish to the restaurant at a certain low price. The fishermen got angry and refused to be blackmailed. They chose to bring ice down from Half Moon Bay or up from Morro Bay. Only the unsuspecting fisherman who pulled in from beyond our "neighborhood" bought ice there and got stuck selling his catch for the low price the restaurant boss would pay. I felt guilty as if I were a turncoat, working for the enemy.

After only a few weeks on the job, I was elevated to full-time chef, selecting the seafood we would use, prepping humungous whole fish into single-portion fillets, and creating nightly specials. Next, the manager wanted me to be the stool pigeon and tell him who was stealing food from the freezers and walk-ins. A dilemma… how could I rat on co-workers? It wasn't just a few tomatoes or handful of shrimp… ten-pound buckets of Alaskan king crab and big bags of lobster tails and even of whole lobsters were disappearing. I began to feel really weird working with culinary pirates. The next week I got a part in San Francisco Opera's production of *La Bohème* and had to drive 90 miles one way to rehearsals. I asked the restaurant manager for certain rehearsal Saturdays off and he wouldn't let me switch with the other chefs although they were always switching with each other. He made the excuse that while I was there, the till always had the right amount in it and less food was missing. Soooooo, the job would have to go. Anyway, it was autumn and soon would be time to move back to Moss Landing for the winter.

The second season I made the move from Moss Landing up to Santa Cruz for the summer, as crew, I took a guy, Michael, along whom I had met at the Elkhorn Yacht Club that winter. He was thinking about buying a sailboat, and eager to witness, first-hand, life as a live-aboard. It was about a five or six-hour sail and halfway there, I had to reef (shorten) the main as the wind was starting to get a little snotty. Michael looked scared and even a bit green, but I felt fine as I had good control of my boat. Then, out to sea, I saw an odd configuration. I couldn't quite tell what it was but it just didn't look right. After you sail a lot out there, you get to know the look of the sea and anything irregular sticks out like a hairless dog in an upscale beauty salon. It's fascinating how one's eyes get attuned to what is normal, safe and OK, and what isn't. The longer I was living on the sea, the more intimate we were becoming. I felt like I knew all her moods, all her patterns. In many ways, we were alike…calm, serene and peaceful at times, tempestuous, wild and unpredictable at others.

"Hey, Michael, we've got to head over that way... I think someone's in trouble."

"No, way, Sandra. We've got to keep going -- this is too bad out here to be helping anyone and besides, we're past whatever it is."

"Michael, it's the laws of the sea… you've got to help someone in trouble and that's what it looks like over there."

We began arguing about whether or not to go back when, without warning, *Sérenta* made the decision and jibed, coming about. I had taken my eye off the sails for a split second, arguing with him and she came about by herself. As we got closer to the strange configuration on the horizon, I could make out the shape of an overturned multi-hull and a man hanging on, waving frantically.

"Go below and call the Coast Guard," I shouted to Michael. He wouldn't go. He looked about ready to throw up and had a death-grip on the lifelines.

"Get over here and take the helm if you won't go below. I'll go call them, myself," I hollered racing down the steps to the radio. "Coast Guard, Coast Guard…it's me again, *Sérenta*, but this time it's serious. I think another boat is sinking. I'm about three hours out of Moss Landing heading towards Santa Cruz out here in the middle of the bay."

"*Sérenta*, you're going to have to go to the vessel alone -- it will take us more than an hour to get to your destination," said the Coast Guard officer responding from Monterey. "We haven't got a vessel closer."

"I don't think I'll be much help to him, Sir. I can barely handle my own boat in this wind," I said as we whizzed past the disabled vessel. "It's an overturned Hobiecat, I think. I see one guy aboard but can't bring my boat about to get to him without fear of going over myself. The waves are about 30 footers out here. You'd have two boats to rescue."

I couldn't help the guy as I knew it was crucial to keep trying to control my own boat. He must have thought me nuts not coming back to help him but I just didn't know enough about heavy-weather sailing yet to be able to do more than keep my own boat aright. I heard later his crew person had been washed overboard and drowned hours before I had even come across him and called the Coast Guard. Their cutter got there in time to rescue the skipper who, by then, was suffering from severe hypothermia. Thank goodness I called them as it could have been worse

After Michael got off in Santa Cruz, I began to think about all the other guys I had invited to day-sail with me. It was progressively more and more annoying -- they would get on *my* boat and immediately start trying to order me around.

"This is all wrong, that's not right. Do it this way, do it that way."

"Listen, I tried it that way three months ago and it works better for me like this. Do you mind?"

There was the guy who came aboard and was appalled I had square knots on a lot of my lines. "What? You've used a square knot on the jib sheet?" he hissed with disdain as if I had committed some heinous crime. "You need a bowline here, a clove hitch there, and my God, you've got a granny knot on this line."

"I haven't learned all those fancy knots yet. I'm still struggling with getting the sails up and down. The square knots have held up just fine thus far. Tomorrow, I'll learn more knots," I said, looking out to sea and feeling like Scarlett.

I don't know what it is about men and boats, but put the two together and it's a dangerous combination especially for the salty old broad I was becoming. I took a macho guy fishing out of Moss Landing one morning. As soon as he stepped on board it was the usual…this was wrong, that was wrong.

"You shouldn't tie your dock line like that," he chided.

There's that nasty "shouldn't" word again, I thought, squinting at him in the early morning sun and trying to avoid "accidentally" bumping him overboard.

"The jib sheet needs to be wrapped the other way around the cleat," he sneered.

Big deal, I thought.

"What you using for bait? Chicken fat?" he bellowed. "You're never gonna get a fish with that shit."

So now this guy is going to show me how to fish after I've been catching prize salmon with chicken fat or skin almost daily since I started this gig? Less than a half-hour out of the harbor, he started to look a bit piqued, a bit green behind the gills.

"You look a bit verdigris, my dear. Need to head back?"

He just nodded affirmatively… too macho to admit he felt seasick. I motored back to the harbor and was I ever glad to be alone again on my beach-front floating condo. I lay down in the cockpit to watch the clouds playing and realized I had finally had it with these guys' know-it-all attitudes, but what to do? I watched mama bear cloud playfully chase her cloud cubs out of sight and then came up with a solution… something that would let these guys and the world know this was a woman's boat… owned, paid for, and operated by a woman who knew exactly (most of the time) what she was doing. Aha! I would remove every last piece of damned blue canvas, blue trim, blue anything from the boat and replace it all with hot pink!

"You can't get hot pink canvas, dear " the chandleries all said. (I hated it when anyone called me "dear" as if I was some old suburban Southern matron.) "Blue, brown or green -- that's your choice, like it or not, dear."

Yeah, men's colors. That began the Great Search. I spent weeks researching and calling all over the country for hot pink sailing canvas. No chandlery carried it. When I was about to give up, I hit on the idea of going beyond the sailing circles and called the manufacturer of Sunbrella material in Brooklyn.

"So how come you want this hot pink so bad, huh girlie?"

"Well, I'm the only woman big-boat owner on the entire central coast of California and I just want to have pink, that's all. I'm tired of these men telling me what to do on my own boat. I need to make a statement."

"Only woman, eh? Well, that sounds pretty plucky. OK, for you, we'll rustle up some hot pink pronto... but you'll have to buy the whole bolt, agreed?"

"Hip hip hooray," I shouted. "You better believe it's Ok! It's fantastic! When can I have it? Here's my credit card but please don't run it for 13 days or it'll decline."

"It'll be out there in three weeks."

I lined up a fellow who could work with the canvas and he measured my ship from stem to stern. Had him make covers for all my sails, covers for the toe rails and handrails, got a new clear plexiglass dodger which he trimmed in hot pink, new flotation seat cushions with hot pink piping and ice white leatherette, and a hot pink cover for my barbecue that hung out over the stern and one for my man-overboard pole! To complete this pretty pink picture, when the local sail-maker said he couldn't put a hot pink edge down my mainsail's luff, I took it to the Santa Cruz Windsurfing Company. Most of the guys working there were either old hippies or punk rockers and they couldn't stand the "White Pants". When I told the guys that none of the chandleries would accommodate my needs, they almost knocked me over as they jumped right onto the pink bandwagon and agreed to sew a wide hot pink strip all along the luff of the mainsail.

Next, I plastered my gray Avon rubber dinghy with pink anti-slip rubber daisies that you put in the bottom of a bathtub, painted the cover of the outboard hot pink, and sprayed with great care to avoid damaging it, most of the insides of the motor pink. No self-respecting thief south or even north of the border would dare steal my hot pink outboard! *Sérenta* looked terrific! I heard through the grapevine that when I took her out for her hot-pink maiden voyage, the Italian fishermen on the other side of the harbor dubbed her the titty-pink boat. Who cared! I loved how she looked!

I was salmon-fishing about three miles out a few mornings later, when a dangerous fog bank came creeping up behind me. It was just before 5:00 a. m. and I'd already caught a salmon the perfect size to fit on my barbecue. I started heading back towards the Moss Landing harbor and realized nothing was visible…not even the mile-out channel-marker buoy. I was engulfed in a huge white blanket of deadly fog. Now was the time to rely on what I learned those early days when a lot of time was spent sailing with my eyes closed and picking up on sounds the way a blind person becomes keenly aware of what is going on around her. This foggy morning, I sent a prayer up to You-Know-Who to please help guide my little vessel safely to the harbor, then put my "blindman's talent" to good use, following the shoreline by the sound of the waves crashing up onto the beach. If the sound of the waves was loud, I knew I was too close to the beach and I'd head out a bit farther. As long as I kept heading in an easterly direction towards the rising sun, I knew I'd sooner or later come to the harbor entrance. There it was! I steered *Sérenta* into the harbor and tucked her neatly into her slip.

"Cheated Death again," I chanted, and lay down in my bunk to send a gratitude prayer up to my able Captain, knowing I had just passed a major milestone in my maritime career.

About 45 minutes later, Big Tony, the leader of the fishermen, sauntered up to my boat. I was on deck trying to scrub off the little spots put out by the Moss Landing generating plant. If you didn't get the black dots off in three days, they turned to red rust and ruined the deck. A few weeks before, when

I was fed up with all the time spent on those darned dots, with defiance, I marched up to the Pacific Gas and Electric Company office. Told them they owed me $250 a month in cleaning and maintenance fees, and they better throw in a new cover for my Avon dinghy as the rust had ruined that, too. Without batting an eye, they complied and in a week, a new cover was sitting in my cockpit and each month, I collected a check for "Cleaning Services" which, the whole time I was docked there, kept me in locally-grown flowers, Lady Godiva chocolates, divine croissants and bear claws from Gayle's Bakery in Capitola, and sinfully rich hot fudge sundaes from Marianne's Ice Cream, a Santa Cruz institution founded in 1947 and where Mother and I always enjoyed a reward-stop after an unpleasant trip to a doctor.

I wondered what Tony was up to over here on our side of the harbor where fishermen seldom if ever trod.

"Hey, *Sérenta*," (they always called me by my boat name). "We decided we ain't gonna call it the titty... I mean…. we ain't gonna call it that no more."

"What's the sudden change of heart, eh, Tony?"

"Well, we was all out there this morning when that dang fog come in sudden like."

"Yeah, it was a doozy, wasn't it?"

"Yeah, and we was out there cruisin' back and forth hoping for a break in the fog when I spotted the tit...uh, your pink neon boat heading in. We followed you and I told the boys, `Well, maybe we ain't better call it that no more'. They agreed, so c'mon and have a little red with us."

"I don't drink anymore, Tony, but I'll sure take you up on a cup of joe. This was a pretty hairy morning, if I do say so myself'. I managed to land a nice one in spite of those darned sea lions out there tryin' to steal it off my line."

Taking out his hand-held radio, he hailed his fishing buddies on the other side of the channel and said, "Get the pot on…she's coming back with me to have a cup of joe with us."

I gave him a big wink and then we waltzed off, arms linked, heading in the direction of his dinghy for a trip across the harbor. We walked down the fishermen's dock and when we got to Tony's boat, I stepped into the cockpit of his Monterey, the typical classic little fishing boat used for generations by fishermen families in both the San Francisco and Monterey Bays. Its original hull design was introduced into the area by Italians in the late 1860s, many of whose descendants still fish the Monterey Bay. The boat is often called a "Puff-puff" for the sound of its small single-cylinder gas engine which had been added to its upgraded design in the 1920s.

I was welcomed by the other fellows in the cockpit, a jolly handful of wise and well-worn old fishermen. When they asked why I was living aboard and especially alone, I explained about my mother being paralyzed and how I had moved there to help her. It seemed to strike a sympathetic note in their momma-lovin' Italian hearts. After that, any morning I wasn't out fishing with them, they must have figured I was off taking my mother to a doctor or for groceries and when I'd return to *Sérenta*, I'd find a salmon just the perfect size for my barbecue tucked into my cockpit. I always wondered how they managed to slip undetected over to our side of the harbor.

That afternoon, I fired up my barbecue attached to the stern rail and invited Darryl over for dinner. I turned my day's catch which I had grilled whole on the barbecue into a salmon feast. First, salmon sushi for appetizers, then salmon salad with capers and Russian dressing, next salmon with fresh dill and lime for the entrée, and of all improbable offerings, pureed salmon custard for dessert! I forgot all about that morning's tough battle with the fog. That's an odd thing about all this... it's sort of like childbirth. When you have finished the battle, you soon forget how bad it was and you go back again for more. After dinner, we watched the gigantic blood-red sun sink into the steel-blue Pacific with all the seabirds dancing their farewell-to-the-sun ballet. A bellyful of fresh salmon sure helps you forget scary moments. I spent much of the next couple of years tending to my mother's needs and lining up home healthcare nurses to come three times a week to bathe her. I had a regular schedule of helping her with chores around the house and garden, taking her shopping, to medical appointments, out for lunch one week, dinner the next, to local concerts, movies and often to San Francisco to see Broadway musicals. I even managed to take her sailing with her new puppy. Strong and muscular Darryl had simply lifted her out of her wheelchair, over the life lines and onto the cockpit bench. In spare time, I was perfecting nautical techniques daily out there in the bay.

My proudest moment was one afternoon when I wheeled Mother into her doctor's office for a check-up. He had been one of the many who said paraplegics couldn't have a dog, couldn't do this or that. I tossed onto his desk a photo I had taken of her sitting in *Sérenta's* cockpit holding a mug of tea with her new puppy in her lap, the beautiful Monterey Bay's Irish diamonds sparkling in the background.

"That's what paraplegics can do," I said with triumph. "And besides that, Mother and I just inaugurated California's first State Park handicap campsite a few weeks ago, we've been twice up to San Francisco to cultural events this month, and had three picnics on the beach since we last saw you. Tonight, I'm taking her out to dinner and then to a play over in Palo Alto."

He just smiled. He knew I was justifiably chastising him and his colleagues. By this time, I was comfortable sailing in and out of the slip by myself and even sailing in all conditions back and forth, single-handed, from Moss Landing or Santa Cruz to Monterey. I got a kick out of hoisting the sails, trimming them just right so I could lie down on the long seat in the cockpit soaking up rays for a fabulous tan while watching whipped-cream clouds create storybooks in the sky. *Sérenta* glided along past the Army's Fort Ord Officer's Club which was slowly but inevitably sliding down the cliff towards the sea, and past the miles of what had been a gunnery range. It boggled my mind that if I tweaked the sails just perfectly, because the boat was so beautifully designed and balanced, she could follow a course by herself without any adjustment to helm as long as the direction of the wind didn't change.

The third summer I spent on the fishermen's dock in Santa Cruz Harbor was the last I'd spend there. San Francisco Bay was calling. Elkhorn

Yacht Club announced a club trip up to Baghdad-by-the Bay in late August and I signed on to join the fleet rather than attempt the daring trip alone. Eight boats would be buddy-boating all the way. I invited two friends, John and Nancy, to join me as crew--they just bought a 36-foot Catalina sailboat in Moss Landing but hadn't yet sailed out of the Moss Landing area. They felt too novice to take their own boat up to San Francisco so said they'd love to go with me. I knew they would be good company. John was a genius NASA engineer and had something to do with space shuttles; Nancy was a wild-haired motorcycle-riding momma he met somewhere and married -- a most unlikely couple but happier than any other married couple I had ever known.

A few weeks earlier I'd taken them on a sail from Santa Cruz around to Capitola to see the U. S. Navy destroyer that always showed up in Capitola's small anchorage for July 4th celebrations. This was a controversial event with left-wing Santa Cruzans hollering, "Go home, warmongers" and right-wing Capitolans shouting, "God bless America." Folks started with bumper stickers months before the event and usually had to peel off last year's sticker before affixing the newest one to their cars, front windows, public bathroom mirrors and boat transoms.

For the July 4th festivities, *Sérenta* joined the sailboat flotilla which called itself the Peace Navy. All had huge signs hung from lifelines to that effect and we spent the afternoon circling around the warship while Navy tenders brought crowds back and forth for tours of the ship. On our last pass around the Navy ship, with gangs of white-uniformed sailors standing on deck looking our way, Nancy suddenly jumped up and bared her breasts. John just smiled nonchalantly with his scientific-observer look, studying her bountiful breasts as though they were instruments on a shuttle dashboard.

For the trip to San Francisco, we left Santa Cruz Harbor at sunset, having plotted and timed the trip to enter under the Golden Gate at high tide going in as it would be difficult trying to get in under the Gate if the tide was running out. This was to be a three-day trip with a one-night stop-over in Half Moon Bay. Our little armada consisted of seven mono-hulls and one

49-foot trimaran. Three of the skippers were well-seasoned having made the trip many times.

A few hours out, the wind kicked up. We were heading north against the current, just like the last nightmare trip with Darryl. It was a full moon and I could see the other boats in close proximity. Every so often, someone would get on the radio to see how we were all doing. John and Nancy disappeared below deck early on, both feeling seasick even though I tried to explain it was better to stay top-deck in the fresh air. After almost six hours of being bashed around, members of the fleet were calling on their radios back and forth, starting to sound dismal and discouraged. The skipper of the "tri" announced he was heading out to sea with the two other boats with veteran skippers. The rest of us didn't have the courage to go offshore that far and plodded on for a few more hours until we all finally decided to return to Santa Cruz and wait for more favorable conditions.

When we were safely tied up, one of the skippers came over to see how I was. Nancy and John had been white as ghosts first, then pea-green for hours, and now color was slowly returning to their cheeks. They had spent the entire trip below trying to sleep through the hellacious experience, probably wondering how fast they could sell their boat—which is exactly what they did the next week, trading it in on a "prairie schooner" RV!

"How are you doing, Sandra?" asked the skipper. It was the first time any of the men had addressed me by my given name rather than just as *Sérenta*. I detected a hint of respect there.

"Oh, I'm doing fine. It was a bit snarly out there, wasn't it?"

"Well, I can tell you this now. When we were running alongside you, your boat was coming up out of the water so high as you left each wave behind that we could actually see the full moon under your hull!"

The next morning, inspecting my boat, I discovered a number of spider cracks in the fiberglass deck. *Sérenta* had been through a lot that night. It would be six more months before I would even consider trying that harrowing trip again, but I knew I eventually would. The boaters all said if I could sail the

San Francisco Bay with all its varying conditions of wind, waves, tides, plus heavy traffic of freighters, Navy vessels, recreation boats and windsurfers, I could sail anywhere in the world. Faraway harbors and exotic anchorages were now tugging at my anchor lines. San Francisco Bay would fit the bill for my sea trials.

Chapter Fifteen

We're Not Lost...We Just Don't Know Where We Are!

It was late September and almost three years since I bought the boat. My fisherman friend had returned from fishing herring and now needed his Santa Cruz slip, so I single-handed *Sérenta* back to her slip in Moss Landing. The next week, I put Mother in the hospital as she developed bed sores and no matter what we did, they wouldn't heel. She was even changing her position in bed every two hours through the night, but it didn't seem to be helping.

I had heard about bed sores, but didn't realize how critical they could be to the well-being of an invalid. Her doctor decided he had to operate and she was to spend two weeks in the hospital beforehand to get bolstered up and well enough for surgery. I went to visit her daily and her spirits seemed good the morning of surgery.

As they were wheeling her on a stretcher towards the operating room, I leaned over to give her a kiss and said, "I'll be praying for you, Mother."

She took my hand. "Well, you never did have enough time for me", and off she went, through the O. R. doors. I was stunned. How could she say such a thing after I had given up my happy and rewarding life in Philadelphia for her...left my children, my jobs, all my friends in recovery, sold my beloved little historic home ? Three hours later, she was in ICU and they told me she was in a coma.

"My God! What went wrong?" I stammered in disbelief.

"We're not quite sure," was the doctor's response. "Her heart stopped and we attempted resuscitation but she slipped into a coma."

"My mother would not have wanted to be brought back," I stammered, following him into the ICU. I saw her lying on the stretcher, her eyes closed.

"You can stay in here next to her as long as you wish. If you see her eyelids flutter at all, it's a good sign she'll come out of it," he said and walked off which her doctors always seemed to be doing, anytime there was a problem or a complication.

I was there all day and all night, holding her hand at times, mopping her brow at others. The next day, after spending almost 30 hours softly talking to her, hoping she was hearing me tell her how much I loved her, the situation seemed hopeless. With my mouth close to her ear, I muttered something Scottish I had often heard her say: "Ah, mither, 'tis a sair fecht." This was the equivalent of "Mother, this is a difficult fight" or "This is a hard life." Her eyelids flickered and she opened her eyes, acting as if nothing had happened and as if she had been awake the whole time.

"You need a break," the ICU nurse said. "Go down to the cafeteria for something to eat and we'll be here for her." When I came back an hour later, Mother was sitting up sipping a cup of tea.

It was difficult, but I said, "Mother, I feel terrible because when they were wheeling you into surgery, you said I hadn't had enough time for you."

"I said that?"

"Yes."

"Well, I can't imagine saying that, Sandra," was all she could say.

I was wishing she would express a little gratitude for all the help I had been giving her, but that was not to happen. It reminded me of my childhood when I never did anything quite right for her. Mother then lay back, closed her eyes and died. For several moments, I just stared at her lying there.

"Thank you, Mother, for the unmitigated spirit of adventure you've given me...no one can ever take that away," I said aloud. I had no wish to kiss her farewell nor a need to shed a tear. I had done the best I could as her daughter and she had done her best as my mother.

The next morning, I called my brother to tell him Mother had died. Since she was being cremated, he didn't see any need to rush out to California and asked me to scatter her ashes, myself. He said he'd fly out in a few weeks to put the house up for sale and to tag some of her things to be sent to his home in North Carolina. I then made the difficult call to Ian and Sandi to tell them their grandmother had died.

"I know Obi didn't like being paralyzed, Mom, and she's in a better place now," said Sandi who always seemed far wiser than her years.

"I'm sure she's happy now," said Ian.

"We'll all miss her but as you said, Ian, she'll be happier now where she is. You don't have to fly out as she didn't want a funeral service and will be cremated. I'll scatter her ashes under the redwoods way up in the mountains where my father's ashes are. I'm going back to the boat now to rest for a while. It's been a stressful time for me, but I'm OK, so no need to worry."

In honor of my mother, I engaged a local composer to create a short classical piece and invited everyone I could think of who had ever known Mother for a concert at her house. Her heavy oak dining table was laden with silver platters of food I prepared for the occasion. Several dozen of her old friends and other newer ones showed up. I knew Mother would have been pleased. Music and elegant parties that she was so well-known for had always been a prominent part of her life.

Bruce arrived in time for the concert, identified the furniture and other things he wanted from the house and arranged to have them picked up by a moving van. The next week, several of my artist friends helped me pack up all the rest and move everything to a storage unit where it would sit undisturbed for several years.

Eight months before Mother died, I applied for a county job, and out of 418 applicants, was awarded the post of Cultural Affairs Specialist for the County of Santa Cruz and Executive Director of the Santa Cruz County Arts Commission. It was a one-man office, I didn't have a boss other than answering to the board of the County Arts Commission, and best of all, I could set my own hours. My office was located within the purview of the Santa Cruz County Parks, Open Spaces and Cultural Services Department. After Mother died, days seemed empty without duties to attend to for her, anymore. I threw myself into my new job.

One afternoon after work, I stopped in the Moss Landing office of the Pacific Gas & Electric to pick up the monthly maintenance check they owed me for the previous month of pollution they had spewed out onto my decks. The guy behind the desk asked me if I had met John, the new live-aboard.

"He's a mighty fine guy. You two might really hit it off," he said.

Oh, boy…. now the PG&E is trying to play cupid, I thought, but simply said, "Nah, I don't really have time to meet him."

"Listen," the guy persisted. "He's kinda new at this sailing shtick and I'm sure he'd love to talk to you. He was some sort of advertising executive, then retired, sold everything, and bought an old sailboat. He's teaching himself just like you did. Bet you could give him some helpful tips. How about I send him around to your boat later this afternoon?"

"Alright," I said, figuring the guy probably wouldn't show up.

Wrong! About 4:00 p. m., John called me on the ship's radio and asked if he could come over and chat.

"Just look for the hot pink boat," I said, a phrase I would find useful in future harbors when telling people how to find me. It wouldn't be too long before friends would locate me on their own just by scanning the harbor where they knew *Sérenta* and I were hanging out and looking for the hot pink glow.

John arrived wearing an ascot and a cloak of courtliness and charm. He was tall and skinny – looked like he needed a few days near a bakery! He was about 60 and I figured during our preliminary get-acquainted chats that he was an educated man for he was extremely knowledgeable about literature and classical music. We had fun discussing a variety of books and authors. After an hour or so, he invited me to his boat, *Onera,* on Saturday for lunch, admitting he loved to cook especially when he could share his culinary delights with others. It would be fun to have someone to chat with who was familiar with the Arts and good literature, so I accepted, making my way to his boat the next day in my dinghy. He had prepared a feast which included one of my old-time favorite lunches from student days in France… Salade Niçoise with dilled white albacore tuna, chilled red- skinned potatoes drizzled with olive oil, real Kalamata olives, fresh-from-the-fields radicchio and arugula, and a marvelous boat-made cherry balsamic vinaigrette. We had a wonderful afternoon talking about our new lives as sailors. Towards the end of the afternoon came the hook when he asked if I would consider sailing with him south, as his crew.

"We can just be buddies," he said. "No sex. I need a good crew and you seem to know what you're doing. Plus, I think we'd have fun together. Will you consider it?"

"Gosh, John, I am totally honored, but the problem is I really want to go sailing away someday on *Sérenta*. I've been outfitting her with all these neat gadgets and looking forward to one day taking off, myself."

I hit on a brilliant idea. I had a friend, Mariella, whom I met a while ago in Santa Cruz. She came over from Germany some months before to be an *au pair* and when she got to San Francisco ready to start work, they had already given her job to someone else. She took the little money she came over with and bought a one-way ticket to Hawaii. There, on the beach, she met an older man from Carmel who was vacationing in Hawaii. He was now living on a large sailboat in the Moss Landing harbor although I had never met or even seen him. He needed to get some painting and varnishing done on his boat and invited Mariella to come back to Moss Landing with him. He would pay her return fare from Hawaii to California in exchange for the painting and varnishing. She could live aboard rent-free. She jumped at the offer and they arrived together in the harbor who knows how many months before.

I'd see her from time to time walking along the Moss Landing docks. You couldn't help noticing Mariella. She was 22 and although born at least 10 years after the last flower child had moved on, she was a carbon copy of those young women of the '60s with wispy blonde straight hair, steel-blue eyes rimmed with wire Ben Franklin specs, and an inviting impish smile. She had few clothes and mostly wore a white sleeveless undershirt, no bra--you could see her breasts through the low-cut armholes--and a pair of cut-off shorts. She never went anywhere without her macramé braiding material. I'd see her sitting on Pacific Avenue downtown Santa Cruz with the rest of the hippies making multi-colored friendship bracelets and anklets which she'd give away free to any passerby who'd take one. As it was about a 45-mile trip one-way and she had no car, when I saw her downtown, I frequently gave her a ride back to Moss Landing since bus service was almost non-existent. There was a refreshing innocence about her I enjoyed.

It was one of those blustery late autumn Sunday afternoons when Mariella stopped by to invite me over to the boat she was living on to meet her benefactor. As we approached the boat five docks over from mine, I was surprised to see it was one of the few completely covered with a huge boat cover…. the kind you put on your boat when you are going to leave it unattended for months or sometimes even years. I wondered how they were living aboard under the cover as it would be very dark and dank below. Mariella announced our arrival as we stepped on board and a man about 60 popped his head up to see who was with her.

"Hello, I'm the barber of Carmel," he announced formally, extending a hand and motioning me to come below. I expected to hear Rossini filling the cabin below but instead, it was Jimmy Hendrix. The main salon was in a state of total disarray with odd mismatched boat parts, used paint brushes, and varnishing supplies strewn everywhere.

"I put all those things away last night. What are you doing with them all out again?" Mariella chided, hand on hip.

You could tell she was more than a bit frustrated with him. He ignored her and picked up a guitar and started strumming an off-key rendition of the Eagles' song, *Hotel California.*

"So you work in Carmel, do you? Are you really a barber?"

"Oh, yes, and the best. People come to learn important things from me. I just happen to cut their hair in the process."

At that point, he pulled out a small piece of paper and started rolling a cigarette. As soon as he lit it, I knew it wasn't Turkish tobacco. Ah-ha! So that's the reason for the boat cover.

"Are you planning to sail away soon?" I asked.

"We just have to get this painting and varnishing done. I'm waiting for a new engine to arrive and then Mariella and I are taking off."

"Doesn't the engine work?"

"Nope, hasn't for years. I've been saving for a new one and any day now it'll be here."

When he looked at Mariella, his lust-filled eyes showed the effect of pot-loosened passion. I felt uncomfortable and after a very short visit, returned to *Sérenta.* The next week, she stopped at my boat several times and invited me over for dinner. I finally accepted as I loved being with her, but listening to the host's pot-invoked distorted dissertations on Enlightenment and his skewed version of the Zen way of life was tedious and boring. I watched as she managed to avoid any close contact with him even though he tried his hardest to caress her. He reminded me of an old anaconda I met once on an island in the middle of the Amazon River. The natives always put a big chicken in the snake's cage in the morning, and the serpent slithered with stealth and cunning towards the innocent chicken who probably didn't have the slightest idea she was soon to be breakfast. A few weeks later I mentioned to Mariella that her skipper was head-over-heels for her but she emphatically refused to agree.

"Oh, not at all. He just like how good I varnish," she said in her cute German accent.

"Mariella, let me tell you something else…. that guy isn't ever going to leave the harbor. I've been watching him these last few weeks and as soon as he gets home from Carmel he goes below and lights up. You can smell it all over the harbor. He probably hasn't even ordered that engine. I'm telling you…that guy is a loser and he's never going to leave Moss Landing."

"Oh, Sandra, do you truly think so?" she asked in her little-girl-lost voice. "I was counting on sailing away with him. My visa expires soon and I don't have any money to get back to Germany. I don't know what I will do if we aren't really going to leave."

"Well, I have the perfect solution for you. There's this really nice older man named John over in the other harbor. He's a perfect gentleman so you wouldn't have to worry about any inappropriate behavior from him. He owns a 28-foot sailboat called, *Onera,* and guess what! He wants to leave for Mexico next week! He's actively looking for crew and it would be a fabulous opportunity for you to get outta Dodge before your visa expires."

The next day after work, I took Mariella over to meet John. The moment he saw her, I knew he was pleased. In less than fifteen minutes it was all settled… they would take off in three days. He asked if I would go with them for the first leg of the journey, down the coast to Avila just beyond Morro Bay and near San Luis Obispo. He had an appointment to have the boat hauled out there. It was the cheapest (and smallest) marina on the West Coast and he'd been on the waiting list for a haul-out for over a year. He explained he didn't quite feel comfortable enough to go out in the open seas alone with Mariella who had never been sailing. If I would go with them for that leg, he would feel a lot better…and safer! He'd give me bus fare back.

It felt odd to realize for the umpteenth time I no longer had Mother to worry about, that I was free now. I also knew I could easily get off work. I agreed to join ranks and packed a few things in a duffle bag, ready for the trip.

We took off Saturday morning at first light to get out of Monterey Bay and over to the first anchorage, Stillwater Cove, before the wind might die. *Onera* was a gaff-rigged sloop with a tiller for steering…quite different from my vessel which was more conveniently outfitted with a big wheel for steering. We anchored in the cove about 1:30 p. m. that afternoon and John fixed a fabulous early dinner. We passed on going ashore as Mariella and I didn't want to unpack his stowed dinghy. At dawn, we readied for our second day out there. It was quite windy when we weighed anchor. John was nervous. Once out of the safety of the bay and into the "Big Blue" as I liked to call it, almost every twenty minutes he'd holler, "Watch out for the boom!"

I was getting a bit tired of his mother-hen behavior and said, "Listen, John. I've been sailing almost daily out here for three years. I'm well aware of the boom and I think Mariella has it figured out by now. We're not going to let the boom hit us on the head, OK?"

Aeolus, keeper of the winds, finally decided to call his subjects in so we could rest a little after breakfast. The sea was behaving herself and the morning was going to be uneventful. I pulled out the <u>Coastal Pilot</u> to figure out where we were. John was in the cockpit tinkering with some zincs to hang off the stern to ward off corrosion. Mariella was getting an early start on a tan up on the foredeck with nothing on but a little lace hanky spread across her privates. About 11:00 a. m., I went below to make coffee.

"Hey, John…how do you get this stove to work? It's not the same as mine."

The contraption made me feel apprehensive, remembering, when I was a little kid, how my Aunt Margaret had died after being severely injured when the alcohol stove on her sailboat exploded in her face.

"Come up and take the tiller. It's an alcohol stove and I have to prime the burner," he muttered coming down the steps. I wasn't a minute back at the tiller when from below, he began yelling and screaming. I looked down and saw the curtains over the stove ablaze.

"Mariella! Quick, get below and put out the fire! I'm stuck on the tiller," I shouted to her still sunbathing up at the bow.

She scampered down the ladder bare-naked and started swatting with a chart. They finally got it extinguished. John announced the stove was now useless which meant no hot food or coffee until Avila. He came up to take over the helm, and as he clambered up the ladder into the cockpit, ran smack into the boom, knocking himself to the deck.

For those not familiar with boating terminology, the boom is the spar (long thick pole) attached to the lower part of the mast via a gooseneck which swivels horizontally and pivots vertically. It holds the bottom edge (foot) of the mainsail fast during raising and lowering operations, greatly improving control of the angle and shape of the sail. Often, if the skipper is not in control when the wind makes a sudden shift in direction, the mainsail will violently pull the boom across the cockpit at a break-neck speed. Worst case scenario… the boom can be fiercely snapped off of the mast and tossed into the sea, taking the mainsail with it and capsizing the vessel in a matter of minutes. As it is coming uncontrolled across the cockpit at skull-cracking speed, if you don't duck, it can take your head off! With a lot of practice in Monterey Bay, I taught myself how to manage a controlled jibe which can be a tricky maneuver for novice sailors. It was ironic – here John had been shouting at us for two days about the boom and now he ended up being knocked down by it. Not feeling well, he went below to lie down. I would have to take over the helm.

"Keep heading south," he murmured as he threw himself into a bunk. "You're going to have to take her around Point Sur, yourself."

Never having met a tiller before let alone managed a vessel with a gaff-rigged mainsail, I wasn't looking forward to this and especially not happy at the idea of skippering someone else's boat around that infamous and dangerous Point. Mariella would have been a worse choice as helmsman. She had no clue how to steer her own life let alone a sailboat. The wind was getting gustier as we approached the Point and now there were whitecaps...definitely not weather for a beginner like her. Even I was having difficulty handling this oddly rigged vessel. I looked down the coastline and focused on a big mountain. It was easier to steer towards something than stare bleary-eyed at a compass. We made it around Point Sur without incident and I thanked God and the entire Universe. Towards late afternoon I could hear John moaning below. He soon began upchucking.

At 4:00 p. m., as the sun was dipping towards the horizon, he weakly called out, "You better call the Coast Guard. I think I have a concussion," which was something I knew absolutely nothing about. Mariella took over the tiller while I went below to call for help on the hailing channel.

"Coast Guard, Coast Guard. This is the sailing vessel *Onera* calling."

"Switch to channel 22, *Onera*", said a welcome voice.

"22," I replied.

"Coast Guard here, *Onera*. What's your problem."

"I think the skipper of this sailboat has a concussion. He got hit on the head with the boom about seven hours ago and he's been throwing up for hours now. He asked me to call you."

"Where is he now?"

"He's down below throwing up in his bunk."

"I mean, what's your position, *Onera*?"

"I'm not sure, Sir. We went around Point Sur about five hours ago."

"Give us your position on the charts, *Onera*."

"I haven't learned yet exactly how to read complicated charts, Sir"

There was a moment of silence and then, "Well, how are you navigating if you don't know how to read charts?"

I paused, then said, "I'm using the O. R. L. L. method, Sir."

A moment of silence and then, "We're not familiar with that method of navigation. Can you explain it, please?"

"Certainly, Sir. It's the "Ocean Right, Land Left" method."

Before he managed to click off the microphone we could hear bountiful laughter and it took a few minutes before he came on again.

"What was the last thing you saw, Miss?" the guy said, trying to stifle a giggle.

"I was reading the <u>Coastal Pilot</u> a few hours back and I think it was *Piedras Blancas* back there."

At that point a man's gruff voice came on and said, "I saw them about an hour ago and they were about 10 degrees north of there."

"You're all wet," chimed in another. "I saw them two hours ago and they were at least a mile south of *Piedras Blancas*."

Great, two boats arguing as to our position. The argument went back and forth until one of them said, "Listen, I'm going to pull up my damned lines and find them just to prove I'm right."

"Listen, fellows," I interjected. "It isn't worth losing fish over this. We're not lost…. we just don't know exactly where we are."

At that point the Coast Guard came back and told us to keep heading in a southerly direction and although they were hours south of us they would be coming up the coast as fast as they could.

It was a long day. I stayed on the tiller steering as best I could even though after a few hours, felt drained and exhausted. Soon it was dark and the wind was howling all around us. I kept reading the <u>Coastal Pilot</u> by flashlight, trying to figure out where we were. Every 15 minutes or so, the fisherman who had offered to pull up his lines would come on the radio to ask if we were still OK. He was very reassuring as he told us which stars and constellations we were seeing, trying to distract us from our alarming situation by offering us the heavens to ponder.

"Oh, look…there's the Big Dipper and that big star is Riegel, pointing you in the right direction, and there's Orion with his belt helping to show you the way," he said.

It was such a relief to hear another human voice from time to time in that dark night. Ever after, when I see the Big Dipper or Orion, I remember how helpful those wonderful fishermen were. For the rest of my life, Orion's belt would jump out at me every time he was travelling through our skies. Each time I'd see Orion, I was comforted for other reasons I'd later learn.

"Don't worry, girls. You'll come out of this just fine," our faithful fisherman would say from time to time. For some odd reason, I believed him as I'd been asking my HP for help the entire time. I didn't even mind that he referred to us as, "girls", a prickly term which, in other situations, I would not have found endearing.

The winds of Aeolus finally died down and I back-winded the mainsail so the boat was barely moving. I just didn't have the energy to deal with heavy-duty tillering. Mariella took the tiller for about an hour but said she didn't really feel comfortable with it and gave the darned thing back to me. I steered all night. There was no moon and the ocean seemed not at all friendly…all that black water enveloping us like Dracula's heavy black cape which I used to know so well. The sounds of waves whooshing past us terrified me, but I didn't dare let Mariella know how afraid I was. Even scarier was the thought that any minute, a gray whale could come right up through the hull on its way down the Baja to San Carlos, the calving lagoon. It might not be as sweet as that big one Darryl and I saw when this crazy sailing life first began what seemed eons ago.

I managed to keep the boat on a steady course all night without any mishaps, catching a few winks now and then when the wind had died down. Mariella was still below sleeping when Apollo peeked his head around the corner of the mainsail. I wondered where the Coast Guard was.

Our loyal fisherman greeted us on the radio with, "How are my damsels in distress this beautiful morning?"

"Boy, am I glad to hear you. It was pretty lonely out there in the dark, but we're doing OK now."

"Would have called you sooner but was afraid you might be trying to get some shut-eye. Hang in there, girl. Everything's going to be just fine."

Ah, he had just put out my favorite mantra. If we made it safe into a harbor, I'd track that fisherman down and give him some sort of little giftie – just knowing he was out there with us somewhere was reassuring. About 7:00 a. m. I was relieved to see a U. S. Coast Guard cutter heading towards us. They came alongside and one of the sailors jumped onto our bow. "Our Captain says we're going to tow you in to San Simeon," he explained. "I'm going to tie this line around your bow cleats, alright?"

"Whatever you say, buddy. Am I ever glad to see you guys."

They towed us for about an hour into the same spot at San Simeon where Darryl and I had anchored when the Coast Guard had boarded us for one of their "safety inspections". I was worried about how to anchor the boat because it had such a convoluted system of anchoring.

"Do you think we could tie up to your beautiful big buoy over there? I don't have a clue how to anchor this boat. Oh, and could you possibly help us inflate the dingy and get it into the water? We haven't had anything hot to drink or eat since the skipper blew up the stove two days ago."

He asked his Captain on a hand-held radio, and we were given permission to use the buoy until the next morning. The officer also said his mate would help us with the dinghy operation. They took John off the boat in a stretcher hoisted into the air on a block and tackle system.

"Sandra, what about my appointment at the haul-out?" moaned John mid-air from the stretcher. "I waited for over a year for that slot. If I don't get the boat there as arranged, I'll lose my slot and won't get her bottom-painted in time for my voyage south. Any delay now, and we'd be getting into winter storm weather which means I'd have to hang around here all winter."

John was right…they would have to wait until spring, definitely a problem with Mariella's visa expiring. He'd end up losing her as crew and she'd be in big trouble with immigration.

As they hoisted him up and away, I shouted, "Don't worry, John. I'll get your beloved boat to Avila."

I instantly realized what a foolish promise that was, envisioning being alone out there with a dizzy flower child on a boat I didn't know how to handle and no idea where Avila was. We were moored to the big orange floating Coast Guard buoy, our newly-inflated dinghy was tied to the stern cleat, and the Coast Guard was steaming away.

"Hey, let's go ashore," I said. Looks like a hot dog stand up there and I'm dying for a cup of hot coffee."

We jumped into the dinghy and I treated Mariella to a quick lesson on rowing. San Simeon was a sweet little harbor. You could vaguely distinguish parts of Hearst's incredible castle up on the mountaintop. We tied the dinghy to the little pier, climbed the ladder and walked along to the food stand. They didn't have any "real" food…just crackers, cookies, plastic-wrapped things, but they did have hot coffee. I ordered four big cups to go. We were both exhausted and decided to head back to *Onera* to rest, rowing past a large sailboat anchored in the harbor. A fellow on board was going through the motions of preparing to weigh anchor so we rowed over to him.

"Morning, Skipper. You taking off?"

"Yep. We're going to try to get around this little point past Morro Bay before the fog sets in. If it's too foggy, though, we'll pull into the bay and head for San Luis Harbor for the night."

"I need to get that boat tied to the buoy over there to Avila for a haul-out. Will that be very difficult?"

"Well, it's pretty windy getting around Point Buchon…kinda like going 'round Sur but a lot worse. More like going around Conception. If you want, follow us to Morro Bay entrance and if it isn't foggy, you can continue around Buchon to Avila. But if there is even the slightest hint of fog, you better tuck into Morro Bay and San Luis – it can be hellacious trying to get around Buchon in the fog."

"Great! We'll be ready in a few minutes to follow you out."

There wouldn't be any time for a nap. It was more important to have someone to follow than going out there all by ourselves. I managed to stow the dingy on deck, get the gaff-rigged mainsail up, the jib hoisted, and untied our bow line from the buoy without having to start that darned engine. We followed the big sailboat out of the harbor under sail. Once out to sea, our fearless leader started pulling away from us…. we just didn't have enough canvas to keep up with him.

"I'll put a reef in my mainsail," he said over the radio. "That should slow us down a bit so you can keep up with us."

"Gosh, I really appreciate this. We're both absolutely exhausted and to be out here alone would be dismal. Just knowing that you are up ahead is comforting."

We kept radio contact with him throughout the morning. At 1:00 p. m., he hailed us on Channel 16.

"*Onera*, I'm pulling into Morro Bay. My weather-fax shows fog and bad weather beyond Morro. I'm going to have to pull out that reef and hustle in there. I don't want to be caught in this snarly weather coming our way. Good luck to you and sorry I can't help you more!"

"Thanks for the help so far. Maybe we'll see you in there. By the way, how do I find, Morrow Bay?"

"Just head for the big round rock you'll see in a few hours," and that was the last bit of advice we got from him or anyone.

Once he had taken the reef out of his mainsail, his boat took off like a rocket out of Canaveral as he headed towards Morro Bay. We were totally alone again to fend for ourselves. I decided to heed his advice and head into Morro Bay as the wind was now beginning to scream in my ears and I could almost smell the creatures living on the bottom of the sea. Mariella was of no use. Feeling seasick, she was lying on the bench in the cockpit. Inside the bay, waves were mounting and white curls were careening off the top of every wave. I looked behind where a mountain of water was about to engulf us. I still hadn't figured out what kept the water from crashing over our stern and swamping us. It was best not to look back again.

It took a herculean effort just to steer the boat. Before this adventure, I had never used a tiller, never even read up on tillers, and didn't know any of their idiosyncrasies. It soon became very stiff and hard to move as I tried to force it against the incredible power of the water. My arms felt like they were being rammed through Mother's old-fashioned Sears laundry mangle, but I knew if I gave in to the pain, we would be lost. I wasn't sure where I was supposed to be heading as the boater hadn't given me any compass points. The fog was now closing in on all sides. Soon, we would surely be swallowed up and smothered in fog and misery. I grabbed the radio and tuned in Channel 16, the hailing channel.

"This is the *Onera* to anyone listening. Can you please tell me where Port San Luis Harbor is located? I'm out here somewhere in the middle of the bay."

"Hey, *Onera*, this is your old fisherman friend. Just keep heading southeast and when you're about three-quarters into the bay you should be able to spot the big round mountain. Head straight for it – the channel into the harbor is dead center of that big round mountain."

"Boy, am I glad to hear you. We're really getting blown around out here."

"I heard your skipper was rescued by the Coasties. Not to worry, girl. You'll make it."

I just wanted to hug him. I couldn't hold on to the radio cord stretched from below-deck and steer at the same time, so signed off to concentrate on trying to keep the boat heeled at an efficient degree. While peering into the distance for that round mountain, I prayed out loud that God still loved us and would help get us into the harbor safely. I felt seasick but knew our lives depended on me keeping level-headed and not getting sick. I couldn't afford to be seasick. I remembered the saying I had heard in meetings, "There ain't no disbelievers in foxholes," but in this case, it was "no disbelievers in force 9 waves" and I prayed over and over that we would make it into the harbor.

Through the mist, I saw my mother's tiny Scottish handwriting on the yellowed slip of paper she always kept by her bedside. It was taped to her reading lamp since ever I could remember and were the first words of an Old Breton fisherman's prayer: *Oh, God, thy sea is so great and my boat is so small.* I once read that the same prayer was inscribed on a block of wood that rested on President Kennedy's desk in the Oval office. Admiral Hyman Rickover gave it to the President and always gave a copy of the prayer to all new submarine captains. I wasn't exactly captain of a submarine, but I kept repeating the words silently, over and over, to keep fear at bay. Each time I was in a frightening situation at sea, or for that matter, anywhere, I would recite that prayer followed by as many things as I could think of to be grateful for. The gratitude list was a bit short that night. I was having trouble concentrating on being grateful when I didn't have a clue as where we were, where we were going, and exactly how we'd get there.

Chapter Sixteen

Is The Sky Falling...Or Was That Just Another Earthquake?

It seemed an eternity before I saw, looming ahead, a huge round mountain and knew we were home free.

"Praise the Lord!" I shouted, waking Mariella from her own private nightmare. "Get up, girlfriend. We're about to be saved!"

It truly felt like both a spiritual as well as a religious experience. I was so thrilled to see that mountain, I wished I had arms long enough to reach all around it with an embrace. The only thing left to do was head for it and find the channel entrance to the Morro Bay harbor. As we got closer, the wind seemed to subside…another blessing. Soon, I saw the entrance and sailed over to it and then had the strangest experience yet in my new sailing career. I was in the dead center of the channel entrance just like where you're supposed to be when entering the harbor. All the sails were up and filled with air, the engine was running full throttle, but we were standing still not making any headway at all.

"This is weird. I'm going to call the Harbor Master," I told Mariella who looked like a drowned little kitten. "Harbor Master, Harbor Master. This is the *Onera*. Come back, please."

This wonderful masculine bass voice replied, "This is the Harbor Master. I've been expecting you two lovelies and I'm in my boat about halfway down the channel to greet you. Just keep on keeping on and I'll be there to tow you in. You've managed to arrive on one of our record fiercest high tides running out the channel and you won't be going anywhere."

Splendid! He was expecting us. In a few minutes, he was rafted up to us, telling me to pull down the sails and turn off the engine.

"You a member of any yacht club, Skipper?"

"Yes, Elkhorn in Moss Landing," I replied proudly as if it were the St. Francis Yacht Club in San Francisco and thrilled to be hailed as "Skipper".

"Good. Then I have a guest slip at our yacht club waiting for you. I'll tow you up to it and then let you go. You can just slide neatly in---she's an end-tie."

As he towed us down the channel inside the harbor, I looked to the right and there in the public anchorage were our friends who had led us there from San Simeon.

"Hey, *Onera*. Channel 22."

"*Onera*, here."

"Glad you made it. How would you like to come over for dinner once you've tied up? My wife makes a mean clam chowder and she's just about to put some of her buttermilk biscuits in the oven."

"Tell you what! We'll trade you guys a hot shower at the yacht club for dinner. Fair deal?"

I knew they would be thrilled. It's not often cruisers use their precious limited supply of fresh water for a shower unless they can stop at a reciprocal yacht club and refill the tank right after showering.

"That is a fantastic deal! We'll be over to pick you up in our dinghy in five."

After glorious showers, we had a wonderful meal aboard their gorgeously carved vessel. Must have been made in Taiwan – those boats always had incredible carving below-decks. After dinner, Bill (I never did learn their last name) took us in his dinghy back to our boat and we both gave him a huge goodbye hug. As Mariella and I walked down the short length of the dock to *Onera* , I noticed a dark shadow on our bow.

"Mariella, do you see someone sitting on our bow or am I hallucinating?"

"It's a handsome man, Sandra", she replied with her usual innocence.

"Hello. Can we help you?

"Well, you finally made it in, did you?" It was one of our fishermen!

"Oh, how happy I am to meet you," I shouted, running up to him and giving him a cuddle. Mariella joined in the group hug. "You're the one who kept talking to us last night, aren't you?

"No. I'm the guy who spoke to you early this morning. The one last night was Joe on the big fishing boat *Lightning*. I'm a party boat skipper and took the first trip out this morning. The whole harbor knows about you two."

"No kidding! They all must think we are really dumb broads."

"*Au contraire!* You're being hailed as heroes."

"Is *Lightning* in the harbor?"

"Yep, down at the main fishing pier."

"Can we buy you a beer or something?"

"I was about to invite you both to a café for a cappuccino and a piece of cheesecake. Thought that might be a little appropriate," he said while checking out Mariella in her come-grab-me undershirt.

"We'll treat," I said and we followed him to a darling little place in the center of town.

The next morning Mariella, all fitted out in leopard skin tights and her usual low-cut undershirt, walked with me towards the main fishing pier. I bought a little bouquet of daisies and a card along the way and wrote, "Many thanks to our Knight in Shining Fish Gear!" When we got to the fishing dock, we saw the humungous *Lightning* tied up and all hands on deck unloading fish.

"Is the Captain aboard?"

"Nope. He's off on errands."

"Darn. Well, will you please give him these? Oh, do you happen to know a good place for breakfast?"

"Yeah. Lefty's down there at the other end of the pier."

"Great. Many thanks."

Lefty's was a fun place filled with fishermen and other interesting types who hang around the world's wharfs. We ordered pancakes and about ten minutes later, the door opened and in came a big hulk of a fisherman who walked right up to our table.

"You the damsels in distress?"

"Why, yes. But how on Earth did you know it was us?"

"My crew said you were looking for me and there's only one woman in this town gussied up like that," he said, pointing to Mariella who looked puzzled while the fisherman and I had a good laugh.

"Have a seat and let us buy you breakfast," I said

"Sorry. Don't have time. I'm outfitting *Lightning* to take off on the tide going out. Just wanted to stop by and see you two brave women…wild crazy women, I should say. Fair winds and following seas to ye." And off he went, probably not truly realizing how much gratitude I felt for him and his crew.

The next morning we got a message via the yacht club steward that John was OK. They were going to keep him in for one more day of observation and he would be released in the morning. We got the boat as shipshape as we could and early the next morning, a cab pulled up and out popped John looking friskier than ever.

"Am I ever happy to see you two," he said, giving us each a bear hug. "And *Onera* looks just wonderful. Thanks so much for getting her here. We can easily get around Buchon today in time for my haul-out. I called them from the hospital and told them what had happened and they are holding me a space. They had already heard all about you two."

We made fast all the things below-deck that might fly around during the voyage, warmed up the engine and pulled out of the slip. As we sailed down the channel, I got on the radio.

"Hi. To everyone out there. This is the two damsels who were in distress aboard *Onera* . Thanks to everyone for all the help. We're heading out to sea again with our skipper safely at the helm. *Adios.*"

As I was about to put the mike back on its hook, a voice came over the radio. "Is that you, Sandra?"

"Gosh, who is it?"

"It's me, Dick, from Moss Landing. I'm out here with a couple of my pals on our annual domino run. I might have known you were one of those damsels we kept hearing about. Where are you headed?"

I couldn't believe it. This was the guy whose gorgeous antique trawler Darryl had spent months repairing and rebuilding back in Moss Landing. Dick had always been real friendly every time I saw him on the docks.

"We're just leaving the harbor to head around Buchon to Avila," I said. "I'm on a friend's 26-foot sailboat. A pal is coming down from Santa Cruz in his little plane to fly me back tomorrow."

"Well, I think we'll get to Avila a bit before you as we've just gone around Buchon. We'll save an anchoring spot next to us and have the martinis ready."

Going around Buchon was literally a breeze...we even had to put the engine on to keep up with the friendly seagull who had decided to lead us around the point. We arrived about 5:00 p. m. and headed into the little bay looking for the domino players.

As we sailed in closer to shore, Dick's voice came on the radio, "Hard a-lea. We're over here and we've got a spot warmed up for you."

We anchored next to them and saw they had the cocktail flag flying. As we were about to step into the dinghy, someone hailed on the radio. "To the new arrival, this is the Harbor Master. Is there a Sandra Smith aboard?"

"This is Sandra."

"There are two gentlemen here to see you. Here's one."

"Sandra, this is Lance. How are you?"

I explained to John that Lance was a friend who had volunteered to come down as a back-up to pick me up. Before leaving Moss Landing, I'd told Lance another friend from San Jose was going to fly down in his Cessna to pick me up but in case the weather was foggy, I would need a back-up. Lance was to check with Jack in the morning and come down only if the weather was too bad for flying.

"I'm fine…this has been quite an adventure. I'll tell you all about it."

"Jack is here, too," said Lance.

"What? You both came?"

"Yeah. He said he'd fly down and get you, but I just had a sort of pre-monition. Are you sitting down? We've just had a terrible earthquake about 30 minutes ago. Most of downtown Santa Cruz is in rubble. They are saying it was a 7. 2 on the Richter scale. Pretty bad. Jack was flying over at the exact moment the main quake ripped and he is quite upset…saw many buildings downtown collapse in a matter of minutes."

I couldn't believe what he was saying. I told him friends were anchored next to us and we'd all see him in a few minutes.

I hailed our buddies on the radio. "Hey, Dick. Guess what! There's been a huge earthquake in Santa Cruz. The town is in rubble."

"Naw, you're joshing. Here, c'mon over for a chocolate martini. I've got a world-famous cardiologist and a former State Senator aboard…. you'll love 'em both."

"I'm serious. We've got to go ashore and get to a TV. Santa Cruz is in disaster mode. Is your dinghy big enough for the six of us?"

He realized I was serious and said they'd be right over for us. We met Lance and Jack in the Harbor Master's office. Lance said he had a funny feeling the night before that something was going to happen and even though Jack had assured him he was cleared for the hop to fly down and pick me up, Lance had decided to drive down anyway in his Winnebago.

When we all walked into the office, both men rushed up to embrace me as they had already heard tales from the Harbor Master about the damsels in distress.

"Sandra, you won't believe it – I flew over Santa Cruz about 45 minutes ago and there was smoke everywhere downtown," said Jack, talking 100 miles a minute. "The city is in flames and downtown looked wiped out! Let's go find a TV and see what's happening up there."

Arms linked, we all walked out on the pier to the Olde Port Inn restaurant where diners were crammed into the bar, staring at the screen. Newscasters were reporting how the San Francisco Bay Bridge had fallen into the bay while the World Series was going on, some of the Nimitz Freeway in Oakland had caved in on top of its lower level, Highway 17 leading over the mountains from San Jose to Santa Cruz was completely blocked by a huge mountain that had come down in a massive landslide. The quake had wrought an incredible amount of damage. They were calling it another San Francisco quake, but we were soon to learn that the epicenter was Loma Prieta just a few miles from the center of Santa Cruz and my mom's house.

Just to set the record straight and stop those darned San Franciscans from persisting in calling it *their* quake, less than a week later, a bunch of us rebellious Santa Cruzans printed T-shirts with the words, LOMA PRIETA 7.

1 QUAKE, OCTOBER 17, 1989, 5:02PM on one side and on the back, IT'S OUR FAULT! Well, that's cheeky Santa Cruz for you!

Jack couldn't reach anyone at the Watsonville Airport, the closest to Santa Cruz where he had planned to drop me. His only choice was to fly directly back to San Jose. With Highway 17 blocked, I might be stuck indefinitely over there at his place. I opted to drive back with Lance. Trying to listen to the news coming from the bar, we all had an almost silent dinner together. Following a heartfelt farewell with a promise to drive the sailing community's Christmas mail down to Cabo San Lucas and meet John and Mariella at the Cabo Marina for Christmas Eve dinner, Lance and I pulled away in his Winnebago for a most eerie journey north. There was no electricity anywhere – gas stations were dark, no street lights shined, no traffic signals worked. Lance filled both his large gas tanks before leaving Santa Cruz, so no worries there. We pulled into a Denny's for coffee. The place was alit with candles and the coffee was cold. Everyone was talking in whispers, afraid if they raised their voices, the walls might come tumbling down. We took off again and there were places where little bridges over small viaducts were actually separated apart. Lance would make the Winnebago take a flying leap to get us across the cracks.

We arrived in Santa Cruz about 1:00 a. m. and went straight to his apartment. There was no electricity and when he pushed open the door to his second floor apartment, we were greeted with a total mess. That was when I learned earthquakes always move back and forth in the same direction…the San Andreas Fault in our area apparently was one that made its quakes move north to south. If your kitchen cupboards faced north to south, everything would be on the floor; if they faced east to west, things would still be in the cupboards. Unfortunately, Lance's apartment faced north to south. We were greeted with a pile of broken bottles of ketchup, mustard, milk splashed every-where, pickle relish on everything and all his china smashed in the middle of the kitchen floor. The bathroom was worse with umpteen bottles of medicines, shampoo, lotions, splashed everywhere and broken bottles lying all over the floor. I took one look at the mess in the living room and immediately wanted to get back to my boat to see if she had suffered any damage. Lance agreed to drive me over to the harbor.

We passed through Downtown Santa Cruz which was a disaster…no street lights or traffic lights worked. Young and old were wandering around in disbelief as they stared at where their houses had stood or at their wrecked vehicles crushed under trees. Facades of buildings were lying on their sides like a Hollywood re-creation of Atlantis destroyed. I couldn't face going up to my mother's house. I was still reeling from the shock of her unexpected death two weeks before and just couldn't bear to see her place in ruins. We drove through Capitola, parked and walked out on the pier. It was incredible…. at the end of the pier we peered into a huge swirling hole in the water and saw the bottom of the sea. It was a whirlpool and the pier started to shake. We scampered off to the safety of his car and drove to my boat which was still tied to the dock not showing any ill effects of the earthquake. I didn't feel like inviting him aboard. I just needed to lie in my bunk and thank God for once again, being there for me, for saving me and *Sérenta* from harm. Climbing into the bunk, I slept for hours until the phone woke me up. It was the secretary at the Parks Department office asking if I was back and coming in to work that day as I was needed. When I took the job, they didn't tell me my "cultural services" was connected to the Parks Department which meant in times of disasters like this, I would be part of the County Emergency Squad. I checked *Sérenta's* mooring lines to make sure she would be OK while I was gone as I knew there would be after-shakes. When I walked into the Parks Department, they slapped a badge on my shirt identifying me as a member of the Emergency Squad and told me to go downtown and search for bodies in the rubble. No one was allowed downtown without a badge, so there weren't many in that area where bricks were scattered everywhere. Where once beautiful historic buildings stood were now piles of rubble. A young college girl had last been seen working in the coffeehouse next to Bookshop Santa Cruz and everyone was desperately trying to find her in all the chaos of broken glass and twisted metal. I had grown up as a kid being rocked in the night by little quakes, but nothing had prepared me for this scene out of a horror movie.

I spent until dark picking up pieces of blood-stained bricks and adobe tiles, listening to people wail and dogs bark in the distance at each after-shock. The dogs always knew first…they could hear that awful rumbling way below the surface as Mother Earth began to shudder and tremble. We had tremors for weeks. Residents refused to stay inside their homes for fear of being buried alive, preferring to sleep in their cars or outside on blankets on their front lawns. It was a way, too, of letting their friends see that they were safe and alive. Those whose homes had been destroyed moved into the elementary school.

I waited three days before going up to Mother's, afraid of what damage I might find. Back in 1968 when my Dad was dying of cancer, my parents had bought a high knoll surrounded by redwoods in Scotts Valley, cut off the top and designed a house that would fit on the very top with fabulous views in every direction. I could just imagine the whole house down the bank as happened to so many others I saw and heard about all week. I called Lance and asked him to come with me for moral support. The house was still standing . We went inside to see what might have been damaged or destroyed.

To our total amazement, nothing was amiss except for Mother's large china cabinet which always sat against the wall in the dining room and was now standing in the middle of the floor some nine feet out from the wall. How had it gotten there? More to the point, how had it managed to arrive at its new location without falling over and breaking all the family heirloom china and crystal on the shelves behind the glass doors in the top half of the cabinet? We figured out it had slowly slid, with each tremor, from north to south, on the hardwood floor Mother always kept shiny and clean. It hadn't fallen over during its "journey" because Mother had stored all the priceless family sterling silverware in the drawers midway down, and behind the doors of the bottom half of the china cabinet the shelves were filled with sterling serving pieces, trays and heavy sterling candlesticks. The weight of the family silver had kept the cabinet upright and saved the china and crystal which many years later, I would still be enjoying the use of.

The only damage the quake did to her property was to relocate the narrow little sidewalk that was built around the perimeter of the house. It was now in pieces at the bottom of the hill. My father would have been proud to know that his chimney was one of the only 8% in the entire county that hadn't been destroyed.

The next day when I went in to work, I thought about Watsonville to the south of Santa Cruz which had also suffered severe damages. It was the southernmost part of the county and home to many Mexican migrant farm workers. No one from Parks had thought about Watsonville, often the step-child of our activities. I asked our Director if I could handle Watsonville since everyone else in the department was concerned with Santa Cruz, Capitola, Aptos and the wealthier areas of the county. He was glad that someone was even willing to go south. I drove to the county fairgrounds where large tents had been erected. They were filled with people sitting on little cots but what plucked at my heartstrings most were the children wandering around aimlessly and afraid.

"I've got to do something for these kids," I thought. "They really need even more help than the adults."

I drove to the Watsonville Public Library which was only slightly damaged and asked the woman at the check-out desk to help find me some children's books in Spanish. She looked at me rather oddly while squinting at my Emergency Squad badge.

"I need to help the kids out at the fairgrounds," I said. "No one seems to be doing anything for them."

The librarian smiled and hurried around filling two huge bags with children's books in Spanish and I headed back to the fairgrounds. I hadn't spoken Spanish for more than 20 years. In the 1960s, back in Philadelphia, I took a course at Berlitz so I could help Cuban refugees buy houses. They would come to the real estate office my husband and I were running. At the time, I was the youngest woman licensed in real estate in Philadelphia, 22 years old and full of enthusiasm. We were one of the few if not the only real estate office in downtown Philadelphia helping the Cubans who were mostly former professors or intellectuals who had managed to escape from Castro's purges. I always had a pot of dark coffee going and would sit around drinking coffee with prospective clients while we chatted about what a great life they would soon have with their very own home. I loved working with them – they were so grateful for anything you did for them. Plus, they loved good coffee as much as I did after all the time I spent in French cafés during my student days abroad.

I also helped a lot of low-income Black folks buy or rent homes. I remember the time when a young Black couple came into my office looking for a house to rent. She looked like she was going to have her baby right in front of me! Larry McElroy, the district constable, always stopped to visit when he was in our neighborhood and was sitting on our leather couch at the time, enjoying some coffee. I told him to watch the fort and I'd be right back as I wanted to take the couple over to see a little $35/month house I had bought and fixed up in historic Germantown and which was now ready for rent. The couple loved the sweet house with its tiny garden. We returned to the office and I typed up a lease. They left beaming with enthusiasm and hope for their new life together as a soon-to-be family.

"You shouldn't take these people in your car places, Sandra. You make them give you a $5 key deposit and send them on their way. You don't waste time taking them places."

The constable, so used to pinning eviction notices on people's doors, was so callous, while I, on the other hand, experienced great pleasure helping less fortunate people get a new start in life. A week later, Larry was sitting on the leather couch by my desk and in walked our newest Black tenants with the tiniest baby I had ever seen.

"I wanted you to see our new baby, Mrs. Smith," said the proud mother. "We're just taking her home from the hospital to the little house you helped us get for her. I wanted to name her after you but I didn't know your first name so we named her Luzerne. You were so kind to us…. we'll never forget you."

Our office was on the corner of 9th and Luzerne. I got up and gave the baby a hug and wished them blessings as a new family. As they left with their precious little bundle, I looked at McElroy and sure enough, there was a tear in the old Irishman's eye.

"I guess I'll never tell you how to run your business again," he said, walking out the door with a little more humility than he had when he first came in.

Every morning following the earthquake, I got up early and drove directly from the Moss Landing Harbor to the Watsonville fairgrounds. The kids were always waiting for me…. a huge group of them ranging in age from about two to ten. First, we'd do our exercises outside on the lawn. I taught them some tai chi movements I always did on my boat which they thought were a hoot! Then we'd sit in a circle while I tried to read stories to them in my best Spanish. They'd giggle and laugh as I mutilated their language and when I told them they could correct me anytime, they loved it. This was a learning experience for all of us. I went there every day for about two weeks until the Director told me there were "other more important things to do." So I went to the fairgrounds after work on my own time. I couldn't erase the sudden fearful looks that crept across the faces of those adorable kids every time Mother Earth shuddered as the tremors continued. When I'd show up, they'd come running up to hug me as if I were a long lost friend or their favorite auntie. When a tremor jolted our playful moments, some would hang onto my arms or legs, afraid to let go until the earth settled back down again.

Helping these little children somehow made up for all the times I hadn't been able to help my own children when they were young, to hug them when they had little hurts, to console them when they had disappointments, to gently stroke their hair when they were afraid, and to whisper, "God loves you and everything is going to be alright." Amidst the chaos after the earthquake I was being given another chance to comfort a child, something I had so missed all those years when my children spent more time with their father than with me.

My brother didn't waste a minute in listing Mother's property with a local realtor even though I protested it was not the right time to sell – so many were fleeing Santa Cruz like rats from a sinking ship and home values had plummeted. The house sold in less than a week. Three weeks later, the day before the buyers took possession, I went back to snip what would be my last sprig of blooms off Mother's huge daphne bush that she had dug up and brought with her from her last home and transplanted into this garden. It had supplied many small boxes of blooms wrapped in wet paper towels Mother used to send to me no matter which far corner of the world I was in. I was astounded to see what had been a beautiful healthy plant reaching up to the edge of the roof only a few weeks before was now reduced to broken leaves and limbs lying on the ground. When I examined the daphne's remaining root structure, I saw that the gophers had taken over and chewed it to death. How odd, I thought. Guess they knew Mother was gone and wouldn't be there to care for and enjoy it anymore.

Chapter Seventeen

Anchors Aweigh, My Gals

Once I was able to get back to my Arts Commission projects, I realized what a tremendous effect the earthquake and all its destruction had had on me. I felt there must be something more meaningful, more significant I could do with my life but I didn't know what that could be. And I was, tired...tired of keeping up a happy face amidst all the chaos and sadness, tired of watching the City Fathers (and, Mothers, too!) thinking only of the deals they could cut and not about how they could help the people. I sat in the lantern-lit salon of *Sérenta*, meditating one night for two hours, trying to find out what my Higher Power might next have in mind for me. As usual, I had no clue and no amount of prayers brought an answer. Had God decided to move on? Had He moved back to Armenia again to help all those starving kids over there?

Early December, with a three-day window of calm weather predicted, Lance and I sailed *Sérenta* up to San Francisco where I secured a slip on Pier 39 next to Fisherman's Wharf. We had an easy trip north, motor-sailing most of the way. I then began commuting back and forth from San Francisco to Santa Cruz, spending most weekends in the City. Hanging out in San Francisco and sailing around the bay was fun and exciting and worth the commuting. I was honing my nautical skills but becoming increasingly restless -- it was time to move on with my life. This was just like what would happen much later when I'd have spent some time in an anchorage and wake up one morning with the restless feeling that it was time to weigh anchor and move on to the next anchorage.

For fun, I invited friends from Santa Cruz up to San Francisco on weekends to sail with me. One woman, Patricia, came up almost every weekend for a month or so. She had never been on a sailboat before and really seemed to enjoy the sailing. I wondered if she would make a good crewperson if I ever decided to cut the umbilical mooring lines and sail away. One Sunday night, alone on the boat, I was lying in my bunk looking up at Coit Tower silhouetted against the skyline of this fabled city. Listening to the rhythmical sound of the lines gnawing on the dock cleats, I began to meditate to find out what the Universe had next in store for me.

"OK, God," I murmured aloud. "I've taken care of my mother these past three years, her ashes are scattered and all her affairs have been laid to rest. Bruce has his share of what she left and I've paid him back what Mother loaned me for the boat and the rest of my share is invested. Ian and Sandi seem to be doing just fine with their father. I've done everything I can think of to help cheer up post-quake Santa Cruz. I've created music festivals with generous contributions to the musicians, held art competitions with huge monetary prizes for the artists many of whose studios were destroyed. I've designed new Arts education programs for the school kids to take their minds off the disaster, and started workshops for the writers. I have stayed smiling and sober through it all. I am weary, Lord, and need to know what You want me to do next...maybe a plan of something nice to do, just for me this time?"

Silence. I continued on, speaking aloud as I was pretty sure my HP was sitting beside me. "It's too late to go back to Philadelphia and try to resurrect my career – all the politicians in Harrisburg whom I used to hound for money as a lobbyist are probably out of office and I would be starting all over. I love my job here, but I can't stand what they are doing to Santa Cruz, or rather what they are not doing. Blue tents are still serving as retail shops, most of downtown is still chained off, and the politicians are wheeling and dealing with the heartstrings of our town, trying to turn our downtown over to deep-pocket developers. Why, I heard one night they were considering an offer from a company in Japan to buy up downtown to turn it into a theme park! What is in the stars for me next?" Silence. Perhaps, I need to go off on another tack. "OK, it's me down here again, God, and I need Your help. Please tell me what You want me to do next."

"Break your ties, go out there, and take off on the spiritual odyssey you're finally ready for," came the instant message.

"Sail out there in the Big Blue? It's so dangerous, so scary out there. You don't really mean that, do You?"

"I told you before I'd help you," came the booming reply.

I started formulating a plan to leave the area and head south, following my nose like my father had always said we were doing when we took off on vacation in some unknown direction. I couldn't decide if I should go it alone or find crew, not realizing how difficult it would be to find good crew. My first step towards "interviewing" for crew was to approach Bill, a fellow I knew from the 12-Step meetings, and a friend of his, Marilyn, whom I met at West Marine while working there. They were both in their 50s. Bill had never sailed but had a dream to sail the South Seas. Marilyn had owned a boat with her recently divorced husband and grew up around boats as her father had been an avid sailor.

To see how we might fit together in close quarters, I invited them to help sail across the San Francisco Bay from Pier 39 to the boatyard in Alameda where I was to have a new anchor winch installed on the bow. We would sail over, leave the boat at the boatyard, hang out at the marina until the job was done, then sail back to San Francisco. The sail across went fine and I soon realized they were a bit chummier than I initially realized. That wouldn't matter as long as they didn't let romance get in the way of their crew responsibilities. On the way back, about 15 minutes before we arrived at Pier

39, they both said they would love to sign on. I was thrilled as they seemed responsible and were both a lot of fun.

Marilyn then nonchalantly said, "I think I need to tell you something. If we are really going to go cruising together, it won't be the three of us…. it will be five."

"Five?" I queried.

"Yes. It'll be you, Bill, me, Maria and Mary."

At first, I didn't get what she was talking about until she said, "Yes, you see, I have multiple personalities and most of the time the three of us get along just fine. But sometimes, Mary acts up and can be really mean and scares the hell out of the rest of us."

Good Lord, I thought. This is too much…on board with a wacky weirdo.

Bill's reaction, however, was unbelievable as he said, "I don't see a problem with that at all…it will be two more people to share turns on the helm," and he burst into raucous laughter.

I steered *Sérenta* towards the harbor entrance and to my slip where I said, "I want to thank all of you for helping me with this little jaunt. I've decided I don't really think it will work out for the three of us -- or I should say the five of us – to go cruising as there just isn't enough room on board for five."

The next Saturday when the usual gang came up from Santa Cruz to sail, Patricia was with them. While we were out sailing around that day, she asked me if I was ever going to go out cruising. I contemplated mentioning I was about to start looking for crew. She had recently received a divorce settlement and had money to cover her personal expenses which was a plus. But she didn't know diddly-squat about sailing. I decided to wait and not mention crewing possibilities quite yet. Monday after work, I stopped at the yacht broker's office to chat about cruising. Did he think I knew enough yet to head way out there? When was the right time of year to leave? Should I go alone or take crew?

"I know a young lady you might consider for crew. She once worked for me selling boats and knows a lot about them. Debra isn't into wild carousing…you won't have to worry about her disappearing in some port. She's quite brilliant and can figure things out for herself. I think she'd make good crew for you."

Thus the idea began to gel that maybe the time was right to weigh anchor and move on. I met with Debra, and after much thought and deliberation, ended up asking her and Patricia as well if they would like to head south with me as crew. We set up a meeting to discuss all the ramifications. After three hours of delving into everything I could think of, they agreed to go, dubbing it "The Great Adventure."

I flew to Philadelphia to close some accounts and complete unfinished business, and while there, set up an appointment with the astrologer I used to occasionally consult. He wasn't an ordinary astrologer…he had a degree in physics which he taught at Temple University and was also the first astrologer ever permitted into the Soviet Union. They had given him official authorization to give a talk in Moscow earlier that year. It was so heavily attended, they extended his permit and he spent six months traveling around Russia giving talks on all aspects of astrology. He told me the Russians were starved for this sort of information and during breaks in his talks, they would run home, then return, covering the stage with flowers from their gardens, loaves of dark bread, pelmeni, bliny, bowls of borscht and anything they could grab in a hurry to show their appreciation.

I explained my plans to go cruising and asked him to check my chart to see when would be a safe time to set sail for this adventure. He said to leave no later than Oct. 15th of that year as after that, it would be dangerous. I picked October 13th as departure date since 13 was my lucky number. I phoned Patricia and Debra back in California and told them we needed to leave Monterey Bay on October 13th for a variety of reasons including the fact that hurricane season would be over by then and the seas wouldn't be plagued yet with winter storms. This would also give them two months… plenty of time to get used to the idea, to set their things in order, and to study up on sailing.

When I got back to California, Patricia and Debra came up to San Francisco to crew the trip south from Pier 39 to Monterey Harbor. Before I moved my boat to San Francisco, I ended a short-lived romance with Darryl and needed to find someone else to help ready my boat for cruising. I made arrangements for a slip in the Monterey Municipal Marina to get all the final outfitting of the boat done. The marina was handy to a big shipyard where I'd have an extra foresail for heavy weather installed (changing *Sérenta* to a ketch-rigged sloop), have a new compass put on, haul out to have the bottom painted again with anti-fouling paint, plus have a zillion other projects done to make her as safe and seaworthy as possible.

I used the three sessions of psychiatric counseling county employees were given to help get over earthquake stress, not for that reason, but rather to help me find the courage to give up my beloved job. With the counselor's help, I was able to give the County notice I would be leaving my job in 30 days. Another aid in this decision was the fact that almost a year had gone by and Santa Cruz was still in utter turmoil over how to repair all the damage done by the quake. The same day I turned in my resignation was the day City Hall decided to destroy Cooper House, one of the landmark buildings downtown. It was built in the last century, had been the city's first courthouse, and its ornate architectural design was a testimony to the bygone days of Santa Cruz elegance. Years before the quake, it had been tastefully turned into an Arts "mall" with lots of little shops filled with art and crafts made by locals. The beloved landmark's outdoor patio was a well-known meeting place – you could sit there for hours sipping a cup of java or an exotic fruit smoothie and watch people all day. They wanted to tear it down, claiming it was too damaged to repair. Unofficially and not as the Arts Commission, I formed a committee, "Save Cooper House", and almost every artist in town made a painting of it to be displayed around town with the bold statement printed beneath every painting, "Keep developers from destroying our landmark."

With the help of some sympathetic legislators, we even managed, in record time, to get it registered as a National Historic Landmark but the greedy jerks got around that. We all tied yellow ribbons to the construction fence put up around it after the quake, an expression of grief at the thought of losing our Cooper House. That dreadful afternoon, artists all dressed in black, sat at the fence sketching and painting images of it so we would never forget it. It seemed the entire town was standing with their fingers grasped onto that fence as the wrecking ball moved into position. The ball was set loose and hundreds of people held hands crying, "No! No!" as wall after wall came tumbling down. Lost was any remaining respect we had for the politicians, those movers and shakers who wanted to sell Santa Cruz off to the highest bidder. As I stood at the fence wiping away tears, the decision to sail away was knotted firmly in place.

The maiden voyage south from San Francisco to Monterey with Patricia and Debra was fairly uneventful, but they would only take the helm when there was hardly any wind. Patricia was feeling seasick, Debra uneasy with the frisky wave action but we made it safely, without any problems, to Monterey. I spent from mid-August to October in the Monterey Harbor slip while a shipwright put all the pieces together for an extended cruise. The two women spent evenings at their homes, tending to final personal details, showing up irregularly to help. I had no idea how long we'd be gone, nor where exactly we would even be heading. It all depended on how the weather treated *Sérenta*, on how I actually enjoyed the adventure, on how well the crew handled their responsibilities, and most importantly, on how well we got along. Always in the front of my mind was what I learned early in recovery: I didn't get sober to be miserable, I got sober to be happy, joyous and free, just as the recovery program's Big Book promises.

When they agreed to crew and before we left San Francisco, I told both I would not be flexible on the October 13th departure date from Monterey. I explained it was the best date to leave based on the hurricane season ending and would give us plenty of time, about seven months before the next hurricane season would begin, to leisurely cruise down the coast of California and then down the Baja Peninsula. We'd have time to make stops along the way to explore the little bays and coves and to snorkel, fish, and dive for shrimp and lobster. We'd also see the whales heading down the coast for mating. By June 1st, at the very latest, we would have to be in the first safe hurricane hole after San Diego which was Escondido Bay, located by sailing around the bottom of the Baja then up to La Paz where we would anchor for a little while to resupply and repair. We'd then continue about a quarter of the way up the Sea of Cortez to Escondido.

The Monterey shipwright worked ten to twelve hours a day getting the boat ready. I had bought the boat for $48,000 and at the time had been appraised at $52,000. It was worth quite a bit more now with all the upgrades I'd already made and the new ones I was making for this voyage. At the first haul-out, I had put in a new head, new intake and exhaust system for heavy seas; replaced the water tank vent and gas gauge; rebuilt the water pressure pump and hot water heater; retrofitted the refrigeration system and added a new fan; replaced the bilge hose with a heavy duty one; put in a new exhaust system including muffler and new insulation. In Santa Cruz the previous summer, I hired a marine electrician to replace all the interior electrical lights as none worked properly. During the process, we discovered most of the interior electrical system had been wired with lamp cord...the former owner must have fancied himself a handyman. I decided to have the entire boat rewired.

Before taking off from Monterey, I had the engine completely over-hauled, all the exterior teak oiled and interior teak repaired where it had gouges from that first trip out in the Pacific with Darryl, a new knot-meter installed and all the cables, blocks and stanchions replaced. To aid in radar reflection, I had the shipwright install stainless steel steps all the way up the mast to the top. This was done with the hopes that in addition to *Sérenta's* own radar reflector, freighters would be more likely to pick me up on their radar. I could also climb the mast steps to repair lines or sails (which I did once, totally terrified, when I was sailing alone under full sail and a line got tangled). I would also later find the steps handy for spotting whales, dolphins, obscure buoy markers and distant lighthouses. To help bring in better radio signals for possible future Ham reception, I had the full length and breadth of the bilge and alongside it lined with copper. By the time all the various repairs and renovations were completed, the boat was worth about $90,000. I put most of these repairs on my loyal first credit card and spread it out on several new ones. I didn't want to have to sell any of my American Funds shares which gave me monthly dividends I could use to pay expenses during the cruising. I figured I would have the rest of my life to pay off the credit cards in monthly installments.

I had a pretty slim budget for cruising. Fortunately, when I was working in Philadelphia as a lobbyist and also part-time for that very successful developer, I had set aside a certain amount of my pay each month to buy shares in mutual funds and would not deviate from the plan. I was lucky to have met an honest and savvy young stockbroker in my travels with the developer and his high-roller buddies. When I sold my historic house, although I didn't realize a very large profit, the money I did end up with went into more mutual fund shares. That same year, the divorce was final and what I got for my share of some of the houses I had bought and renovated went to buy more shares. When my mother's house was sold, after paying my brother what I owed him for the money Mother gave me to buy the boat, my share from the sale of her house went into yet more mutual funds. Staying within an allotted monthly budget was not my strongest suit although some months when I didn't have unexpected repairs or expensive parts to buy, I did have some money left over.

Next came the decision about boat insurance. This was always a big debate with cruisers – many maintained it wasn't going to do them any good south of the border so why have it? I opted to keep it until leaving San Diego when I cancelled it, and at the insistence of crew, used the refund towards the purchase of a GPS device. It was during the Gulf War and the Army had taken command of all the GPS devices. After a quick call to my old boss at West Marine, through his various channels and with the help of Randy, the owner, they managed to acquire a stray GPS for me which gave up working after the first month of use.

A week before our October 13th scheduled departure from Monterey Harbor, Patricia announced she was going in for a tummy tuck because, "I won't look good in a bikini with this big stomach." The surgery couldn't be done until after October 15th and there would be about a week of recovery before she could come near the boat. I couldn't believe this…how could she decide to delay our departure when I had given her two months advance notice about the optimum date? As it was too late to line up a replacement for her, I acquiesced. I felt nervous after what the astrologer said, but had no choice but to delay our departure the two weeks. Her attitude was an ominous foreshadowing of what was to come.

In spite of Patricia's surgery delaying our departure, my dearest friend in Santa Cruz, Sam Patterson, went ahead with a "Bon Voyage Shindig" he planned for Columbus Day night, Friday, Oct. 12th, in the courtyard of The Crest on the cliff above the village of Capitola. Sam had a condo there where I had rented one for awhile when I moved *Sérenta* to Pier 39, knowing I wouldn't always feel like making the commute back and forth. I gave the condo up right after the earthquake as it just didn't feel safe in a condo hanging out over the ocean. In fact, they had to evacuate and then close half of the complex for safety reasons.

It was to be a potluck and Sam sent flyers around Santa Cruz inviting one and all to the party "to send Sandra and her all-female crew off on their Grand Adventure to the Sea of Cortez and beyond." Before the party was over, most everyone ended up in the pool…it was so crowded they couldn't help but fall in! I had to go upstairs to Sam's condo for a short while during the party as I was hit with a combination of unbounded fear, terrifying anxiety, sheer panic and utter sadness. What did I think I was doing, anyway, going off into the big blue ocean with a couple of women who didn't even know an inkling of what I knew about boats and engines, navigation and sailing maneuvers? And what would I do if we got hit by a freighter and sank or rammed by a whale and sent to the bottom? Well, it would be too late by then to do anything! I lay down on Sam's couch alone and cried while everyone outside was singing, dancing and having a great time. It reminded me of the loneliness I used to feel in the drinking days.

A few days before our original departure date, I decided to get my Ham license so I could keep in touch with Ian and Sandi back in Philadelphia via Ham phone patches. The Ham association in Santa Cruz was having an exam for the license and I had two days to cram into my already bewildered mind all the Morse code dots and dashes. Amazingly, I passed with flying colors and got the license I would be able to use to get a talkie license down in Mexico. In the U. S. A., that initial novice license only permitted the licensee to use Morse code over the radio; in Mexico, they were less stringent and for $52 cash paid at the border one could get a Mexican license and actually talk over the radio. The call letters assigned to me were KC6PMP and when the Ham operators in the area found out I was on a boat decked out in hot pink, hailed me by the traditional Poppa-Mike-Poppa, and immediately dubbed me, "Peppermint Patty", a moniker I was to be recognized by throughout the marine and even land-based Ham community.

Once we had finally taken off cruising, Ham operators (I called them 'Hamsters'), sequestered in their little Ham shacks across Mid-America's farmlands, or in the deep South, or way up in Seattle, or all the way down to the Galapagos and even across to Fiji, would keep track of *Sérenta*'s position. Each morning, when I was able to check in on the 1600 Zulu time (8:00a. m.) Pacific Maritime Ham net, they'd all be arguing over exactly where I was. All had maps in their Ham shacks and would follow me, sticking pins along my route on their maps. Sometimes it was difficult to tune in to the net, especially during certain weather conditions. Heavy clouds overhead, for example, sometimes helped the signal; other times, hindered it. The Hamsters all used a lot of technical jargon like "angle of propagation", "skip-effect", "signal reports", all of which were beyond me. Either I found the net or I didn't, and after moving the tuner miniscule degrees on my single-sideband radio, if I hadn't found the net in ten minutes of fiddling, I'd just give up and try the next day. I did have as an advantage the most expensive state-of-the-art single-sideband radio, courtesy of a West Marine discount. I could not just take off without knowing I'd be able to contact my children and they, too, could reach me if they wanted to. I set up a schedule so they would know the various times of the Ham nets I would be checking in on. At the time, Sandi was in college in Pennsylvania and Ian at Virginia Tech.

Before graduating from high school, Ian had become an Eagle Scout and without being prejudiced, I considered him the best-behaved youngster I had ever known. But he managed to discover a different world out there when he went to college. I could imagine what his life was like when I learned he was playing the tuba in the college band and living in "The Tuba House" with nine other tuba players, and had dropped Engineering as a major and changed to Psychology with a second in English.

Conversations with my kids over the Ham net were available to all ears as they were being "patched" from one Ham operator to another and several more across the country, ending with a phone call to Ian or Sandi from the last "patcher". I devised a code so I could ask over the radio how Ian was doing with his attempt at keeping alcohol and marijuana from interfering with his studies. Alcohol was "Rasputin", marijuana, "Robespierre".

On the Ham net patches, I'd casually toss into a conversation with Ian that everyone in the world could hear, varieties of, "And have you seen that rogue Rasputin lately?" or "Are you managing to keep that rascal Robespierre at bay or is he still hounding you?"

Ian would guffaw and respond, "Nope…Rasputin hasn't been over to see me for a month now. Isn't that great?" or "Well, I'm sorry to say, Robespierre came over last week to help me with my homework and he's still camping out in my room every night."

I would come back with something like, "He's a devious one, alright. Just tell him to get the heck out and leave you alone! You can say your finals are coming up and your mother doesn't want him distracting you," and we'd both laugh.

Ever since Ian was young and living with his father, if he had to phone me or I had to call him, at the end of our conversations, because neither wanted to say, "goodbye", we'd always end the conversation with a simultane-ous chorus of, "one…..two….three…" with each number being held as long as our breath would allow, and then right after "three", we'd hang up at the same time. This carried over into our abbreviated Ham conversations when I was able to set up a phone patch. Ian continues the one…two…three tradition to this day even though he's in his fifties. Sandi would always just say, "Bye, Mom", but she always answered the patches whereas with Ian, it would often take many days, sometimes even several weeks, to get a patch through to him.

Two nights before we were to leave Monterey Harbor, I woke up just after midnight with a foreboding premonition that something terrible was going to happen to the boom. I called the shipwright on the radio…woke him up, actually…and asked him to come right over as I needed his help to weld a steel collar for where the boom connected to the mast.

"Sandra, your boat is already maxed out for strength and safety. You don't have to do this. That boat is a floating Sherman tank!"

"Please, trust me…just get up and come over here. You're only two docks over and we already have the material you'll need left over from the last welding job you did for my bicycle rack on the stern."

Reluctantly, but probably inspired by how well he was going to be paid, he came over and together in record time, we devised a collar that would hopefully eliminate any danger of the boom departing the ship and capsizing us during a storm.

This same feminine intuition (or since getting sober, what I preferred to think of now as messages from Above) played a large part in the deci-sion-making process for the entire voyage. If I had a feeling of impending doom, I'd heed the warning and either scurry into the nearest safe harbor or cove and drop anchor or stay put. If I was hunting for a protected place to tuck into for the night, I would sail back and forth along a stretch of the beach until just the right spot would leap out at me. I would then steer the boat in and drop anchor. I knew my HP was taking over the helm and leading me to these safe anchorages. Before weighing anchor, I'd always draw the outline of the shoreline or mountains in my logbook for each of these places so I could find them again later if ever passing by on a return voyage and needing a safe anchorage. I would end up with a lot of drawings for my Sea of Cortez anchorages.

While *Sérenta* was still in Monterey, I met a couple of fellows aboard another sailboat getting ready to weigh anchor the same day we were. The owner of the boat, a seasoned cruiser, was heading directly to the South Pacific after rounding Point Sur. I chatted with him every day about the route he was taking to get around the point, how far off he'd take it, when he'd start back in, and when he'd actually head out westerly towards the South Pac. He said without much enthusiasm that we could follow him as far as his westerly jumping off spot and agreed to keep in radio contact every two hours. I felt a lot better about our first venture "out there", knowing we would at least have a buddy to check in with -- rounding points could be tricky and dangerous as erratic current patterns and heavy winds were almost always the norm.

We planned to leave at dawn on the morning high tide. I asked the two women to be on board early the night before so we'd be well-rested for the rigors of departure and the long day ahead. That last day before departure, I went to the supermarket and purchased food for the first leg of the journey. Another boater in the harbor told me I didn't have to refrigerate eggs, so I bought ten dozen of them. About a week in the heat, they smelled godawful and we had to throw them all overboard... protein for the fish. The boater had neglected to explain I had to turn the egg cartons over every other day to keep the eggs from sticking to their shells which would cause them to spoil.

The shipwright helped stow the foodstuffs and supplies while I made explicit notes in a spiral notebook as to where everything was going so I could find anything in a matter of minutes. Late afternoon, I raced to the hardware and bought about $250 worth of small tools – pliers, wrenches, every size and type of screwdriver, chisels, a pair of channel locks, a small saw, a hacksaw with spare blades, several sizes of hammers, and whatever else I came across in the tool aisle. I didn't know what half the things were or how to use them but I figured before this journey was over, I'd know most of them intimately. The clerk at the hardware asked why I was buying so many tools. I told him I was taking off in my hot pink sailboat with two women as crew and didn't know when I'd ever be back again. He looked incredulous and gave me a 50% discount on everything. He was one of the many nice guys I'd meet along the way which was helping me get over a prejudice against and mistrust of men I'd developed not long after I was married.

About 6:00 p. m., Sam met me at Santa Cruz Storage where I'd leave Mother's Ford van for an indefinite period. He drove me back to the boat in Monterey and I kissed him farewell. When I climbed aboard, I found Debra below studying the chart. She said Patricia had a friend pick her up that afternoon and she returned late that night after Debra and I had already hit our bunks. In the morning, I saw she had acquired long bright purple Vampira nails to go along with her new tummy tuck. How she was going to pull lines to get the sails up with those claws was beyond me!

November 8th (almost three weeks after the safe date I had originally set for departure), as Apollo came up out of the sea and balanced perfectly atop the dock piling, we were all set to untie our lines when Sam came running along the dock to wave goodbye and wish us Godspeed. He handed me a bagful of my favorite breakfast indulgence, bear claws from the Carmel Danish Bakery.

"I stayed over last night in a motel in Carmel so I could pick these up for you, fresh out of their oven. I know how much you adore them."

From behind his back, he whisked out a beautiful posy of fresh pink carnations in a plexiglass vase. "I wanted to put these in my antique crystal vase but figured that wouldn't do well out at sea. I've weighted this vase with river stones I picked up out of the river in Santa Cruz last week. Thought you'd like a bit of "home" along with you. Hopefully, the flowers will survive at least until you get around that ominous Point Sur. I also put a lot of prayers in with the stones."

I was grateful and happy for Sam's friendship and his farewell blessings while at the same time, feeling anxious, wondering if I was doing the right thing to just take off like this with two women who knew zilch about sailing. Was this an alcoholic ego trip that would come to a bad end? Standing on the dock alongside *Sérenta*, Sam joined me in reciting the Serenity Prayer. I started the motor and we slowly cruised through the harbor gates into the bay where we were immediately surrounded by a pod of about 15 small black and white orca whales. They were so close to *Sérenta,* I could practically reach out and pet them.

Since these were the first sea characters we were to come across, I grabbed my file box of info I had earlier put together about all the neat creatures I might meet on this adventure and read what truly amazing creatures orcas are (also known as killer whales). According to the folks at onegreen-planet. org, "Orcas possess brains four times larger than our own, and MRI scans have revealed that the lobes that deal with the processing of complex emotions are also larger in an orca's brain than our own. In the wild, they swim up to 100 miles a day and typically live in tight-knit matriarchal pods, spending their entire lives close to their family members. The compassionate bonds that these animals share run deep."

The article continued to say that a series of heartwarming pictures emerged recently which showed a group of orcas looking after their disabled brother who was unable to fend for himself. I later heard how a momma orca had carried her dead baby on her back for 17 days before letting go of it. According to marine scientists, the average life expectancy for wild orcas is 46 years for females and 38 years for males; however, their lifespans can extend considerably longer than that. When Granny, the head matriarch of J-Pod, was spotted off the coast of Canada in 2014, marine scientists studying the pod believed her to be 103 years old.

How fitting that it would be orcas who surrounded us in a dance of farewell. As my little pink sailboat was leaving Monterey to take off on The Grand Adventure, I knew the orcas had come to wish us a safe journey. I remembered the three whales that followed Darryl and me more than a year before and knew these beautiful creatures of the deep were carrying good signs to me, little messages from Above.

Chapter Eighteen

Good Heavens! What Have I Gotten Myself Into?

We sailed along the Monterey Peninsula and then set a course south. Passing Stillwater Cove, I remembered that frightening first voyage with Darryl and realized how far I had come as a sailor even though there was still a knot of fear in the pit of my stomach. There were still those memories of nearly drowning three times in the ocean as a teenager which haunted me.

The worst near-miss encounter with Dame Death occurred at Pescadero Beach. It hadn't been the ocean's fault. I was the one who decided to cut high school that day and drive through the mudslides to get to the beach after the big storm, wanting to be the first to discover neat things washed up. Yes, I was the one who climbed down the steep cliff to the beach and then crept on my knees through the cave to get to the beach isolated on the other side and stayed too long hunting for treasures. It wasn't Poseidon's fault when high tide came in and flooded the cave and the one way back to safety. The only choice was to force my way through the cave between waves, relying on only the few inches of air at the ceiling to get me through. I made it, and yet, for years, I had blamed the ocean for that and other near misses. Now, in my new sober life, I was learning to accept responsibility for my actions and not to point the ugly blame finger out there to everyone and everything else. What a change this was making for me and how I was now relating to others.

Standing alone at the helm, steering *Sérenta* safely along on top of playful waves, my mind began to wander. What a great chance to think of all the blessings I was receiving since that night almost ten years before when I admitted I was powerless over the disease of alcoholism that afflicted me and turned my will and my life over to a Higher Power of my understanding. Ah, life was wonderful!

As my time on watch passed, keeping *Sérenta* on the correct heading towards Point Sur was becoming increasingly difficult. The wind began to blow so hard I was forced to reef the main and shorten the jib. Thank goodness I spent the $3,000 to rig *Sérenta* with an auto-furling jib to avoid having to go up to the bow to bring it up or down. Then came the fog billowing around us, severely dropping the temperature. While manning the helm, I could see that the two women were not feeling well. Whereas Patricia had started the afternoon sitting on the deck in her bikini, she was now huddled in a jacket and wet-weather pants complaining about the cold. Debra was sitting in the cockpit all bundled up, not saying a word, but she had at least taken the wheel for two hours in the afternoon. Then, as it got windier, she said she had had enough and gave the wheel back to me. As evening closed in, I tried to reach our buddy-boat on the radio as we had lost sight of him in the fog. Their response was difficult to understand due to poor reception but at least we exchanged a few words. It was a relief to know they were still out there somewhere. We weren't completely alone.

Another hour passed. When I had been on the helm four hours, I asked Debra to take it for an hour and she refused. Her face was the white pallor of Death and I realized the yacht broker had greatly overstated her boating abilities. Patricia only had a few hours on the helm coming down from San Francisco and hadn't done well, so it was up to me to continue even though I was totally exhausted. I was grateful I had splurged and purchased the brass ship's clock and barometer. At least I had the comfort of hearing the ship's bell ringing out every 30 minutes above the din of the sea and I could keep track of how many hours I was on the wheel.

Two hours later, I called to them below to make radio contact with the guys we were following and they both refused to move from their bunks. I couldn't leave the helm to go below to check the chart as the seas were too rough and so asked Debra to at least plot the chart for a position check. She refused. Was this what sailors called, "mutiny on the High Seas"? Whatever it was, I sure didn't like it. About 45 minutes later, I made a mad dash to grab the radio mike and attempted to call our buddy-boat but no response. I felt alone in the black and angry sea with no one to look to for help or consolation. I forgot to call on my HP.

Thankful to have been able to grab the mike, I looped it around the cleat closest to me.

Even if the buddy-boat wasn't in sight, if we crashed into the many outcroppings along that coast in the darkness and fog, at least someone might hear over the radio my final words on Earth which would be, "Help, we're sinking! God save our souls!"

Despair was setting in with the realization I was basically alone on the boat without assistance of crew. I tried to remember what the coast line looked like when I went along it with Darryl, but the fog obscured everything. Another couple of hours steering and trying to keep the boat on course, and I could no longer even remember any details of the coast line. This had me wanting to give up sailing and if things got much worse, I would even consider going back to life in the suburbs! The situation was that desperate!

"Hey, will one of you get up here to steer?" I yelled. "I've been on this helm for 12 hours and I'm exhausted. I need to check the chart to see where we are."

"No way," came the answer in unison.

"I'm throwing up," added Patricia. Debra gave no explanation.

For a moment, the fog opened up and I could see the faint beam of the Point Sur lighthouse off the portside and already behind us. Whew…at least I've gotten us safely past that dangerous point but which compass bearing should I be steering now? I decided to maintain the same bearing I was currently on. Even though it would be taking us out to sea, at least it wouldn't be putting us onto the beach.

I was cold, I was tired, I was hungry, but most of all, angry. How could they lie down there without doing anything to help? How could they leave it all up to me? Didn't they realize our lives were at danger sailing without a new course to follow? And why the heck had they signed on in the first place… did they think they would only be hanging out in ports, downing free rum drinks and carousing with handsome cruisers? I started singing, *Moon River*, envisioning Audrey Hepburn as Holly Golightly waltzing into Tiffany's to look at all the gorgeous jewelry. I remembered how, in the old days when I was a teenager travelling abroad, I had brass luggage tags engraved with "Sandra, Travelling" and attached to all my bags, just like my heroine, Holly. Over and over again, trying to stay awake, I sang, "*Moon River, off to see the world. There's such a lot of world to see. We're after the same rainbow's end, waitin' round the bend, my huckleberry friend….."*

My mind started playing tricks on me. I saw a specter sitting on the boom, nestled into the mainsail. It was small and dark and wore a black shroud pulled over its head. I wasn't startled…it seemed perfectly normal to see it sitting there.

"Who are you? What do you want?" I hollered, wanting to be sure it heard me above the roar of the sea, the screech of the wind. I doubted the women below would hear me so I shouted again, "Who are you?"

It didn't reply, just sat there staring back at me, staring, staring. I began to cry as I realized it was the ghost of the marriage past. Tears streamed down my cheeks as I mourned the demise of the once hopeful marriage I thought would never end. Next came a great emptiness inside me. All the broken dreams, the sadness, disappointments, disillusionment, even anger that I was apparently still holding within was now being carried off by that specter who, as suddenly as it had appeared, was now sliding off the boom and slipping away into the mist, never to return.

I continued on the same course for the rest of the night. As Homer's *rosy-fingered dawn* welcomed Apollo up out of the sea, I shouted, "Hallelujah! Thank you for the glorious sunlight, Lord!" I knew He was listening and had been standing beside me at the helm all through that frightening night.

The ocean always seemed a lot friendlier in daylight. Still glued to the helm, my mind travelled back to when I was about 10 and already a Greek mythology junkie, reading stories in bed under the covers with a flashlight when I was supposed to be asleep. Eos, the Titaness and goddess of the dawn, was one of my favorite heroines back then. She lived at the edge of Oceanus and opened the gates of Heaven each morning for the sun to rise and shine. Looking out to sea that morning, I imagined her teasing Apollo because she had wings and he had to depend on his chariot.

The wind died down to a gentle breeze and I was able to tweak the sails enough to keep *Sérenta* on a steady course while I ran down to check the chart. In calculating the time we had been sailing since we went around Sur and our approximate speed, I realized, to my horror, we were way far out to sea. In the light of day, I discovered the mainsail traveler was all screwed up and part of the track had even ripped off in the heavy winds in the night. The oven below was ripped out of its mounting and hanging by one screw. I didn't have the expertise to fix either nor the desire to even try.

"We're going to head inshore to Avila to get some things fixed," I announced to the two who were now sitting, bedraggled, in the cockpit. "We're out to sea more than 100 miles off course because neither of you would look at the chart for me last night. We won't get back in to Avila until tomorrow."

They didn't answer which was probably better as I might have yelled at them if they had dared to open their damned mouths. As we were making our way towards shore and the Avila Boatyard, no one said a word. For more than the almost 100 nautical miles it took, I wrestled the entire time with the idea of confronting them and kicking them off *Sérenta* when we arrived at the boatyard. Reality prevailed, however, as I truly didn't feel I could handle the boat by myself even though that was basically what I had been doing all night. But the image of going around notorious Point Concepcion alone was too overwhelming. I decided to keep quiet and put up with them.

The owner of the boatyard remembered me from the time I came in on *Onera*. He said he could get the stove and the mainsail traveler fixed in no time. He didn't even charge me his full fee for the work and I was grateful for his generosity and kindness.

The next morning, we left Avila before dawn as I wanted to get around Point Concepcion before the heavy winds came up. This Point had the worst reputation of all those along the California coast. I'd been fearing the rounding since I first thought about sailing south. To my surprise, we had to motor around Concepcion as the wind had completely died and the seas were as flat as the back of my already sunburned hand. Cheated Death again, I murmured as I looked back at that infamous point thrusting herself out into the sea, just waiting to seduce the next roving buccaneer.

Continuing on south of Point Concepcion, the weather was fair with gentle following seas and for the next two days, crew took turns on the helm. We pulled into Santa Barbara Yacht Club while the sun was still high on the horizon. The club had reciprocity with Elkhorn Yacht Club and we were allowed a few days in the courtesy slip, a real boon. I felt sure there was a leak in the main water tank which would take time to fix. The club manager gave me the name of a good shipwright and he was able to get right on the job. Unfortunately, he had to pull the hatch in my beautiful new sole to get at the tank and damaged a few of the purple-heart planks in the process.

Debra said she would help him dry out the tank to see if there were any holes in the metal. For my sanity and to get re-centered, I hunted up a meeting that wasn't a costly cab ride away. I left the two women on the boat saying I would be back by noon the next day when we could share the tasks of a good cleaning of the boat, inside and out. Much salt water and sea-debris had come aboard during the night's rough trip around Sur. We were at a dock with fresh water and electric and it might be a while before we had those two luxuries.

I met an interesting old Russian fellow at the meeting who imported Chinese acupressure balls and other odd things. He invited me to spend the night on his couch as a little escape after he heard me share during the meeting about the developing tense situation aboard *Sérenta*. After the meeting, new friends I made that night hugged me and said, "Just don't drink and keep coming to our meetings." Ah, something comforting and familiar, I thought.

The Russian's apartment was a wreck and the couch dirty, but I welcomed the escape. When he brought me back to the boat at 11:00 a. m. the next morning, the women were nowhere to be seen and the shipwright was still working on the water tank.

"I thought you would have the job long since finished," I said, rather annoyed at the time he was taking since I was paying him by the hour.

"Well, I think you should know that one of your wacky crew members spilled a quart of acetone into the water tank and wasn't even going to tell me. It's lucky I have a good sniffer and a better memory of the supplies I bring to a job. She was going to have me fill up your tank without flushing the acetone out of it. You would have had pretty unhealthy drinking water. That's what's taken me so long – the acetone ate all the lining off your tank and I had to re-line it. Gonna cost quite a bit more than I told you."

I was livid but decided once again not to bring it up to the crew. I kept hearing the words of my Fellowship buddies saying, "Pick Your Battles" and "Let Go and Let God". It was new for me and a bit difficult to be in such close quarters with others. Maybe I was in the wrong for expecting more help from them than they were willing to give. Whatever the problem was, they were becoming increasingly more argumentative, aligning over every issue. Each decision turned into a divisive debate. When I wanted to leave Avila real early to get around Point Concepcion before it got too windy, they both said they weren't about to get up before dawn. I had to insist. When I wanted to put in to Santa Barbara to have the water tank checked, they said they wanted to keep going on to Newport Beach. I had to point out it would cost at least twice as much to do repairs in glitzy Newport. On this day when we were supposed to all be cleaning the boat, they had gone off somewhere without even leaving a note and didn't return until after 10:00 p. m. Rather than do the cleaning by myself, or worse, drink over this nasty situation, I paid the shipwright extra to scrub down the decks and non-skid and was in my bunk facing the wall when they came back aboard. I was afraid if I turned around and spoke to them it would be to say, "Get the hell off my boat!"

The next morning I found a payphone and called Sandi in Philadelphia. I was so glad to hear her friendly voice. "Oh, Mom, I was just thinking of you this morning and wondering where you were. I miss you and I have good news – I'm captain of my college's women's soccer team. Isn't that great?"

"Sandi, that's fabulous. I'm so happy to hear that and so proud of you… way to go. Hey, I wondered if you might like to fly out and sail with me to Catalina Island if you haven't yet made other more exciting plans for your Thanksgiving break."

"Mom, it's freezing here in Philly and I can't think of anything I'd rather do than sail with you but I only have five days off. Guess I could cut an extra day to make it six. But worse, I can't afford the tickets."

"Here's my trusty credit card number – put the tickets on it and I'll worry about paying for them later. Book a flight to San Diego as that's the closest cheapest place to fly into. I'll call you back tonight about 8:00 p. m. your time so you can tell me which flight you're coming in on. In the meantime, I'll plot a course to San Diego and if *Sérenta* and I can't make it there in time, I'll rent a car and drive down to get you. See you in about a week. Yippee, hooray!"

While enjoying lunch by myself the next day at the Yacht Club sushi bar, I met a few other boaters who all said to be sure and check out the nearby Channel Islands. I asked the crew if they would like to sail over and they half-heartedly agreed to the side-trip. After plotting a course from Santa Barbara to Santa Cruz Island, we left early the next morning. Again, weather was perfect and we took turns at the helm, two hours on, four hours off.

We arrived that afternoon without a "challenge", my favorite word, preferring to try and stay positive by avoiding the word, "problem". Santa Cruz Island was large enough to have an inviting park but the Coastal Pilot said anchoring close to the beach was forbidden. To get off the boat other than by diving overboard, we'd have to assemble the Avon dinghy now securely stowed away on deck. This would have been a tedious task I wasn't up for as it would also involve lifting the heavy 35hp dingy motor over the side. We motored *Sérenta* around the islands and set anchor in the lea of Santa Cruz, protected against the winds and waves coming in from the open sea and close to the smallest of the islands, Anacapa.

Neither of the crew offered to cook dinner so I opened a couple of tins of sardines, broke out some crackers and opened the first of many jars of chunky peanut butter which was to become one of my staples for the next few years and often the only thing I could grab during long bad-weather passages. It was handy my brother was high up on the ladder at Procter & Gamble when I was ready to take off on this spiritual odyssey which was also becoming an emotional odyssey to discover myself. When I was outfitting the boat in Monterey, Bruce had UPS deliver to *Sérenta* some bon voyage gifts which included four cases of that wonderful nutty stuff, a case each of Folger's coffee, Charmin toilet paper, Bounty paper towels, and a few other cases of P&G products. Took quite a trick to get the glorious stuff all stored away. I even had to give away a stash of Scott-brand paper towels to make room for my brother's gifties, remembering anytime he came to visit me or Mother, he would immediately toss out anything we had anywhere in the house that was made by "Brand X" and replace it all with P&G products. I also remembered when Bruce's cousin had named his son, Scott. Bruce immediately dubbed the baby, "Brand X", privately calling the kid that for years.

What a rather unpleasant evening of zero conversations with the crew who stationed themselves way up at the bow and whispered to each other the whole time. I worked out the dead-reckoning for our next destination, Newport, and calculated we would have to be up before dawn to weigh anchor and head out to sea. The two of them groused and grumbled about having to get up early. I explained that I didn't want to be entering an unfamiliar port after dark and especially without a secured slip. We got up at 5:00 a. m. and Debra said she'd take the helm. I went forward to winch up the anchor which to my chagrin, wouldn't budge. What could possibly be keeping it stuck down there? The sun hadn't yet come up so the water was black and offered no clues. Debra started the motor and was jamming the stick into reverse, then into forward, then into reverse, then forward. She was doing this at such a fierce speed that the gears were grinding and I feared for the transmission.

"Hey, can you take it easy on that, please? You're going to damage the tranny," I called back to her from the bow. She chose to ignore me and continued to thrust the gear shift back and forth. I shouted again, "Hey, watch what you're doing—you're going to damage or break something."

"I think you better come back here," she said. "I'm not getting any response at all now from the engine."

I tried to put the boat in gear to move forward and nothing happened. I tried it in reverse, nothing happened. Oh, hell, what's wrong now, I thought as I prayed for some help from Above – any help at all, for we were completely alone in the anchorage and hadn't seen any other boats since arriving. It was mid-week and Californians seemed to limit their sailing to weekends. I was frustrated because I didn't even know what was wrong. I was also furious that she had so callously ignored my instructions to take it easy on the shifting and now had us in this helpless situation.

And then came another of God's miracles – one of many to occur during this journey. Off the starboard side was approaching a small fishing boat. I scampered below, grabbed the radio and on hailing channel 16, said, "To the fishing boat…help! This is *Sérenta*, the pink sailboat ahead of you in the anchorage."

"Switch to channel 52," came the baritone voice of a knight in shining wetsuit. "What seems to be the problem?"

"We're stuck here. I can't seem to pull up the anchor and now the gear shift isn't engaging and I can't move the boat in any direction."

"Hold on a minute. I'll anchor, get my gear together and dive down to check it out."

I couldn't believe my ears – a diver just when we needed one! Turned out he was one of those rare fellows who dive for sea urchins and later told me he only came over to Anacapa once every ten days.

He was only down for a few minutes when he surfaced, took off his mask and said, "Well, first off, you're anchored in a huge bed of kelp that came swirling around your boat last night at high tide and has your anchor completely ensnared. It'll only take me a few minutes to cut the seaweed away from your anchor with my urchin knife. That's the good news. The bad news? It's your transmission – she's about to shoot straight out the back of your boat. One of you must have really manhandled the gear shift and you won't be able to use the motor at all. I can't really help you with that problem as I've got to get down there and grab all the sea urchins before the tide comes back in. Best to call the Coast Guard. You'll have to fudge a little. I can't suggest this, but you might tell them you're stranded out in the shipping lanes or they won't help you. Want me to cut the kelp and free your anchor?"

"Gee, that would be fantastic! I can't tell you how grateful I am! I'll have some yummy homemade cookies from my stash for you when you come up for air."

I switched back to channel 16 to hail the Coast Guard and they came right back with, "Is this an emergency?"

"Not exactly, Sir, but I'm stuck out here in the shipping lanes with a disabled engine."

"What's your exact position?"

Not thinking, I told him the latitude and longitude from my last plot on the chart the day before. There was silence for a few minutes.

"You're not anywhere near the shipping lanes– you're right behind Anacapa."

Caught in a fib. So much for that attempt for a rescue. The Coast Guard wasn't as friendly here as they were up in Monterey Bay. That's Southern California for you, I thought, my childhood prejudices surfacing. As a pre-teen, I was forced to wear a hat and white gloves when going up to San Francisco with my mother to buy school clothes while I heard girls were wearing bikinis into restaurants in Los Angeles! Many of us up North refused to accept the existence of that "lower half of the State".

"All we can do is call a towing service for you," replied the Coast Guard. "Gosh, how much will that cost?"

"We can't answer that – this is an emergency channel. You'll have to figure this out for yourself. Coast Guard out."

At that point, I felt like either sitting down and crying or just jumping overboard and leaving my boat to rot there like a dock bird. The two women offered no suggestions. Debra didn't even apologize for having manhandled the gear shift and causing the problem.

"*Sérenta, Sérenta*. Switch to 32," came a man's voice through the darkness.

"Don't call the derrick – they'll charge you $600 minimum. Plot your way to Balboa, get your sails up and come out around Anacapa. I'm just getting my motor started here in the Balboa anchorage and I'll meet you half way."

"Are you a real angel? If not, you're definitely a Godsend! Do you know anything about transmissions or anyone over there in Balboa who can fix this?" "Don't worry, Skipper. I'm in the Navy and I've taught Diesel Mechanics for years. Just grab a cup of joe, put on a happy face and I'll meet you out there in a couple of hours. Stay tuned to 32 so we can keep in touch. My name's Joe and my sailboat is a Catalina 22."

The urchin diver popped up and gave me the A-OK sign and I reached over and handed him a sealed baggie with some of my famous brownies. I set the sails, ran up to the bow to finish hauling up the anchor, and cruised out of the anchorage without having to ask those two for any help at all. It was the first time I had sailed off the anchor without use of the motor and was probably grinning like a kid. The two were sitting in the cockpit stony-faced like a pair of grim reapers. I tried to think positive thoughts -- I didn't want their foul moods to spoil my latest nautical triumph. The sun was up and the airs were light enough to make it a sweet little sail. About noon, I heard Joe's voice on the radio saying he could vaguely see us through the haze.

"I'm looking through my binoculars. Is there a lot of pink on your boat?"

"Yep, that's me, alright, but I can't see you yet."

"Look off your starboard, maybe 10 degrees."

"Hey, I see ya! This is so nice of you, Joe. I can hardly believe it."

"That's what sailing is all about – we help each other."

When we were a couple of boat lengths from him, he came about and we followed his boat to the Balboa harbor. Via radio, he instructed us to pull alongside the end-tie at the first dock as he had already gotten permission for our disabled boat to dock there while we made the repairs. As soon as we were tied up, he came aboard and wanted to get started immediately as this was his only day off to help us. He wasn't thrilled with the lack of maneuvering space available to work on the Yanmar, but by the end of the day had everything back ship-shape. He refused to take even a bag of cookies for all his help, simply saying he believed in "giving back." I wondered if he knew Dr. Bob and Bill Wilson, the two founders of my recovery program. I didn't ask. Kissed him on both cheeks and waved goodbye as we pulled out of the harbor feeling gratefully blessed.

Newport Beach was our next port of call and I radioed ahead to the Bahia Corinthian Yacht Club to request a guest slip for a few days. I figured I'd never get the boat to San Diego in time for Sandi's arrival and would have to make arrangements for a rental car. The Yacht Club offered a reciprocity slip for three nights and said we should radio them when outside the harbor. Their steward would meet us at the end of the dock to point out our slip. I cruised into the small harbor after reconnecting with them on the radio. Standing on the end of the dock was their silver-haired steward wearing a navy blue blazer with shiny brass buttons, spotless white pants with the *de rigueur* crease down the center of each pant leg, and traditional white leather docksider shoes.

As I coasted *Sérenta* with ease into the slip, pleased with my maneuvering, he said in a stiff upper-lipped pseudo-British accent, "My, my. If it isn't the Mary Kay boat."

I ignored him and once docked, told crew I would be leaving the boat in the morning to drive down to San Diego to pick up my daughter and bring her back for Thanksgiving. The crew had previously agreed it would be fun to spend Thanksgiving on Catalina Island as I had told them it was a holiday when many cruisers would head over to Two Harbors on the far side of the island, some dressed up as Indians, others as pilgrims. For many years, the Harbor Reef Restaurant, the only restaurant in Two Harbors, had been putting on a Thanksgiving feast for all who showed up.

I didn't feel bad leaving them in Newport Beach as it was just a short walk from the yacht club to all the artsy-fartsy shops and eateries. I told them I'd be back in two days, rented a car (decided I needed to lift my spirits and splurged on a convertible), and zoomed south to San Diego. The ride back to Newport Beach was fun as Sandi and I had months of news to catch up on. She was back with her old boyfriend she had dated in high school. Although I was disappointed – he hadn't worked for years and was on some sort of disability pay – I didn't say anything. Sandi had received a soccer scholarship to Kutztown College and not only was she a fabulous soccer player, she was also extremely bright and talented. I hoped once she got away to college, she would hook up with someone with a little more ambition. Before we got to Newport, I warned her that the situation on board was a little tense (putting it mildly) but maybe things were better now that the two women had had some shore leave.

They were polite to Sandi, addressing comments directly to her, totally ignoring me and acting as if I were a pink elephant in the middle of the cockpit. I decided we could sleep in the next morning as there would be plenty of time to get to Catalina before dark. The sail over was beautiful in spite of the negative attitudes of the two women. We got safely around to the other side of the island and hailed the anchorage on the radio.

"Take any of the available moorings you see," the guy said. He mumbled something about the mooring buoys. There were anchoring tethers under the surface, and sticking up from these were fishing pole "blinds" to be grabbed to pull up the tethers so the actual buoy line attached to the tether would be accessible to tie around the boat's bow cleat. I dropped the sails, put the engine in neutral, and at a snail's pace, we glided up to the only available mooring buoy we saw. Sandi reached out and grabbed the fiberglass "blind", clutching it tightly in her hand. *Sérenta* hadn't completely come to a stop and I couldn't see what she was doing up at the bow, but apparently, the fiberglass "blind" was slipping through her hand while *Sérenta* was coming slowly to a halt when she was finally able to reach over the side, pull up the tether, grab the buoy line and loop it around our cleat. As she came back towards me at the helm, I saw her hand was bleeding. She hadn't let out a peep, but the "blind" was so old, the fiberglass had perished and Sandi's hand was imbedded with shards of needle-like fiberglass. In several places, her palm was actually punctured. The anchorage boss came out in a dinghy and I showed him her hand and asked his advice on what to do.

"No hospital 'round these parts 'cept way down in Avalon. Here, hop in and I'll take you quick like to the Harbor Master and we'll see what he says."

"Can the other two women come with us? I don't want to take precious time to tackle the job of getting our dinghy and its motor overboard and into the water."

"Sure, that's what I'm here for ...to shuttle boaters back and forth, but tell 'em we don't have any time to waste. The Harbor Master leaves at 4:00 p. m. sharp and that's in a few minutes, but more important...the last bus heading to Avalon leaves at 4:30 p. m."

We all jumped into his shuttle, and once ashore, Sandi and I ran up to the Harbor Master's office and showed him her hand. He said we better take the bus to the hospital in Avalon which would be a two-hour ride. I said the harbor ought to pay for our bus tickets (which weren't cheap) because it was their fault we had to go. He agreed she needed a tetanus shot and paid for both our roundtrip tickets. The bus was already at the bus stop ready to leave, so no time to eat. I figured we'd go right to the hospital then get dinner afterwards. The two women said they didn't want to spend their own money on bus tickets. I didn't offer to pay since I didn't feel it my duty to pay for crew side trips, especially since we weren't going to Avalon for pleasure but being forced to go because of Sandi's medical emergency. Besides, they hadn't even got up off their bums to help Sandi with the buoy-line task.

"My daughter and I'll be back tomorrow. There's only one return bus and it gets back about noon. Will you please make reservations for tomorrow's Thanksgiving dinner – there's only one seating, at 5:00 p. m. and I can treat us all." They both walked off without even a "will do" or a "thank-you".

Once at the hospital, I decided to have a tetanus shot as well just so Sandi wouldn't feel so bad. We had fish 'n chips in a cute little outdoor eaterie overlooking the harbor, walked around Avalon, gorging ourselves on ice cream and fudge, and peeking in the windows of all the quaint Victorian cottages. For our overnight stay, we chose the least expensive of the numerous B&Bs. After a hearty breakfast, we hopped onto the bus back to *Sérenta* and the "Sisters Grim" (a name Sandi dubbed them after only an hour in their presence). Thanksgiving dinner was wonderful – real comfort food. The entertainment provided by the Indians and pilgrims, with a few pirates thrown in, was a relief from the otherwise totally silent meal. As expected, the two women didn't even thank me for dinner which had been quite pricey and way beyond my budget.

The next day we sailed back to Bahia Corinthian Yacht Club to another complimentary stay. That night, Sandi and I went to what was for me, a well-needed meeting. Turned out, much to my surprise, she had been going to meetings herself back in Philadelphia. When we got back to the yacht club, I told her I wanted to stop at the club's bathroom before walking down to the boat. She followed me into the ladies' room and I began to bawl.

Sandi put her arms around me and recited some of the things we both had been learning at our meetings: "This, too, will pass" and "As long as you don't pick up a drink or a drug over this, things will get better." It was as if she were a stand-in for Marjorie, my program sponsor, who had died after a lengthy battle with cancer and just after I left for California. Sandi and I hugged each other, the first real woman-to-woman hug we ever shared. It felt really wonderful. The next morning, as I drove her back to San Diego, I asked if it was my paranoia, or did she think the two women were acting belligerent and nasty.

"Mom, I thought you'd never ask. I don't know how you've put up so long with those two winged death-spirit harpies. Get those damned bitches off your boat!"

Sandi got on her flight home after our fun top-down ride along scenic Highway One to San Diego. When I got back to the boat that afternoon, I told the women it wasn't working out for me and probably not for them either. They had two options: either get off *Sérenta* right then and there in Newport and I would give them money for bus tickets back to Santa Cruz, or stay on and disembark in San Diego where they would have a better chance of finding other crew positions. Bus tickets were not included in the second option and I was crossing all my fingers and toes they would choose the first option. Thank goodness they took the bus fare and got off without a word. Whew, what a relief to have my beloved *Sérenta* tranquil and peaceful, all to myself once again. I thought I heard her breathe a sigh of relief, too!

As soon as I got rid of those two women, I left Newport that afternoon and single-handed the approximate 70 nautical miles down to San Diego, navigating my way through the Saturday night traffic-infested waters off Los Angeles, steering clear of oil derricks by night, and dodging freighters, submarines and pleasure craft by day. The only real tense moment was when the wind had died down and I heard men talking to each other, their conversation somehow bleeding through to my single-sideband radio. It continued for a few minutes. No vessel of any kind was anywhere in sight, and I realized they were on a submarine directly beneath me.

I got on my radio and said, "Hey, you guys better move your sub away from my sailboat. You're right under me and I hear everything you're saying, and I sure as hell don't want you coming up through my hull, either!"

"My, God!" was the only reply, and I didn't hear them anymore.

The single-handed sail to San Diego was tough, but not nearly as bad as it would have been if those two women were still aboard. Yes, back in Newport, a thousand-pound barbell of stress had been lifted off my worn out but beautifully sun-tanned shoulders.

Somewhere off Laguna Beach, I heard my Captain say, once again, "Don't worry, Sandra. Everything is going to be alright!" And I believed Him this time, too.

Chapter Nineteen

A Salty Pup Signs On With Peppermint Patty

I arrived the next day outside the entrance to the San Diego Harbor, totally exhausted. Because of all the maritime activity around L. A., I hadn't been able to grab any shut-eye. I dropped sails, turned on the motor so I could control my approach to the harbor, and got on Channel 16.

"This is the sailing vessel *Sérenta* outside the harbor. To any marina…I need a slip for an indefinite period. Anyone have something to accommodate my 35-foot Ericson? Come back, please."

Silence, so I repeated the message. "*Sérenta* here looking for a slip. Come back, please."

"You're never going to find a slip in San Diego," came a reply. "It's the America's Cup trials. O'Connor is stunning everyone and San Diego has been booked solid for at least a year, even two in some marinas."

"Switch to 32," came another voice.

"Are there no slips at all?" I queried on 32.

"*Andiamo*, here. None in the entire harbor. Even the free anchorages are full. I'd say you're up shit's creek without a slip. Better head back towards Santa Monica."

"But I'm totally bushed – can't hardly keep the peepers open. I've just single-handed from Newport and had no idea the Cup trials were going on. Doesn't anyone have anything at all?"

"This is Harbor Island Marina," came a woman's friendly voice. "I'll check with our Harbor Master. Stay tuned to 32."

Her reply was taking forever, forcing me to aimlessly motor back and forth outside the harbor. I felt like I'd rather scuttle *Sérenta* right there than sail north against wind and tides back towards Los Angeles. This whole sailing adventure was turning into a dismal disaster. Why did I ever think I could do this? It must have been a moment of complete madness when I came up with this scheme but I had so much invested in the boat, I owed so much on the credit cards, that it would be ridiculous to abandon ship before the voyage had even really begun. What would I do, anyway, if I gave it all up? Try to start all over back in ice cold Philadelphia? Go back to living aboard in Santa Cruz amidst the blue-tent city rubble and political polemics? No way!

"*Sérenta*, Harbor Island here. Our Harbor Master has found you a temporary slip for a few nights. Head into the harbor and anyone can steer you to us – we're kinda across from the airport."

"Thank the Lord," I shouted into the mike. "I'll need a live-aboard permit as well until I can decide what to do with the rest of my life."

"Oh, no!" she said. "We have a 14-year waiting list here for live-aboard permits."

"This is awful. I can't just sail around in circles and I don't know what I'm going to do next. I left Santa Cruz almost a month ago and this has not been easy."

"Stay tuned. I'll get right back to you."

More tacking back and forth, trying to stay awake while I awaited the answer that would define my destiny for at least the next few days.

"*Sérenta*, he's issued a temporary live-aboard permit. We're here ready to welcome you."

I knew that as long as I lived, I would never forget the warmth in that woman's voice and the name of that wonderful Harbor Island Marina. I motored into the harbor where boats were tied up in every conceivable space and facing every possible direction. They had even built new docks to accommodate the Cup crowds. As I motored along past other sailboats, boaters on deck would wave, then shout, "Welcome, *Sérenta*" and point me in the direction of the marina. I wanted to cry. These were the first kind and friendly gestures I'd received since I took on that mean-spirited crew. Maybe sailing away wouldn't be that bad after all. The Harbor Master was waiting to help me tuck *Sérenta* into her new slip. I accepted his assistance with pleasure and gratitude.

"I can see you're not up for signing documents. Stop by the office in the morning and we'll take care of the paperwork then. And above all, don't worry, *Sérenta*. Everything's gonna be alright," he said, putting an arm around me and giving me a warm squeeze. His hug was as comforting as when Mother would rarely cuddle me as a kid when I'd fallen out of our apricot tree trying to reach that fat juicy one.

I splashed on some of my precious Arpège perfume (my talisman ever since those glorious days in France), climbed into the V-berth, pulled the flowery comforter across and let the tears cascade onto the pillow. I didn't know why I was sobbing – for joy, for fear, or for sadness – but somehow the salty tears were just fine. I remembered what seemed eons ago back in Philadelphia when I first heard the words, "Everything's going to be alright", whispered to me when I was meditating on my Victorian chaise. I wondered if God had been teaching those same words to all the people I would meet on this adventure. Just like back then on the chaise, I drifted into peaceful sleep, not worrying about whether to continue to sail or not to sail, but knowing I was exactly where I was meant to be

I woke up an hour later with someone banging on my bow. This was when I first learned you knock on the bow as a doorbell signal rather than walking down the dock alongside a boat where you'd see everything below deck and possibly catch the skipper nude or in a compromising position. The banging persisted. I got up and popped my head out through the forward hatch to see a woman standing there with a big old dog on a leash. She was wearing spring-a-lator heels from the '50s with clear plastic sandal straps and rhinestones embedded in the stiletto heels. I remembered in 8th grade going to a school dance wearing the same glitzy heels with my black-felt pink poodle skirt. Why someone would wear skinny heels on a wooden dock was a conundrum. It would be tricky to keep the heels from slipping into the cracks between the boards. As my eyes wandered up, next came fake suede pants as tight as if sprayed on and a cotton knit V-neck shirt plunging practically down to the navel with a bright-sequined blue and green peacock embroidered on each breast. Then came the face, almost all hidden behind huge black Hollywood sunglasses, and all this topped off with 1960s-style black big-hair teased and frizzed to the max. I later found out it was a wig.

"Where's your dog?" she growled with a deep Boston accent.

"I don't have a dog," I stammered, still half asleep.

"Well, you shouldn't be alone on a boat without a dog."

I looked at the big beast she had beside her, half Dingo and half German Shepherd, and trying to sound diplomatic, I said, "Oh, that's a really nice dog you have there, but I wouldn't have room for such a big one."

"This is Bandit, my baby. I wouldn't dream of parting with him. I mean you need your own dog. So you come from Santa Cruz, eh? I heard the whole thing on the radio. Where you going next?"

"I'm not sure I want to continue this madness and mayhem. So far it's been pretty awful. Are you on a boat here?"

"Yes. Well, sort of."

I could tell she wasn't about to go away so invited her on board and climbed up to sit beside her in the cockpit. Her name was Clare and she explained when her mother recently died, she inherited some money and bought an old Ericson 26 in the harbor because her husband hated boats and wouldn't come near it. I didn't quite understand until she explained they lived about two hours east of San Diego.

"I have to spend weekends with the old man but then I can hardly wait to get back down to my boat Tuesday mornings and have some time away from the old codger. I actually left him this morning after church because he was acting so beastly. So that means I get some extra days on my boat this week...don't have to be back home 'til Friday. Yippee!"

She broke into a fit of hearty laughter which her dog completely ignored – he must have been used to it. This was interesting – a reverse from the scenario where White Pants had a boat to get away from The Little Lady and have a martini-sipping love nest for his mistress. From that moment, I knew I was going to like this eccentric old gal.

"Hey, what you doing for dinner? Want to join me? Then after we eat, if you like, I'll show you my boat. It's about five docks over. Nothing fancy, you understand, but it's freedom.

Are you ready? We can walk to the restaurant. Has a great view of the harbor and the food is wonderful. If we get in before 5:00 p. m., we get the blue-hair discount."

Even though I could probably sleep for at least 24 hours and needed it, I knew after all I'd been through for the past few weeks, to be in her convivial company would be far more nourishing and healing than any amount of sleep. Ah, what a delight...the smell of simmering clam chowder, garlic, and real sourdough French bread greeting us as we entered the restaurant. I splurged and ordered some of the incredible thick chowder followed by lobster and shrimp thermidor and then a huge slice of luscious key lime pie ...all beyond my budget but oh, so worth it and, not to mention, well-deserved!

Clare and I walked back to her boat where we sat and gabbed for hours. She invited me to go shopping with her the next day. As I hadn't been inside a boat-unrelated store for almost a month, I accepted and said I could be ready about 11:00 a. m. as I had to stop by the Harbor Master's to sign papers first. As promised, he had the papers all ready and I was thankful to learn I now had a slip for six months and it was renewable, plus a one-year live-aboard permit, also renewable.

On the dot of 11:00 a. m., Clare was knocking on my bow, and the first of many "Clare Escapades" began. I soon teasingly dubbed her, "Thrift Store Queen of San Diego" as we established a habit of spending almost entire afternoons driving from one store to another with Bandit hanging out in the backseat. She said over the years, she had found lots of antiques at the Salvation Army and other such humble havens and her garage back home was filled to the rafters with treasured finds. She admitted there was even a vintage Rolls-Royce covered with a blue tarp sitting in her driveway which she hadn't driven since the day it was towed there from the auction house over a year before. What eccentricity! What delight! When Clare left on Friday morning to return to her connubial commitments, I felt a bit lost. I knew if I ever left San Diego, I would miss her jovial outlook and her devil-may-care attitude which was getting infectious.

I spent that first weekend in San Diego tidying up my boat, reading the chapter on anchoring in my nautical "Bible", the <u>Annapolis Book of Sailing</u>, and listening to classical music on the local NPR station. Thank goodness my little radio picked up the station, loud and clear! On Monday I realized I didn't have any plans for fast-approaching Christmas now that I wasn't going to be cruising. The thought of spending Christmas alone was depressing. To avoid falling into a pity-pot which is always a convenient place to pick up a drink, I called a friend who had moved to Tucson from Philadelphia about the same time I left for California. We had kept in touch over the years but never managed to arrange a visit.

"I can't believe it's you," she said. "Where are you?"

"I'm on my sailboat in San Diego. I've kinda come to a temporary or maybe even a full stop from the cruising life. What are you doing for Christmas? Thought you might like to come out to San Diego for a little break. There's plenty of room on board – I got rid of the crew. It would be fun hearing about all your adventures since we last saw each other."

"I sorta have a new beau," she replied. "He's coming over to help me and my daughter cook Christmas dinner. It would be great to have you join us. Why don't you hop on one of the commuter flights a few days before Christmas and I'll pick you up at Tucson International."

"That sounds wonderful. And thanks. I was kinda crying in my alcohol-free vino at the thought of being alone for Christmas. I'll call you when I get the flight lined up."

I could hardly wait for that first Tuesday morning when the clip-clop of Clare's high heels on the wooden dock would announce her arrival. I could tell her of my Christmas plans and ask her if she'd be able to pop by my boat the week I'd be gone to make sure the breaker hadn't blown, spoiling all the food I had in the miniscule fridge-freezer.

After another week of just hanging out, repairing everything that came loose or broke on the voyage, restocking the larder and going "thrifting" with Clare, I began to think I might someday be ready for more solo-sailing. To bolster the finances, I took a bus over to West Marine on Shelter Island to see about a job, explaining I would be gone from December 23rd to the 31st. They hired me right away as they were already into the busy Christmas season and my former West Marine boss back at the main offices in Watsonville had given a terrific reference.

I took my 16 year-old Raleigh two-speed bike off *Sérenta's* stern and pedaled all week along the shoulder of the freeway, to and from West Marine. It was exhausting, dangerous and probably illegal. I then hit on the idea to commute across the bay by dinghy which turned out to be a lot more fun. I just tied my Avon up to the Shelter Island dinghy dock and walked a block to work. Working for $5/hour wasn't too bad but what really got to me was meeting all the boaters coming in to outfit their boats for ports unknown. When they found out I had given up on cruising, they'd chastise me and say I should just bite the bullet and take off. It now started to sound like I was a fearful ne'er-do-well. This was all fine for them…guys with girlfriends or wives to help them. I was a woman alone with hardly any experience to boot!

When Clare knocked on my boat the Tuesday before I was due to fly to Tucson, I looked up to see her cuddling something in a blue blanket.

"Look, I brought you an early Christmas gift. He's five weeks old. I paid $50 for him but if you can't afford it, I'll just give him to you."

She stepped into the cockpit, pulled back the blanket to reveal a Chihuahua puppy smiling up at me.

"Oh, Clare," I winced. "I can't take a baby dog. And besides, you know I've just made reservations to fly to Tucson for Christmas and I'll be gone a week."

"Don't worry. I'll take care of him while you're gone. He's no trouble at all."

The Tucson visit was a disaster. My friend acted as if I was trying to steal her new boyfriend just because he kept plying me with questions about all my sailing experiences. Christmas dinner was dismal. For the next two days, she went off somewhere early each morning with her boyfriend, leaving me to fend for myself out in some neighborhood far from downtown and *sans* vehicle. The third morning when she had gone off early again without saying anything, I left a note explaining I was going back to my boat a few days early and caught a cab to the airport. I could hardly wait to get back to the sanctuary of *Sérenta*. Once I'd gotten rid of the Sisters Grim, I now realized how quickly I'd forgotten what "real life" was like, with all its petty jealousies and ego-driven behaviors. Once back aboard my boat, I felt grateful to have given, at least for the moment, that sort of life the slip.

It was Thursday so Clare would still be in the harbor. *Sérenta* looked wonderful resting calmly in her slip. I opened all the hatches to fill the cabin with fresh air, put some classical music on the tape deck, made a mug of hot chocolate and a pitcher of sun tea to set out on the deck for the next day, and grabbed some cheese and crackers. As I was splashing on some Giorgio and ready to hit the sack for the night, I heard the clip-clops.

"Sandra, Sandra! You're back. Look who I have here," she squealed, holding up the little blanket-wrapped bundle.

"Is that the Chihuahua?" I asked, trying to sound nonchalant and a bit disinterested.

"Yes, and I just love this dog. While you were gone, he slept with me every night. He's so sweet and lovable and I'll miss him now that you're back."

"Why don't you just keep him, then, Clare? He's used to you and won't be happy here with me."

"Oh no you don't. I bought him for you and that's that," she declared, stepping into the cockpit with the puppy. I figured I'd have to accept him for the moment, but then in the morning before she'd leave to go back to her husband, I'd take him to her boat and tell her I just couldn't keep him. I would say he chewed all my lines and tinkled in the bunks.

"I can't stay," she said. "Have to get back to my boat and pack up everything as I'm leaving in the morning. Here's a leash and a bag of food and be sure to put out water. I've already given him his dinner and he's done his you-know-what so he's ready for bed. I'll see you tomorrow before I leave."

The puppy was darling, it was true, but as I'd never owned a puppy, I had no idea how to deal with one...and especially on a boat. The only dog I had ever owned was 30 years ago in high school when I inherited Robespierre, the little poodle a schoolmate's mother had left to me in her will. When I came home from college that first year, to my dismay, Mother, without even telling me, had given Robie to the local pound, claiming he had tried to bite my father.

"OK," I said to the Chihuahua. "It's bedtime. Now, you sleep over there on that bunk and I'll sleep here in the quarter berth. Got that?"

He jumped right up into his bunk and snuggled his head into the corner. Wow, this is easy, I thought, as I covered him with the blanky Clare had left, turned off the cabin lantern and crawled into my bunk. I wasn't in bed three minutes when I heard him softly jump down from his bunk, followed by the pitter-patter of little paws on the cabin sole. Next he jumped up onto my bunk and was stealthily pushing his way down inside my sleeping bag. He crawled all the way down to my toes and lay there as still as could be. Then without any apparent reason, he started madly struggling to get back up and out of my sleeping bag. His little head appeared next to my face, he licked my cheek, and then turned around and crawled back down to my feet – he had forgotten to give me a goodnight kiss. I knew I now had a dog!

He slept the whole night through without a squeak. In the morning, I leashed him up and took him for a walk and he tinkled on the first dock post as if he had been doing it there for years. I decided while he was on board, I would train him to tinkle on a flat, coiled line at the bow which I could then easily shake overboard to rinse off. He learned that procedure in short order as well and even did his "poop" on the coiled line. It was amazing to me later out to sea in huge storms that when he had to go, he'd crawl up the ladder from below, using his neck for leverage against the next rung up, turning around at each step until he reached the cockpit. Then he'd clamber up onto what we boaters call the "doghouse" and do his business atop there. He must have had a second sense it was too dangerous in stormy weather to crawl up to the bow. I'd then just take a bucket later and wash it all off the doghouse, simple as that.

Clare showed up about 10:00 a. m.. I told her the puppy would make a great crew member aboard *Sérenta* and I had named him "Teak". He was the exact color of all the beautiful teak on my boat and if I ever did sail away, I knew I wouldn't be able to take up precious space with teak oil and cleaning products and the teak would eventually turn a whitish grey. This way, I'd always remember how pretty my teak originally was every time I looked at the puppy.

It wouldn't be too long before Teak would be proving his worth many times over. I am sure it was his fierce lip-curled growls as he stood on his hind legs leaning on the stern rail that fended off the drug dealer's ship chasing Sandi and me for two days on our way to Cabo San Lucas. The pirate captain must have had binoculars, and I could just hear him snarling, "We better leave this boat alone…she's got an ankle-biter aboard!" It was Teak who stood guard aboard *Sérenta* anytime I had to go ashore in dangerous surroundings so my boat would be safe for me when I returned. It was Teak who stayed in the dinghy until I got back from an errand, ready to bite anyone who came near the line that held my daisy-decorated Avon fast to a dock or mooring. And it was Teak who, one day in La Paz, bested a vagrant Mexican who made the mistake of opening the side door of my loaded-to-the-gills supply-filled van, letting Teak escape when I had gone into a little *tienda* for a Coca-Cola. When I came out, there was Teak growling as he maintained his challenging stance at the bottom of a tree with the hombre as high up in the boughs as he could climb.

Teak also caught the eye of everyone I met in the Southern Hemisphere. People would stop their cars in the middle of busy intersections and come running over to ask if they could mate their dog with mine. As I didn't know how to say "neutered" in Spanish, I told them in my best Spanish that my dog could no longer have babies. Teak was a huge hit when the full solar eclipse hit the Baja. Everyone was holding up the small piece of welder's glass which the government made us all buy (at outrageous prices!) to protect our eyes. I bought a Mexican puppet just to get its wide-brimmed sombrero, then cut two holes in the hat for Teak's ears. Wearing his new sombrero, my Chihuahua buddy "walked proudly in the street" (as my old Beatnik-days friend Ferlinghetti said in one of his poems) while I explained to one and all that he couldn't be bothered holding the welder glass so he bought himself a sombrero. He was the star of Tokyo's television news of the eclipse. Their camera crew followed us down the *Malecón*, the main seaside esplanade in La Paz, while we wound our way amongst all the other eclipse *aficionados*.

I always got a kick out of telling the locals, *"El hable Español pero el wow-wow-wow in Ingles."* They'd double over with laughter and Teak and I always knew we had just made new friends.

Chapter Twenty

Cruising With A Hillbilly, A Gorgeous Blonde, And A Lovable Pooch

On January 10th, a day before my 48th birthday, I got a letter forwarded to San Diego from my post office box back in Santa Cruz. It was from a 45-year old guy named Billy Joe writing from Kentucky in response to the classified ad under "Crew Wanted" I had placed the year before in *Latitude 38*, a free sailing rag most boaters read in Northern California and beyond.

My ad read: "Seeking M/F crew for circumnavigation departing S. F. October. N/S, no drugs/alcohol. Mechanical aptitude preferred. Opera-lover a plus. Must pay own personal expenses. Minimum 5-year voyage aboard Ericson 35. Contact Sandra Smith, PO Box 9433, Santa Cruz, CA".

Billy Joe claimed he had recently sailed all over the South Pacific with a woman skipper aboard her 70-foot cargo schooner. He was also well-accustomed to the 12-volt life, living for the past eight years in a converted school bus.

"Call me collect. Let's talk," he wrote. "I'm planning to be out in California in about two weeks – maybe we can meet."

This unexpected development threw me into a tailspin. Did I still really want to go cruising? Did I want to deal with crew again? Did I honestly feel up for a long journey where I might not see or even talk to my children for extended periods? What was I supposed to be doing with my life, anyway... frittering it away under sail? hanging out feeling useless in San Diego? One can just go to so many thrift stores a week. What was the point, anyway, of "thrifting" when there was no room aboard for anything bigger than the sterling silver thimble I still owned years later?

The day before the letter arrived, Clare was driving us to thrift shops all around San Diego while Teak remained back on *Sérenta* as he'd had enough of "thrifting". As we passed the San Diego Open-air Market, Clare explained it was the biggest place in San Diego to hunt for neat things but added she'd never been inside the market. Pouting a bit, she said she wished we could go in.

"Well, why not?"

"Oh, they'll never allow a dog and I couldn't possibly leave Bandit in the car that long – it's too hot and he'd die before we got halfway around the place."

"I've got an idea. Head to their parking lot."

"What do you mean? We can't go in there with a dog."

"Not to worry – I have a plan."

We parked the car and I told her to get Bandit out, put him on a leash and to go along with whatever would ensue but above all, not to open her mouth.

We walked up to the gate and the uniformed guard said, "No dogs allowed."

"But, Sir, this is a hearing-ear dog," I replied.

"Hearing-ear dog? I ain't ever heard of one of them?"

"Well, you've heard of seeing-eye dogs, right? My friend here is deaf and this is her hearing-ear dog. He's a service dog so you have to let us in, it's the law."

While the guy went off to check with his supervisor, Clare could hardly contain herself.

"Sandra, we're going to be in big trouble if this backfires."

"Don't worry, but whatever you do, don't say a word."

The old guard came back and said he was told to let us in. We waltzed through the gate and into the biggest collection of booths and stands selling used versions of every little or big thing ever made. It seemed to go on for acres and Clare went into a shopping frenzy. I followed her around doing my best sign language imitation when she'd look at me dumbly holding up some item she couldn't live without. She was sifting through loose pieces of sterling silverware when I moseyed over to look at old books in another booth. When I turned around less than 10 minutes later, I was horrified to see an older woman standing next to Clare making sign language to her. Clare looked over at me with a helpless expression.

I made my way back to her as fast as I could through the avid "thrifters" and mumbled to the other woman, "We're late for her doctor's appointment." We broke an Olympic record dashing for the nearest exit with Bandit loping gaily along after us.

Once in the safety of her car, I said, "Clare, what do you think about this latest development? A hillbilly from Kentucky wants to come out and stay on my boat for a week while he looks for a crew position to go sailing. He saw my old ad for crew and I think he's hoping to talk me into going cruising and taking him with me."

"Sandra, you better watch out. I hear they have a lot of murderers in Kentucky these days."

"Well, I'll be working all day and he only wants to use my boat as a base for a week while he talks to other skippers seeking crew."

"I don't think it's a good idea, Sandra. He might slit your throat in the night."

This was the first inkling I had of Clare's paranoia when any man, for whatever reason, showed an interest in me. More to the point, she probably just didn't want to lose her thrifting buddy.

A fellow I had often seen in the harbor and who had an older full-keeled Ericson in the free anchorage asked me the week before if I would consider crewing on his boat down the Baja, but I told him I wanted to eventually do the same with my own boat. He came up with an idea where he would crew my boat down and we'd leave *Sérenta* safely in a marina slip. We'd take the bus back to San Diego and then I'd crew his boat down. It seemed like a great solution as neither of us would have to single-hand. I told him I'd think about it. He asked Clare a few days later if she would drive him to the supermarket so he could pick up some groceries and in exchange, he'd help clean her decks. He met me at West Marine after work and Clare picked us up and drove us across San Diego to a shopping mall with a gigantic Safeway. As soon as he got out of the car, as I was opening my door, she shouted at me to close the door and off we roared, leaving him standing dumb-founded in the parking lot.

"What's wrong, Clare? We can't just leave him standing there in the rain. It's miles back to the harbor."

"Didn't you see the knife in his boot? He's planning to kill you, I swear. He's a madman. You mustn't let him near you again. He's surely the guy who killed that older woman downtown last week, remember?"

I never saw him again, but a year later, I heard he'd single-handed his boat down the Baja, and halfway down the coast, ended up ship-wrecked on the beach in a storm. While he tramped off in the desert to look for help, the locals came from far and wide and stripped the boat of everything that wasn't bolted down and even some things that were… it was the way of the Baja. According to rumor or legend, in the old days, the Baja natives would re-arrange candlelit channel-marking buoys so boats would go on the rocks or reefs in the darkness, ripe and ready to be plundered.

That rainy night, I phoned Billy Joe in Kentucky. He sounded innocuous enough so I told him he could come out and stay on my boat for a week although I would be working all day. I made it clear I wasn't looking for romance and that he shouldn't be coming with any thoughts of crewing for me. I had long since given up the idea of sailing off. He flew out and stayed the week. I hardly ever saw him. We had dinner out a couple of nights, but in the morning he was still asleep in his bunk when I left to get across the bay in time for work. I really didn't get to know him. He wasn't my type, anyway... big and burly with a fat belly and had never been to an opera. As soon as he got back to Kentucky, he started phoning. He wasn't pushy, but kept saying we'd make a good team going down the Baja and I should reconsider. I made it through January without taking *Sérenta* out. It seemed too much trouble to stow everything and go out there just for an hour or so. Besides, as I hadn't been able to bike to many meetings, I didn't have any friends to invite along.

It wasn't long before I became aware of how much I missed my car. I could ride my bike a lot of places. I could dinghy to work. I could go off with Clare. But I hadn't been without my own car for this long and realized I was going through wheels withdrawal. Plus, there was no speedy getaway car to escape real or imagined demons. When I was still drinking, I used to think it would be neat to put my MGB up on blocks in the garage of our suburban home. When I was home alone, I could simply get in, turn on the motor, listen to the engine purr, and sit behind the wheel dreaming of all the places I was running away to, all in the comfort of my own garage. Plus, I wouldn't have to worry about being arrested for driving under the influence or worse, killing someone.

On the last night in January, with fog enveloping *Sérenta*, I was down in the cabin struggling on the accordion with another Chopin nocturne when the phone rang. It was Billy Joe again.

"Still having fun out there? Tired of working yet? Ready to take off?"

"I don't know what to think, Billy Joe. I feel it is really dumb working for just $5 an hour but it does keep me off the streets and outta trouble. Yet I feel I was cut out for more than this. I know you're not into the God stuff, but I keep meditating and asking what I'm supposed to be doing and there isn't ever an answer. It's totally frustrating – I want the answer N-O-W," spelling it out for him.

Impatience was one of my many character defects that had been surfacing the longer I was in my recovery program. I had been trying to correct this one, working on it over and over, with help from the program Steps. This sailing business was sure a good opportunity to work further on it.

"Well, since the last time we talked, I've sorted through and gotten rid of all the useless junk I've been hanging onto. I've built a still for making potable water and a dehydrator for drying fruits and veggies. Got 'em both workin' real good here. I've also found someone interested in buying the old bus."

"Your contraptions sound, uhhhh, interesting. I wonder if they'd work out on the High Seas."

"Why, not? You'd just have to make sure they were tied down. We could have the water- making machine at work while on anchor. Now, remember, I told you I'd pay my share of the eats and I can pitch in and fix anything that goes bust. I think you need to quit sticking like a hog in mud and get out of that dang fog you're in – we'd have a darned good time."

The next day, February 1st, I called Sandi in Philly to say, "White rabbits, white rabbits." It was an old family tradition my father had introduced to us as kids. The first of the month, before saying a thing to someone, you say "white rabbits, white rabbits" which brings them good luck for the entire month. When Bruce and I were young and always in the same elementary class, on the first of each month, we'd both jump up, run to the classroom windows and shout the good-luck slogan. For a few months, the other kids in the class would run to the windows to look for rabbits until they finally figured out that they were being duped.

When I spoke with Sandi, she confessed she had quit college before Christmas and was working in a print shop.

"What's the weather like back there?" I asked, knowing of course it would be bad.

"Oh, the usual…snow and slush. I spent 20 minutes scraping the ice off my windshield this morning and was late for this damned job."

"What, you're not enjoying the job?" I said, trying to act casual when my heart was pounding like a jackhammer with the thought of asking her The Big Question!

"I've gotten real good at every aspect of it already and now it's bo--- ring. I should probably have stayed in school, but studying Old Masters and designing jewelry wasn't the most exciting thing in the world. Plus, I had to get away from the drug dealer who'd taken a fancy to me. He was showering me with all kinds of free drugs which I'd give away to my friends. It was all getting totally stale, especially since I didn't dare use any of them, myself."

Here goes: "Sandi, how would you like to fly out and go cruising with me? There's this guy in Kentucky who has been out here already to meet me and check out *Sérenta*. He wants to go down the Baja with me. He's a harmless old hillbilly. You could put the ticket on that same credit card I gave you when you flew out for Thanksgiving. You'd have to get out here pretty quick before I change my mind about taking off…it's a tough decision I'm making."

"Mom, I'll grab the next flight and since you said during our last conversation that *Sérenta* is right across the street from the airport, I'll just catch a cab over. Gosh, I can't believe we're going to do this!"

"Think small and don't bring your entire wardrobe. Do bring some sweatshirts and sweatpants as it gets cold out there, one or two pair of shorts, a couple of t-shirts, a slicker for rain, a few bikinis, plenty of sunscreen and a pair of sunglasses. Whatever you forget or need, we can pick up here before we shove off. My friend Clare will be happy to drive us anywhere."

I phoned Billy Joe the next evening and told him Sandi was flying out and I was going to leave within two weeks as I had given West Marine notice that morning.

"I'd like to leave on Valentine's Day – it sounds lucky and it's not a Friday."

"Fannnnn---tastic! I'll be on the next train. And what's wrong with Fridays?"

"Boaters always say it's bad luck to weigh anchor for parts unknown on a Friday."

I wondered why he was coming by train. Six days later, I learned why. Whereas experienced crew would bring along one duffel bag or maybe two at the most, Billy Joe arrived with nine crammed full of stuff, plus four tanks of air for SCUBA diving, a rifle, and two handguns with numerous boxes of ammo for each. He also brought the dehydrator which was way too big for the available space I had on deck, and the water contraption, also too big and not worth the prime space it would take up to collect less than a cup of water in eight hours.

"Billy Joe, the dehydrator and water-maker won't fit – I just don't have room for big contraptions like that. I'm sorry but you'll have to give or sell them to someone or ship them back home. And we definitely cannot take those guns on my boat. South of the border, if they stop you for an inspection and find any weapons aboard, they confiscate the boat and everything on it. Just to go hunting down there, you have to get advance special permission from the Mexican government to bring in a simple hunting rifle. Weapons aboard are a total no-no and totally illegal on board, south of the border."

"Yeah, and how do we defend ourselves against all those drug-dealing pirates out there?"

"I've already bought two of the biggest flare guns available. We shoot them in the belly and their guts will be instantly scattered all over the sea. The rest of the body parts will make a fine meal for the sharks."

Over the next few days, he hadn't made any attempt to get rid of the guns. Three days before we were set to sail, while Billy Joe was at the barbershop, I wrapped up the guns and ammunition and when the post office wouldn't accept them, I took a taxi all around San Diego and found a gun dealer who would. I told Billy Joe I had shipped them back to his daughter whose address he had given me for emergencies. He was livid.

"If you give me any more grief about those guns, you can ship yourself home as well!" And *that* was the end of *that*!

I hired a live-aboard shipwright in the harbor to help with a few repairs I couldn't handle myself and then started checking items off the dreaded "To Do" list, an activity I would become very intimate with as I would later move from one anchorage to the next:

> *Refill on-deck jerry cans with diesel and secure to deck with line. Make sure to mark DIESEL in big letters on all the fuel cans.*
>
> *Top off on-board fuel tank*
>
> *Buy gas for dinghy motor and stow outside in cockpit coaming locker.*
>
> *Flush out on-deck water jugs; fill and secure to deck; stow fresh water hose*
>
> *Clean all decks and stow or secure lines*
>
> *Clean yellow electric shore power cord and have ready to stow at departure.*
>
> *Dig out Mexican flag and mount the flag-mount for forestay and install*
>
> *Mount outboard motor on stern rail*
>
> *Mount my bike on stern rail*
>
> *Wash down dinghy and stow on deck in front of mast on top of emergency survival box*
>
> *Check flares, reflectors, flashlight, water bags and other equipment in survival box.*
>
> *Check snorkel equipment and re-stow under V-berth*

Fix heat exchanger – have Billy Joe look at it to see why it's not working properly

Get spare head gasket, spare belts for engine, water pump & alternator

Install the recently-purchased (not yet used)secondhand self-steering device

Have shipwright re-machine the in-line water filter so it won't leak

Install line on bucket for collecting salt water for deck-swabbing

Take down and stow cockpit awning

Clean out bilge

Clean engine pan

Check engine hours and change engine oil if needed

Mount salt-shaker solar anchor light to backstay

Switch propane tanks and dry out propane locker

Secure spare propane tank with bungee cords

Fix or replace the transducer for the knot log

Lead jib sheet through blocks

Plug waypoints into the new GPS and hope the damned thing works!

Get tourist visas and Mexican fishing permits ($162)

Get Ham license for Mexico ($52)

Buy fresh veggies, meats, eggs, milk, butter and other staples for trip

Buy a couple of large pizzas and assortment of Chinese food we can easily heat up if we get into rough seas the first few days out there and just don't feel like cooking.

Check my on-board "pharmacy"

Call Ian in Philadelphia and Sam in Santa Cruz to say adios

Buy posy of pink carnations to put in Sam Patterson's plexiglass vase

Invite Clare to a farewell dinner

Anything more will just have to wait 'til the next anchorage!

Before taking off on what could be a long voyage, it was important to check my on-board pharmacy to see what was still left since the Monterey departure. Anything we needed to replenish we'd take care of at our first anchorage south of the border where pharmaceuticals were cheap and available over the counter. This whole business of medications was new to me and it seemed silly to take time to buy and stock them, especially since I didn't believe in taking medicine. But almost every sailing magazine and every cruiser talked about all the serious illnesses and situations one could encounter and needed to be prepared for. The list of illnesses was endless, with many I had never even heard of. The ones I did know about were bad enough: malaria, dengue fever, Chagas sleeping sickness (I had to look that one up...a weird infection discovered in 1909 caused by the bite of parasitic sand flies), yellow fever, worms, rabies and even TB, not to mention snake bites, ear infections, non-stop diarrhea, severe sunburn and skin cancer. I had no idea before I embarked on this sailing life I would become an amateur pharmacist. I was equipped with Phosphate of Chloroquine, Bactrim, Amoxicillin Trihydrate, Penicillin and a whole carton of other drugs with instructions I had carefully written out for each. I had a chart for purifying water with a dozen small bottles of Microdyne and a note, "1 drop per liter then Clorox 1 capful per 25 gallons but only if out of everything else to purify in which case best to use the Sodium Hypochlorite and if 1% solution, 10 drops per liter, if 4-6%, 2 drops per liter, and if 7 to 10%, 1 drop per liter." Lastly, the most important thing in this cornucopia of chemicals was the Epinephrine in the Epi-Pen auto-injector which I'd have to jam into my thigh in the event of a bee sting, Over the years,

I had become highly allergic to bee stings and the last time I was rushed to the hospital with a sting, the Emergency Room doctor said it would be my last as I no longer had any immunity. After completing the inventory, it sure didn't look like we'd need to buy anything too soon for the medicine chest.

Sandi arrived and word soon spread throughout the harbor that "the pink boat" was getting ready to depart. I got on the morning Ham net to say goodbye to all my Hamster friends and Tommie, a Hamster and wife of the skipper of *Old Ancient Mariner*, invited Sandi and me over for lunch the day before we were to depart. The White Pants brigade had already made a point of offering unsolicited advice: "Stay within sight of land, don't dare go offshore" or "Whatever you do, don't let them damned Mexicans aboard your yacht – they'll rob you blind, or worse." Their final words of advice were, "And take along plenty of Playboy and other girlie magazines to trade for lobster and shrimp."

Tommie, on the other hand, told me that she had had nothing but good experiences with the Mexican fishing community and found the fishermen to be very honest and friendly.

"If you go offshore to the San Benitos Islands," she said, "there's an incredible population of elephant seals out there. Be sure to take some sweatshirts and sweatpants for the fishermen out there. They'll appreciate it."

The day before we were scheduled to depart, Clare took Sandi and me to the Salvation Army's thrift store where we bought some used sweatshirts and sweatpants in various sizes. We figured some fishermen down the line just might have a use for them. We had dinner with Clare that night in our favorite harbor eatery. I felt sad knowing I probably wouldn't ever see her again, not knowing then that our friendship would endure for almost thirty years. She'd often phone me out of the blue with her favorite opening, "Sandra, do you remember the time we....." and she'd spout snippets of some of our escapades, sending us both into uncontrollable hysterics.

Clare wouldn't come down to the harbor to wave goodbye as she said it would make her too sad, but she would keep us in her prayers. She was a

Jehovah Witness so I knew her prayers would be good ones. I was grateful to her as I was sure we were going to need a lot of prayers as we headed off into unknown waters.

Chapter Twenty-One

Adios San Diego, Hola Baja!

Sérenta sailed away from San Diego on the high tide early Saturday morning, February 16, buddy-boating with a guy from Vancouver who was single-handing his Tartan 34, named *Turleygood*. The skipper was in late stages of diabetes, had already lost sight in one eye, and was suffering with foot ulcers. I felt sorry he hadn't found crew (probably because of his rather dour outlook) so agreed to buddy-boat. One hour out of the harbor, *Turleygood* had to turn back as his autopilot wasn't working. We opted to continue on as he didn't know how long it would take to fix the device. I promised to watch for him but we never saw him again. Late in July, I heard on the Baja radio net he had finally arrived in Cabo as a single-hander. It was like hearing about a long lost friend. The boating community, even though spread across oceans, is very close-knit. We never forget one another.

There are only a few scattered islands lying off Baja's Pacific shore and only three of these (Isla De San Martin, Isla Cedros and Islas San Benito) are visited by cruisers. The San Benitos were less frequented as they are isolated and farther out to sea. In contrast, there is a somewhat continuous string of some 29 islands along the interior coast of the Sea of Cortez (Gulf of California). I wondered if I'd be exploring those later.

Once out of San Diego Harbor, with our sails playfully taunting the breeze, I turned to Sandi and Billy Joe and said, "What do you think about going offshore to the San Benito Islands to see those famed elephant seals? Last night, I checked out the Benitos on the chart – not too far out, about 300+ nautical miles. The chart shows a lighthouse and a lighted buoy which won't be hard to find if we arrived in the dark…which we probably would."

They both agreed it would be fun and I confessed I had already plotted the chart to get there, just in case they'd like the idea. I took the helm for the morning watch and then turned it over to Billy Joe for the noon to 4:00 p. m. watch.

"It is crucial that you don't go more than five degrees either direction off the compass course," I told him. "We're in a downwind situation and it's real easy to jibe which, in case you don't know, if you can't control it properly, can send the boom crashing across the cockpit and could also send us down to the bottom of the sea. So, here's an order! Keep your eye on that compass and the wind tell-tale indicators. Even more important, every 10 to 12 minutes, you have to take a 360-degree scan of the horizon. You must rotate a full circle, looking in all directions for any freighters or other traffic. Only about 12 minutes will elapse from the second you see a freighter as a tiny dot on the horizon to the minute it's on top of us. They hit sailboats and don't even know they have, as they're on autopilot and even their radar often won't pick us up. Down we go to Davy Jones locker in about two minutes and off they go, ignorant of the disaster they've just left behind. We'll be crossing the shipping lanes for about an hour so you've got to keep checking until we are across those dangerous lanes."

I went down below to catch a snooze and Sandi joined me as we were both bushed after all we had done to ready the boat. I was awakened with a loud noise coming from the bowels of my boat and with Billy Joe yelling, "Get up here! Hurry! Get up!"

I dashed up the ladder into the cockpit to see a gigantic freighter heading towards us 100 feet away, coming at us to starboard in a certain collision course. It was so close I couldn't even see its decks above. The loud roar of its screw was what I'd heard down in my bunk below water level. I'll never forget that deadly sound.

"Come about, Billy Joe!" I screamed. "Come about! Turn us to port."

He didn't move. His hands seemed super-glued to the wheel. I flew across the cockpit, shoved him to the side, grabbed the helm and turned it as hard and fast as I could just in time to get us clear of a direct hit. The bow wake of the freighter coming over our stern nearly swamped us. The freighter, probably on radar and autopilot, continued on its course, its crew oblivious to the fact they had almost killed us.

"I guess I forgot to look out for freighters," was all he could say.

That was the last time we entrusted our lives to him at the helm. With that near fatal incident, Billy Joe had instantly become useless and burden-some cargo. We pretty much ignored him for the rest of the voyage. While standing at the wheel on each of my watches, I'd be counting the days until we could find a decent port to put him off our boat. The closest was Cabo San Lucas.

It was just after 2:00 p. m. when we nearly got hit by that freighter and Sandi took over to finish the rest of his shift. She picked up how to handle the helm like an America's Cup champ…she was a natural! What a picture she was, standing behind the wheel with her long blonde hair streaming in the wind, wearing a neon pink bikini, big sunglasses, a dab of white Nosekote to protect her nose from sunburn, and holding a cigarette poised gracefully between two glitzy-ringed fingers. Teak was wrapped up in a blanket sitting in his deck basket right beside her. I decided not to get on her about the smoking – I knew she was already nervous about wanting to please me by doing all this sailing stuff correctly.

At 4:00 p. m., Sandi agreed to finish Billy Joe's watch and would stay on the helm until 6:00 p. m. so I could throw together something for dinner. We were far away from shipping lanes and cruising along in fairly light airs. I managed to tune and tweak the sails perfectly so *Sérenta* could clip along on her own, holding a faultless course without the need of a helmsman unless the wind direction changed. We all went below to have our first meal at sea. Before the watermelon sun disappeared into the western sea, the three of us had chowed down all the take-out Chinese food I'd heated on the galley's propane stove, slurped down cold Cokes from the fridge, and demolished almost an entire bag of chocolate chip cookies from our secret stash of chocolatey treats. I went up to take the helm at 6:00 p. m. and told Sandi to hop into the quarter berth beside the nav station so she could grab some "Zs" before her next watch would begin at 10:00 p. m. since we had agreed on four-hour watches.

"Sandi, if, due to conditions out here I'm not able to leave the helm to check the chart, I'll have to wake you up in two hours to plot our position. OK?"

"No problemo, Mom. I'm sure glad you gave me that crash course on how to read charts and work the parallels and dividers last week back in port. I'm looking forward to doing the charting. It's fun and I won't mind at all if you have to wake me up."

"Great! When I'm at the helm and you're awake, you need to be in charge of the time factor. We need to know every two hours where we are on the chart so if we get lost, at least we can tell someone where we were two hours before. Got that? You have to be aware of time so one of us can mark our location on the chart every two hours. Do you think you have a fairly good grip on this?"

"Sure, Mom. And you know I dig anything to do with numbers so I think I'll be good at it. Not to worry, and if for some reason I get confused, I'll check my notes or simply ask."

"Fabulous! The ship's bell below in the main cabin will ding every half-hour, so you can listen for that and when it's dinged the fourth time, it's time to do your chart work. Do any of your wristwatches glow in the dark?" As long as I could remember, Sandi loved watches. She owned at least a dozen. It had always been part of her need to feel in control...to know what time it was. "Yep, my newest one does," she said proudly holding up a big hot pink watch.

"I bought it in the Philly Airport because it'd be perfect for telling time aboard *Sérenta*. I call it my titty-pink watch," she added with a giggle.

"Right on! We won't have any problems keeping our navigation plotting current. Our lives will depend on this, Sandi."

I wanted her to feel important, to know she was an integral part of this voyage. For several years earlier, she had been battling a case of low self-esteem (something many children of alcoholics suffer from) and I wanted so very much for her to know how wonderful she was, how brilliant and how capable.

Billy Joe finished eating but didn't offer to clean up so I said, almost in a command, "Grab a bucket, haul up some salt water, and wash the dishes. We don't have room for a lump-on-a-log here and there's no free rides, either."

Grudgingly, he did the dishes and then lay down on his bunk in the main cabin, strapping himself in by the heavy-weather bunk harness I had installed in Monterey even though we hardly had any wind at all and no swells to speak of. Maybe it was a subtle indication of the fear he was trying to hide. We never did find out if he really had done all that sailing in the South Pacific he claimed to have done.

The sailing was going well and I was amazed that even though we were no longer in sight of land and were now "out there" in the darkness, I wasn't suffering complete panic or terror. I felt at peace. Although we weren't exactly speeding along – maybe about 3 or 4 knots – we were moving fast enough so we wouldn't have to turn on the Yanmar. I was hoping we could mostly sail as using the engine would bring up a whole different can of worms – keeping close track of engine hours to know when to change the oil and replace fuel filters. I didn't want to have to deal with all that on this first leg of the journey.

Exactly at 8:00 p. m., Sandi poked her head up out of the cabin and announced she had done the plotting and marked our position on the chart. As I didn't want to leave the helm, we shared distant "high fives" and even though I felt she knew I was proud of her, I cemented the fact by blowing her a kiss which she blew back to me. She went back to her bunk for some shut-eye and then came up again at 10:00 p. m. to take over the helm for her watch.

"We're keeping a good straight course, Mom. I just checked us again and we're right on. Used the flashlight with the red light so I wouldn't wake Billy Joe up."

"Wow! You're getting good at all this navigating! We're gonna have to call you, 'Admiral Sandi.'"

As I felt a bit tired, she seemed to just sense it, and came over and hugged me and then took over the helm while I went below to brew up some hot chocolate. After we finished gulping down the divine elixir she said, "Mom, you can go below and get some sleep if you like. I can handle the helm OK by myself. It's not rough out here and with the full moon I can see the compass and the wind tell-tales real good."

"OK, thanks. First I'll take the dog up to the bow and see if he'll go on the coiled up line. I haven't seen him go all day. It's his first venture out to sea and he's probably literally scared shitless!"

We both laughed and it made me feel really good as a very first bond between us seemed to be in the making. I had missed so much of her life and even the tiniest "right on" moments we were beginning to share gave me real joy. I looked up into the star-filled sky and thanked my Higher Power for bringing Sandi back to me, even as brief as the time together might be. I didn't know then that far off, Melpomene, the muse of tragedy, was lurking in the shadows.

It was as if Teak had been born on a boat. No sooner were we up at the bow than he did his "business" and quickly scooted back to the cockpit. All I had to do was grab the line and toss the bitter end over and rinse everything off in the sea. When I went below to the quarter berth, Teak slowly climbed down the ladder, leveraging with his neck while balancing all fours on one step at a time and then he hopped into the quarter-berth with me for some well-deserved rest. He gave me his usual doggie kiss before climbing into my sleeping bag.

Sandi skippered the boat for two hours and at midnight, called down, asking me to plot our course. I was exhausted and sure didn't want to get up but knew it was important to keep us current so turned on the red navigation light over the chart table and figured out where we were. A short nap later, the ship's bell was chiming out 2:00 a. m., signaling time for my watch. Sandi came down and plotted our course before hitting her bunk. She said there was hardly any wind and it had been difficult keeping the mainsail and boom from flapping back and forth. The jib was hanging limp and useless. I switched on the engine and motored for the rest of the night. While at the helm, I noticed the tiny white compass light was shining in my eyes and soon making night vision difficult. After an hour of near night-blindness, I made fast the helm and scooted below to the V-berth where I had all my clothes stashed. I pulled out the only red material I had…my racy red lace bra brought along for special occasions. I tied it over the compass to hide the light and Sandi and I both had a good laugh at 6:00 a. m. when she came up for her watch.

She had looked dead-tired when she got off the helm at 2:00 a. m. so I hadn't awakened her for the 4:00 a. m. course plot. During the night, I had to turn on the Yanmar and was able to turn on the autopilot, keeping *Sérenta* on course while occasionally checking the compass as well. It was awe-inspiring to watch Apollo on his chariot come bursting into view that morning and I realized this would be the first of many such radiant sunrises. From the coral and peachy sky it was difficult to know if it was sunrise or sunset as the sky looked the same in early morning as in early evening.

I noticed many seabirds flying towards Apollo to welcome him back and wondered where they had all come from. After some time into the cruising life, I realized birds always hailed Apollo when he showed up in the morning and then at dusk, flew out to bid him adieu as he sank into the sea. They were probably letting him know how much he was appreciated and begging him to please be sure to return in the morning. Sometimes, even little sparrows and other meadow birds would be among the feathery convocation heralding the sun and I often wondered how they managed to fly so far offshore. Many moons later, when I was lost at sea as crew aboard a Captain Bligh's sailboat, I would learn more about these beloved little hitchhikers.

Sandi was still on her watch, so I got up from resting in the cockpit at 8:00 a. m. to do the chart work and then went back to rest. Billy Joe came up from below about 9:30 a. m.

"Since Sandi and I are doing all the helm, deck-work and navigation duties, it will be up to you to make breakfast and lunches for all of us and to clean up afterwards. We'll do the dinners. You know where the food is stowed. You can make whatever you like, and I definitely like coffee first thing in the morning. It's already past normal time for coffee so please get going on it." He just nodded.

"Oh, look, Mom. Four of our carnations are already drooping and almost dead. Must be the salt air and the heat from the engine at night, the sun during the day."

I had no idea it would be that hot so far offshore. Even under sail with a little wind, the sun was relentless and unforgiving. Thank goodness before I left Santa Cruz, I had come up with my idea for a helmsman's awning, a contraption I designed and made out of leftover hot pink Sunbrella material. Darryl helped me connect PVC tubing to form two arc-like loops, each about seven feet long. We stretched about four feet of pink canvas between the two tube lengths to create a sunshade to install over where the helmsman stands. The ends of the tubes could easily be tucked into fittings mounted into the teak floorboards which allowed me to put it up or remove it depending on weather conditions. It handily stowed in the stern locker. Whoever was on the helm could stand for hours under the awning while steering, protected from the sun while still enjoying perfectly unobstructed vision. When we later made it to Cabo San Lucas, Sandi and I were two of the few if the only cruisers who didn't have sunburned ears so we didn't have to visit the local surgeon, like most all of the other boaters, to have the tops of our ears cut off to remove any evidence of skin cancer. We'd prance around Cabo, with hair pushed back to show our gorgeous and fully complete virgin ears untouched by the surgeon's shears.

That first morning at sea away from San Diego, we performed the first of several flower rituals, dropping the four dead carnations, one at a time, over the stern, several minutes apart. As soon as a flower hit the water, it opened up again as if coming back to life and floated on the surface, waltzing in our wake. As we sailed along, we watched the four flowers dancing in a row behind us for quite some time until they were out of sight.

It was Sunday and we spent the first half of the day motoring as there was no wind. I kept the mainsail up for balance and just in case some wind would gust our way. Sandi and I took our turns on watch and at noon, Billy Joe went below to make hot dogs and baked beans for lunch. We each had a brownie for dessert. About 2:00 p. m. just as I was getting off watch, some decent wind came up out of the east and we were able to unfurl the jib and sail a steady beam reach for a couple of hours before it died again and we were back on the Yanmar. We didn't see any boats, whales or other signs of life all day. At 6:00 p. m. we were famished and as Sandi's watch had just ended, she heated up some of the pizza I bought departure day in San Diego. Sea air sure did increase one's appetite. The engine purred along throughout the night. I was grateful for the four six-gallon plastic jerry cans of extra fuel safely tied up on the foredeck.

I felt a little lonely and even a bit frightened out there on my 2:00 a. m. to 6:00 a. m. watch so I dug out my Walkman and listened to some tapes of Beethoven sonatas. When Apollo came up out of the sea bringing with him the incredible retinue of his loyal feathered friends, any sense of fear disappeared, replaced by joyful exuberance – ah, life was grand again!

Billy Joe made us coffee, squeezed juice from some oranges, and cooked a few envelopes of instant oatmeal topped with bananas already getting over-ripe. According to best estimate, we still had two more full days of sailing before we would arrive at the San Benitos. That day went pretty much the same as the day before…sunrise, sunset, sunrise, sunset. Four more carnations died and we repeated our flower ceremony. We motored quite a few hours as there wasn't any wind until about 1:00 p. m. It died down again at sundown which I began to see as a pattern. Neither Sandi nor I had spoken two words to Billy Joe in that 24-hour period. It was weird, but not nearly as bad as before when I was saddled with the snarling nasty females.

The next day, Sandi did most of the course-plotting which she thoroughly enjoyed. We took our turns on watches. During that afternoon, three more carnations went overboard. We were down to our last flower. Our course- plotting (if we had been doing it correctly!) indicated we would be arriving at San Benitos between 2:00 and 3:00 a. m. and I was glad I'd be on the helm for our arrival in case there were any "challenges". Thinking I could get some Zs, off and on, as we were in fairly light airs, I rigged up the 10-year old Monitor self-steering device I had bought for $750 through an ad from another boater in Sausalito while I was still docked up in San Francisco. I hadn't had a need yet to try it and the seller assured me it worked perfectly. Not! I spent about three hours trying to get the blasted thing to function, but *Sérenta* just would not hold a steady course with it and instead, took to going around in circles. Drat! More money wasted and now no self-steering which would have been handy when under sail as it didn't require the motor to be running. Well, it was a lesson I was learning that not everyone in the sailing community was as honest as expected. I manned the helm under sail for the first half of the watch and when the airs died, turned on the engine and autopilot and tried to catnap in the cockpit for an hour or so. Anticipating our first landfall, Sandi was so excited she couldn't sleep and came up to stretch out on the other long cockpit seat.

The stars were so bold and bright, we both tried reaching out and balancing different ones on the tips of our outstretched fingers. That night, we started our new game of hunting for constellations and picked out the Big Dipper first. No matter where we were, we could always find Sandi's favorite, Orion, with his distinct belt. Every time she saw him she would call out, "Hi, Orion. It's me down here, Sandi." For the rest of my days, I would think of her when I'd see Orion's belt in the heavens. Often, I would almost hear her say, "Hi Mommy, it's me, Sandi, up here" which was especially comforting. Many nautical miles later, I was delighted to see the Southern Cross I had so often read about in my childhood storybooks.

About an hour later, I began to feel a bit apprehensive, sure we should be at the islands by now but not seeing any sign of the lighthouse marked on the chart…no friendly beacon to beckon us to a safe harbor…no sign either of the flashing lit buoy also shown on our chart.

Sandi picked up on my anxiety, saying, "Mom, do you think we're lost out here? I mean, you said we'd be at the San Benitos by now and we're not. Do you think we messed up with our navigating or chart-plotting?"

"Don't worry, Sandi," I said trying to sound reassuring. "We're not lost… we just don't know exactly where we are. If we decide we *are* lost, we can simply turn around and follow all our carnations back to San Diego like Hansel and Gretel, right?"

"Yeah, sure Mom," she replied with that hint of her father's sarcasm I had never gotten used to. My family had never been sarcastic, and it was a little upsetting to see Sandi had acquired a bit of that hurtful habit.

It was almost 3:00 a. m. and still no sign of the lighthouse nor the flashing buoy. Suddenly ahead we saw not one flashing light but about ten. What on Earth could this be? There was only one buoy marked on the chart, not ten. And where was the lighthouse? I closed my eyes and quietly asked God for help, hoping He would hear me way out there in the middle of the ocean. I remembered how helpful it had always been to take some time away from a major challenge and meditate for answers. I asked Sandi if she could take the helm, telling her I just needed about fifteen minutes alone to meditate. I knew she would understand. I then went up to the bow, sat down with my legs dangling over the edge so the sweet water could tickle my toes while I looked up into the skies for an answer that might be attached to a star.

"Oh, Great Creator," I said aloud. "I've been trying to lead a good life, trying to learn how to be the best person I can be. I've tried listening for Your suggestions at almost every turn and been doing my best at following Your advice. Now, here I am, out here in the darkness. Is this where You would have me? Is this what You want me to be doing? Please help me, Lord. I need to know what You want me to do now and once we've got that sorted out, then what I'm supposed to be doing with my life." Silence.

Just as I thought He hadn't heard me or that He might have given up on me, I heard a loud voice say, "Write to glorify My name!"

"Glorify?" I said. "I don't know what that means. Can You please be a bit more specific?"

"Write to glorify My name," came the reply again.

I stood up and walked back to Sandi, thinking that I'd look up that word, "glorify", in my OED if we ever got out of this precarious situation.

Out of desperation but not really expecting a reply, I grabbed the radio mike and shouted into it, "Help! Anybody out there? Anybody at all? We aren't really lost, right? Where are we? Help!"

Over the radio and out of the darkness came a reply in halting English, "This is Ramon, the fisherman. You at San Benitos, but careful. You heading to many dangers.""But what are all those lights I see? Where's the lighthouse, the buoy?"

"They lights on our fishing nets sitting over reef rocks. Lighthouse she died two years ago and buoy last year went with her. Quick, turn to zee right, away from our nets."

"Gosh, thanks. Where are you? I can't see you?"

"I in little boat way over here, but I see light on top of your mast. You can't get to anchorage in dark – many dangers to find the narrow Canal de Peche between the islands at night. You'll must to circle the three islands two miles off and to come into the West Island anchorage from other side."

"But I can't see a thing."

"No worry. I guide you in by watching your light. Now, turn to zee right…good."

And here followed a comical radio show with the fisherman telling us to "go to zee right" and then in a few minutes screaming, "Oh, no.... too far to zee right. Go to zee left" and then in a few minutes, "More to zee right" and then shouting at the top of his lungs, "Queeek.... more to zee right" followed by "Maria, José y Jesus.... more to zee left."

After almost more than two hours of this "show", with the help of Selene, goddess of the moon, we saw that our guardian angel with the funny Mexican accent had guided us right into the "Landing" (as it was called) on West Island. We dropped our anchor, according to our depth-sounder, in 48 feet of water. Billy Joe woke up at the sound of the anchor chain going down and came up to see what was going on. Thank goodness I carried a lot of anchor line and chain. We had racked up 16. 6 engine hours from San Diego and our chart calculations showed we had logged in 331 nautical miles. We all fell into our bunks without even undressing. We were home free and had once again cheated Death, now south of the border whom I'd call Thanatos, that pale horseman of the Apocalypse!

As I drifted off to sleep, I murmured, "Thank you, Lord, for keeping us out of harm's way and delivering us to this safe harbor. Without Your help, I know we would have been lost." In case she had forgotten, I whispered, "And Sandi thanks You, too!"

I was sure I could sleep for days but awoke about 9:00 a. m. to Apollo, without mercy, blazing down on the three small islands surrounding us. They were barren – pure rock and sand with no green anywhere, just beige-grey rock. The sea was as clear as the antique crystal German wine glass I used in days of old, the sand somehow pure white, the water a see-through turquoise and I could almost see our anchor nestled safely below us. I didn't want to wake the other two but was desperate for coffee. I hadn't had any for two days and was going through caffeine withdrawal. I quietly pulled out the stovetop percolator and got it fired up.

When the robust aroma filled the cabin, Sandi crawled out of her bunk saying, "Coffee? It's about time someone made some. I need to find out if I'm still alive."

Billy Joe was turned to the wall and didn't move. Through the port light I glimpsed a small fishing boat going slowly back and forth about 75 feet from us.

"Hey, Sandi, look. There's lunch," I said, pointing to the little fishing boat. "Incidentally, I meant to ask you what you thought about that advice White Pants gave us about the Mexican fishermen."

"Really, Mom, I thought those snotty men were obnoxiously prejudiced. I mean, they had never even met the fishermen and were telling us we'd be robbed and raped."

"Well, there's one thing for sure, Sandi. If we ain't friendly with the Mexican fishermen, we ain't gonna get any of that shrimp and lobster you so love!"

In a flash, Sandi dashed back to the V-berth, changed out of her dungarees and sweatshirt and donned a pink polka-dot bikini, put on bright pink lipstick and to complete the pretty picture, tucked a pink bow in her hair.

"Here I am, ready or not," she squealed as she scampered up the steps to the cockpit, waving to the fishermen. Since age five, Sandi had been a shrimp-and-lobsterholic. When it was my turn to have her stay with me downtown Philly during my starving writer/single mom days, we'd occasionally splurge and go out for dinner to Ralph's, her favorite seafood restaurant in South Philly, a fairly short walk from my house. She'd always order a large gulf shrimp cocktail and then lobster thermidor. I'd have to tell the waiter, "I had a really late lunch. Just bring me one of those darling little dinner salads you have."

The fishermen saw her and brought their *panga* zooming over to us. It was the first *panga* I had seen. I later learned that these 20 to 30-foot fiberglass outboard-powered crafts were designed and originally built by Malcolm Shroyer, owner of the Marina de La Paz in La Paz, Baja California

Sur. Fishermen had been using smaller and shorter wooden boats until 1968, in Ensenada, when The Mac", as Shroyer was lovingly to be called, designed and built the first fiberglass molds in the same machete-like cut of the plywood skiffs used mostly by small-operation commercial fishermen. Also known as "long boat" or "island boat", the *panga* (a Mexican slang word for "skiff") became popular due to their ability to knife through the open water and launch and land through the surf. Mac became known as the father of the modern-day *panga* and went on to open a *panga* factory in La Paz which made fishing a lot easier for the local fishermen. With its flat bottom, the *panga* is more stable than a round hull and allows the boat to be easily driven up onto the beach by its powerful outboard motor after a day of fishing.

Later that year, with *Sérenta* safely docked in either a marina in Cabo San Lucas or on anchor in La Paz, I spent time in the Mexican "artist colony" of Todos Santos, an oasis on the Pacific side of the Baja and some 20 years later, to be known as, '*Todos Gringos*'. The fun thing to do around 4:00 p. m. was to head for the beach and watch the fishermen cruising their *pangas* back and forth horizontal to the beach, judging the waves for the perfect moment to turn and race their *panga* up onto the sand. I was always given first dibs on the fresh fish I wanted to buy for dinner…a favor the fishermen bestowed on me, often even giving me a beautiful fish free. They knew I wasn't one of those *gringos* who never associated with the locals. They had seen me when I first visited Todos Santos that year when I was the only gringa who picked up a brush to help whitewash the town square in time for the annual October 12-13 celebration for the town's patron saint, the Virgin of Pilar.

I would eventually buy a rustic palm-frond thatched-roof "house" atop a hill in that oasis with over an acre of huge well-aged bougainvillea trees in all colors, a fabulous view of the ocean beyond, a separate "kitchen" with open fire pit as stove, outhouse behind, hammock to sleep on, no electricity and no running water. I let the seller's oldest son use the house rent-free anytime I was off sailing as long as he kept the trees and plantings watered with water he had to carry in buckets from quite a distance.

I later learned greedy unscrupulous members of the Baja government, during Mexico's 1983 economic crisis, told The Mac they were going to confiscate his successful *panga* factory. Rather than allow that, he turned the entire business over to his Mexican employees without taking a single peso and he and his wife, Mary, and their son, Neil, continued to run the other business they had established, the Marina de La Paz, as a haven for cruisers. When I drove down the Baja in 2012, the first trip down since I had sold my boat so long ago, Mary was a widow but still holding court at the marina which had become the largest marina in Mexico with over 120 slips and a faithful following of cruisers. She was still an unmitigated bridge-playing *aficionada*!

The fishermen spotted Sandi at once, standing on our bow. When they brought their *panga* up alongside *Sérenta*, I stuttered, "*Ola, como esta?*" trying to remember some of the Spanish I had learned at Berlitz in Philadelphia some 25 years earlier when I was helping Cuban refugees rent or buy homes.

"*Bien, bien,*" said one of the three.

"Radio last night? You?" I asked.

"I am Ramon Castro Redoña," said the tallest who was about 40. "Yes, on radio. I like to practice the English. I studying to being airplane pilot and need knowing English to pass test for *licensia*."

"Thank you so much for your help. We were so tired and I thought we were lost. I didn't know what to do and you were like an angel."

"Everything fine now?"

"Yes, wonderful, thanks to you. Oh, can you possibly sell us some shrimp or lobster?"

"Oh, no. We not allow. The *cooperativo* be very angry if we sell. But can trade you."

"Cool," chimed in Sandi. "I have some Marlboros."

"Yes, or we have some chocolate or peanut butter, or some really good coffee," I added, trying to think of anything that might appeal to them. As a last resort I said, "And we have some Spam, too."

"You have Spam?" he exclaimed, almost at the top of his lungs. "We love Spam. We are here three months eating only fish. Spam be super. We go get shrimp and lobster. Be back maybe 30 *minutos.*" Off they sped in their *panga.*

Less than an hour later, they pulled up to *Sérenta.* We had a barter-bag ready with two packs of Marlboros, a big Hershey bar, six cans of Spam and three sweatshirts and sweatpants.

As Ramon was trying to pass a big bag of shrimp and lobster up, I said, "Hey, want to come aboard?"

They looked at each other. "You mean us to come on to boat?"

"Yes, why not? We can offer you cold Coca-Colas. This is Billy Joe, a passenger."

They acted shy, almost as if they couldn't believe we had invited them aboard. Ramon tied the *panga* off to our bow cleat and he and the other fisherman (Miguel, about 35) and the young boy (Bruno, about 15) carefully climbed aboard. They explained that the three of them and Miguel's wife who was camp cook had been on the islands together for three months, fishing. Regularly, the cooperative's refrigerated boat would come out and pick up what fish, lobster and shrimp they had collected which was waiting and stored in ice the cooperative boat would replenish.

"How do you cook the lobster and shrimps?" I asked Bruno, mostly by gesture. "Can you come below and help show me?" Bruno must have easily weighed 300 pounds and I prayed our little ladder would support his weight.

I pulled out sodas for everyone and while Sandi entertained the two fishermen seated in the cockpit, Bruno came below and started asking me for ingredients for the seafood project. It must have taken about 15 minutes to fig- ure out what *ajo* was…garlic. He wacked the lobsters into pieces with lobster juice and guts flying in every direction. I didn't have the heart to ask him to be a little more careful. I would just clean up the mess after they left. When the pot of luscious seafood was ready, I invited them to join us, but Ramon said they had to get back to camp as Miguel's wife was making them a special din- ner. As they were getting ready to leave, it took quite a bit of charades before we finally figured out Miguel and his camp-cook wife were celebrating their 20th wedding anniversary. I looked at the solitary pink carnation in our vase, then over at the rocky colorless fish camp with not a single blade of grass nor living plant visible anywhere. This was long before tourism would discover the islands and hotels would be built with palm trees and green things and plastic debris brought over from the mainland. As the three of them were climbing into their *panga*, I reached overboard and handed Miguel our last flower to take to his wife. He took it with an amazing gentleness, wiping away a tear as he put the flower with care into a safe corner of the *panga*.

As Ramon untied their boat, he said, "Oh, you want to go San Benito del Centro Island for see the seal elephants tomorrow? Pups borned two months ago are all around there. It fun for you to see. no?"

"Yes, but I don't really want to try uncovering my rubber dinghy and motor stowed on deck and having to lift it all overboard."

"No problem. We have Andreas, the lighthouse-keeper, to pick you up when he go out to work lighthouse, maybe 6:00 a. m. tomorrow morning. Then brings you back at day end."

"I thought you said the lighthouse died."

"Yes, she died, but Andreas still the lighthouse-keeper and still have to go out to her every morning and every night. He needs to keep his job."

Sandi and I smiled at each other--we just had our first lesson in the delightful Mexican way of looking at life. After they left, the three of us lazed about after gorging ourselves on shrimp and lobster. I tinkered with things that came loose during the voyage and retied all the water and fuel jugs on deck that had managed to relocate themselves.

While Sandi studied the chart from the San Benitos over to Turtle Bay on the Baja coast, our next destination, I dug out from under the V-berth my thick file of info I had put together before leaving Monterey. It had all kinds of neat stuff on seabirds, marine life, fish and a variety of sometimes obscure things I might see or need for the upcoming adventure. I remembered saving a copy of a 1988 Los Angeles Times' article about Professor Burney Le

Boeuf, a biologist who had been studying elephant seals for more than two decades and would become head of the department of Ecology & Evolutionary Biology at UC Santa Cruz. I rummaged through the binder crammed with papers and clippings, found the article and spent well into the night pouring over it and other articles I had on elephant seals, learning all about these incredible creatures. It would be info I could share the next day with Sandi as we wandered about.

In the 1700s, the maritime fur trade of the Pacific Northwest depleted almost all species of marine mammals including sea otters, sea lions, seals, dolphins and whales. The elephant seals' fearless behavior almost caused their demise as they were easy targets for 19th-century hunters who sought their oil-rich blubber for tanning, lamp fuel, machinery lubricant, and for making margarine, paint, clothing and soap. Unlike South America's more abundant southern elephant seals, our northern seals were nearly extinct by 1892 and fewer than 100 were still surviving on Isla de Guadalupe, 150 miles off Baja's west coast and about 170 land miles farther west from where we were anchored. All 100,000+ northern elephant seals alive today descended from that Guadalupe colony which, thanks to the Mexican government, had been granted protected status in 1922, a protection also ensured later by the U. S. government. Since protection, the northern elephant seal population expanded northward to islands along the coast of California. They were first seen on Año Nuevo in 1955 and the first pup was born there in 1961. Males began showing up on the California mainland in 1965. A pup born in January 1975 was the first known birth of a northern elephant seal on the mainland. By 1982, elephant seals were all along the Big Sur coastline more than 100 miles south of Año Nuevo. It didn't take long before the colony had spread south and north along beaches adjacent to Highway 1 with more than 1,000 pups born along those beaches some years later where they are now popular tourist attractions.

According to one of the articles, only the biggest and fiercest bull seals get to sire offspring. Natural selection has gradually made the bulls extremely aggressive and given them tools to scare other bulls: stubby elephant-like snouts like antlers on a stag, the ability to trumpet, and body weights three to seven times that of the cows. Males reach 16 feet in length and weigh up to 4,000 pounds; females reach nine feet and 1,600 pounds. A 16-foot bull will dominate a harem of about 50 cows. He quickly overtakes the female, ignoring her growls of protest as he mates. Often, younger bulls sneak toward the nearby harem but are chased away by bigger bulls who rear up and trumpet nasty warnings. During the mating season, bulls engage in battle, biting and trumpeting non-stop for up to 10 minutes. They get drenched with blood as they fight for access to cows. According to Le Boeuf, "Sex and violence…it's the basics of life."

Once a cow has finished nursing, she breeds, becoming pregnant again. Then she swims out to sea for up to 72 days, leaving weaned pups on the beach to fend for themselves and also to learn to swim and dive. Five to 30 percent of the pups don't survive. I thought that was pretty irresponsible of those cow mothers!

"Hey, Sandi, you still awake? Listen, this is really cool! An elephant seal expert, Professor Le Boeuf back at UC Santa Cruz, said that the most famous seal he studied named Adrian had been estimated during his lifetime of inseminating over 250 different lady elephant seals! Le Boeuf said males mate about 10 times a day and will try to mate with anything—dead or pregnant females, other males, even pups. Gosh, they're sure indiscriminate."

"Ooooh, sounds disgusting! Do we need to take our flare guns along for protection in case they come near us, Mom?"

"I don't think so. It's not mating season right now. Besides, Le Boeuf says because a dominant male fights ruthlessly and sometimes kills weaker bulls intruding on his harem, 30% to 80% of the males never mate. So I think we're safe, but we still better watch out. Here's something else really funny. This article says that the professor compares the seal mating scene to "a sleazy singles bar where the female starts the fight, all the males fight, and she goes off with the winner."

The next morning, as Apollo was coming up out of Poseidon's sparkling sea, Andreas, the lighthouse keeper tapped on our bow, his *panga* all cleaned up and ready to take us to the small island where the elephant seals lived. Billy Joe didn't want to go and we were glad to have an entire day away from him. We lowered ourselves over the side of *Sérenta* on our swim ladder and into the *panga*, with our cameras stashed in sealed plastic bags, and a couple of sandwiches and some bottles of water tucked into Sandi's knapsack. It was only about a ten-minute ride over to Central Island. Andreas pulled the *panga* right up onto the beach so we could easily disembark and said he'd be back to the same spot for us when he'd get off work, about 4:00 p. m. After he pulled away, Sandi and I giggled because we knew he didn't have any work to do.

We wandered around the island all day taking photos of zillions of little elephant seal babies, all looking soft and fluffy, totally unafraid of us, and enjoyed our picnic surrounded by the adorable little ones. I knew from my earlier readings that their mothers were out to sea somewhere and I felt sorry for the babies who probably felt so alone just like I used to feel.

At the end of the day, as we reached the top of the ridge to descend to the beach where we were to meet Andreas, we were aghast to see a number of big males fighting each other, lumbering up on their hind legs back and forth through the water and onto the beach at our exact meeting spot. The water was crimson with blood and the beasts were bellowing and trumpeting at each other while females of the harem lay huddled in a protective circle. I couldn't believe how fast these huge creatures could move through the water standing upright. We climbed back up onto the ridge, afraid any moment they might notice and come after us. I was relieved when I saw Andreas approaching in his *panga*, madly motioning us to climb down to the other side of the hill where he picked us up and thank goodness, safely deposited us back to *Sérenta*.

It felt good to be "home" and I immediately got on the single-sideband radio to bring up the *Mañana* radio net or try for the more distant Sandia net to check for a weather report.

"Poppa-Mike-Poppa, you there?" came the first Ham reply.

"Yes, Poppa-Mike-Poppa here…It's me, Peppermint Patty. What's up?"

"We've been trying to contact you all day," said the Hamster. "Wherever you are, get into the nearest safe protected place as quick as you can. There's a bad one coming down the Baja within the next 24 hours and those Santa Ana winds are going to be causing you trouble for about a week."

"Thanks, guys. We're in the San Benitos. We'll weigh anchor right away and head for *Bahia de Tortugas* (Turtle Bay). Poppa-Mike-Poppa out."

I was grateful to those Ham-netters even though we'd constantly hear them squabbling with each other over the air about where we were or where we weren't. I envisioned all those pins stuck into maps on the walls of their faraway little Ham shacks to show our position and many times, I knew the pins were in the wrong spots.

We took time and great care to batten everything down. This would be our first race to beat a storm and find a good place to ride it out. I pulled up our anchor and Sandi and I stood on deck to wave to those wonderful fishermen as we sailed out of our first foreign port and once again, into unknown waters.

After I had the sails set and we were whizzing through the water headed towards the coast of Baja, I went below and pulled from out of its stowed sacred place my tattered notebook filled with favorite helpful life-lesson phrases and quotations. I had carried this book with me through many adventures and for many years. I knew just the quote I wanted to read to Sandi and sat down next to her on the pink-trimmed white leather seat cushion on the starboard cockpit bench. I put my arm around her. The San Benitos were slipping away and my buddy Apollo was retreating with grace into his watery realm.

I began to read aloud something I had written in my notebook back when I was sitting full of questions one lonesome night in that tiny apartment in downtown Philadelphia. It was a quotation from the astrophysicist and astronomer, Carl Sagan, written in an August 1980 interview by Jonathan Cott for *Rolling Stone Magazine*:

"There are two extremes to worry about. One is the extreme in which everything is known and there's nothing left to do. The other is where everything is so complicated you can never begin to do anything. We are lucky to live in a Universe where there are laws of nature and things to discover, but they're not impossibly difficult, so we can understand them to some extent. But they're also difficult enough so that we're nowhere near understanding them all. There are exhilarating discoveries yet to be made. It's the best possible world."

Sandi and I smiled at each other. We both knew there would be exhilarating discoveries and unfathomable challenges awaiting us on our journey through the Universe. We also knew we were in the best possible world and nothing would be impossibly difficult. We had much ahead to discover and learn--we were truly blessed.

"Oh, Mom...look! A seagull just landed on our bow pulpit and he's staring at you as if he knows you."

"He does, Sandi. It's Jonathan Livingston and he's been watching over me ever since I first arrived in Moss Landing."

At that very moment, Jonathan took flight and circled twice around *Sérenta*. On his second pass, he dipped his right wing towards me and whispered, "Don't worry, Sandra. Everything is going to be alright."

And off he flew, heading south. I knew I would see him again.